Shaw, Mark, 1945-
Book report : publishing strategies, writing
tips, and 101 literary ideas for aspiring authors

9000929976

Books For Life Foundation

D1447439

MARK SHAW

Books By Mark Shaw

Book Report

Grammar Report

Poetry Report

No Peace For The Wicked

Let The Good Times Roll

From Birdies To Bunkers

Code of Silence (Melvin Belli)

Miscarriage of Justice,
The Jonathan Pollard Story

Larry Legend

Testament To Courage

Forever Flying

Bury Me In A Pot Bunker

Jack Nicklaus, Golf's Greatest Champion

The Perfect Yankee

Diamonds In The Rough

Down For The Count

Book Report

Publishing Strategies,
Writing Tips
and 101 Literary Ideas
For Apsiring Authors
and Poets

MARK SHAW

Publisher's Cataloging—In—Publication Data

Mark Shaw 1945—
> *Book Report, Publishing Strategies, Writing Tips, and 101 Literary Ideas For Aspiring Authors and Poets by Mark Shaw*
> *p. cm.*

ISBN 0-9717596-6-9

> *1. Shaw, Mark 1945— .*
> *2. Book Publishing*
> *3. Authors and Poets*
> *4. Writing Skills*
> *5. I. Shaw, Mark II. Title*

10 9 8 7 6 5 4 3 2 1

Printed in the United States of America

If there is a book that you want to read, and it hasn't been written yet, then you must write it.

TONI MORRISON
Nobel Prize-Winning
Author

Outside of a dog, a book is man's best friend.
Inside a dog, it's too dark to read.

GROUCHO MARX

All good books have one thing in common—they are truer than if they had really happened, and after you have read one of them, you will feel all that happened, happened to you and then it belongs to you forever: the happiness and unhappiness, good and evil, ecstasy and sorrow, the food, wine, beds, people and the weather. If you can give that to the readers, then you're a writer.

ERNEST HEMINGWAY

Dedicated To John T. Lupton
and To Writers Everywhere

Keep The Faith,
You Will Be Published

Acknowledgments

Book Report evolved from an idea to a book thanks to the assistance of many people. Without them, I could have never completed it.

Thanks are extended to Jodee Blanco, a valued friend, literary consultant, and competent author. She assisted me with the text and wrote the Foreword. Jodee continues to be a leading authority on book promotion and self-publishing.

Mark Dressler, director of education for BookExpo America, and a consultant for Books For Life Foundation, provided helpful suggestions for the book. Donna Cortese , Christina Williams, and Nancy Crenshaw, contributed much-needed editing skills. Their assistance is most appreciated.

Marie Butler-Knight, publisher of Alpha Books, an imprint of Penguin Group USA, literary agent Kimberly Cameron, former Simon and Schuster senior editor Paul McCarthy, former publisher Kent Carroll, author Jodee Blanco, and screenwriter Seymour Englander are thanked for being advisors to the Foundation.

I thank Jack Lupton, the founding benefactor of Books For Life Foundation, for his support and friendship. He is a man of few words with a true passion for one of them. His sidekick Audrey is a saint and his business guru Dave Gonzenbach a treasured supporter of the foundation.

Special thanks go to my brother Jack and his wife Sue, sisters Anne and Debbie, and my inlaws, the Spahn family, Mitch, Sheri, Sam, and Jack, for their friendship and love. I know my mother and father are also assisting me from heaven above.

Thanks are also offered to my canine pal, Black Sox. His companionship at five a.m. is most appreciated.

Above all, I thank the Good Lord for blessing me with the creativity and dedication necessary to become an author. Without his guidance, I am nothing.

Mark Shaw
Author

Contents

If you've purchased this book, chances are you dream of being a published author one day, of having your name in bold letters written across the front of a book jacket. To that end, I have exciting news—your timing couldn't be better since the publishing industry is evolving at an unprecedented rate.

Fresh, new opportunities abound, especially for first-time authors. Traditional self-publishing flourishes. Once considered obscure by the mainstream, it is now one of the fastest growing areas of the book business, generating millions of dollars in sales while introducing countless authors to bestseller lists across America. Self-publishing is the hot new breeding ground for undiscovered literary talent. Dave Pelzer (*A Child Called It*), and James Redfield (*The Celestine Prophecy*) became two of the most successful authors in the 1990s by self-publishing their books.

The Internet has been a blessing for authors and redefined the potential parameters for marketing books. The technology boom has also given birth to electronic books and digital printing. The bottom line—if your fantasy is to become a published author, there now exist many accessible avenues to transform that wish into reality.

Even though opportunities are there to be seized, an aspiring author, to take advantage, must understand the publishing industry. For example, what's the difference between mainstream advance-against-royalty publishing, as opposed to print-on-demand or traditional self-publishing? Does every book need a literary agent to represent it, and if it does, how do you find one? What role do publicity and public relations play in the success of a book? How much does it cost to self-publish? What are the risks and benefits of self-publishing versus signing a deal with a publishing company? What does copyright mean and how do you obtain one?

These questions are just the tip of the iceberg. Discovering answers to them can prevent you from being immersed in a confusing ocean without a life vest.

As a publishing industry veteran of nearly twenty years, I know firsthand the rewards of good agent and publishing decisions, and the heartache accompanying uninformed decisions. Experience as a book publicist (fifteen books on the *New York Times* Bestseller List, five at number one), literary agent, author of a *New York Times* bestseller, and educator (instructor at New York University and the University of Chicago) has confirmed the belief that aspiring authors need guideposts to assist them during the publishing process.

In **Book Report**, my friend and colleague Mark Shaw tells it like it is, straight and to the point. Deftly combining literary acumen with legal experience, he helps you to navigate the path to becoming an author. Whether you yearn to be published by a traditional company, or traditionally self-publish, Mark explains the options and suggests criteria for deciding the one best suited for you.

When he asked me to write this Foreword, I was honored since I know whoever reads this book will be forever empowered. So curl up, start reading, and get ready for a remarkable journey regarding the publishing industry and how you can become a published author or poet.

Jodee Blanco
Author, *The Complete Guide To Book Publicity, The Evolving Woman,* and *Please Stop Laughing At Me*
Tbg32@aol.com, 312-961-3430

Completing a book and having it traditionally published is like visiting Paris in the springtime: Many say they will—most never do. This is unfortunate since I'm certain anyone who works hard at becoming a professional writer can achieve this goal through proper planning and hard work.

Why listen to me? What do I know that hundreds of authors of books on writing and publishing don't? Good question, but one with a ready answer: During the course of having multiple books published, I've learned many lessons and have been through the wars like few others since I possessed no background or education in the field when I began writing for publication in 1992. This means *Book Report* is unique because it provides practical advice about becoming a published author or poet from someone who achieved success in the trial and error trenches of traditional publishing.

Along with my writing adventures, I have consulted with hundreds of aspiring authors and poets through my work as creative director for Books For Life Foundation, our not-for-profit organization that assists writers of all ages and skill levels. This has helped me to appreciate the frustration encountered while attempting to become published. Many talented writers give up, believing the odds are too prohibitive. This isn't true if they follow a few simple rules and a proven strategy.

Authors and poets are a reflection of their experiences. Mine include, among others, being a criminal defense lawyer specializing in murder cases, a newspaper publisher (co-founded the *Aspen Daily News*), a network television correspondent and host (*ABC's Good Morning America, CBS's People, CNN, ESPN, BBC,* and *Entertainment Tonight*), a film producer (two feature motion pictures), a television producer (Fox Broadcasting), entertainment attorney, and a radio talk show host. Based on my checkered background, some conclude that I am an interesting fellow. Others categorize me as a roustabout who can't hold a job!

These adventures have provided memorable moments adding to the education of a small-town (Auburn, Indiana, population 5,000) youngster whose first brush with publishing was selling *TV-Guide* door-to-door. Along the way, I have resided in Chicago, Los Angeles,

New York City, San Francisco, and Aspen while traveling to France, Italy, England, Scotland, Switzerland, Luxombourg, and Germany. Doing so has permitted me to witness many different cultures, providing a background rich in history.

Memorable experiences broadening my horizons include a terrifying flight in an F-4 Air Force fighter jet, walking the streets of London with actor Ben Kingsley, riding with actor/driver Paul Newman in his race car, interviewing rock singer Cyndi Lauper in a dumpster outside the Hard Rock Café in San Francisco, and meeting my look-a-like, John Denver. I also have chatted with Larry King about the infamous Jonathan Pollard case, visited the famed Cannes Film Festival, lunched with astronaut Neil Armstrong, and interviewed Miss Nude California (keeping eye contact was difficult).

More than anything, I love books, including the *Bible*, the greatest book ever written, but I didn't begin to write professionally until I reached the age of forty-eight. Prior to 1992, the only professional writing I had attempted was the first draft of a novel. When one literary agent read the manuscript and sent me a terse letter stating that my writing was "sophomoric," I cursed the agent, tossed the manuscript out a window, and decided writing was for literary geniuses, not me. Less than a decade later, I am proud of my published books. Topics have ranged from boxer Mike Tyson to championship golfer Jack Nicklaus, from famed aviator R. A. "Bob" Hoover to golf course designers Pete and Alice Dye, from basketball star Larry Bird to controversial spy Jonathan Pollard, and from perfect game pitcher Don Larsen to Holocaust survivor Cecelia Rexin. Collaboration on a music anthology called *Let The Good Times Roll* with musical historian Larry Goshen has been most rewarding.

Publishers of my books have included large companies (Pocket Books/Simon and Schuster, Balantine/Random House, HarperCollins, Contemporary/McGraw Hill), medium-sized houses (Addison Wesley, Sagamore/Sports Publishing, Taylor, Paragon House), and small companies (Guild Press and Books For Life Foundation). I've learned much from observing their varied methods of operation.

To date, twenty-one editions of my books, including one translated into Japanese, have occupied bookstore shelves around the world. Two works of fiction, *The Patsy, A Jake Lessing Novel*, and *No Peace For The Wicked*, are works in progress. My personal lack of publication in this arena, and the poetry field, does not cause the advice in this book to be invalid for poets and fiction writers. Publisher research and discussion with numerous fiction writers and poets has confirmed that the basic guidelines outlined in *Book Report* pertaining to becoming published apply to all genres of writing.

During my author journey, most critics have been kind, but my first review was shocking. On the morning after my book, *Down For The Count, The Shocking Truth Behind The Mike Tyson Trial*, was released, a radio talk show host telephoned. "Mark," he began, "nice to have you on the program, but do you want to know the crux of the review of your book in the morning newspaper?" Sure, I said, believing it couldn't be *that* bad.

"All right," the host said, "here's the headline, 'Shaw's Book On Tyson Worthless.'"

As my Adam's apple slid to the pit of my stomach, I attempted to muster a response. I mumbled something that made no sense, fumbled through the interview, and hung up. Resisting the temptation to hang myself, I glared at my sleepy-eyed dogs, rose to my feet, and let out a roaring expletive that could be heard in three neighboring states.

Excellent reviews from *USA Today*, the *Boston Globe*, and the *Los Angeles Times* soothed a bruised ego, but the path to becoming an author had begun on a sour note. Nonetheless, it had begun. Instead of moping about the first reviewer's nasty critique, I used it as inspiration and followed book one with book two and book three, and so forth. When book number five, *The Perfect Yankee,* the story of New York Yankees pitcher Don Larsen's perfect game in the 1956 World Series was published, a *New York Times* book reviewer proclaimed the book, "informative and entertaining." Columnists have dubbed me a "prolific writer," a phrase characterizing those who write at a quick pace and manage to publish books on a yearly basis.

The release of *Down For The Count* provided a thrill like no other. When I teach at seminars about the publishing process, I never fail to mention how wonderful it felt to hold a published book in my hands. What satisfaction.

My journey to becoming a published author could fill volumes. Having no professional training as a writer, no college courses on the subject (during five-and-a-half years at Purdue I majored in golf and drinking), no writing workshops, and no knowledge of the publishing industry, I did what came naturally—I winged it!

This applied to writing skills as well. Only after having written several books did I begin to better understand what good writing was all about. My savior was a tiny book called *Elements of Style*, by professors William Strunk, Jr. and E. B. White.

Like me, you too can wing it when you begin your quest to be traditionally published, but based on my publishing experience, I've learned there is a logical progression toward the publication process. The key is to create a terrific book idea, develop a sound strategy toward publication alternatives, and then work hard to implement your gameplan. No one can guarantee success, but the odds for it occurring can be substantially improved.

To assist your efforts, *Book Report* features an Appendix with sample forms for, among others, Query Letters, Book Proposals, Agency and Publishing Contracts, and Promotion Ideas. Throughout the book, charts outline writing tips, how to evaluate a book concept, proper manuscript form, and the main steps involved with the publishing process.

Companion publications to *Book Report* include *Poetry Report*, designed to aid the creative process as well as provide poetry publication options, and *Grammar Report*, basic writing skills for aspiring authors and poets. The software program, *My Book Proposal*, visualizes the form for Query Letters and Book Proposals by featuring easy-to-use templates permitting the writer to create their book information according to industry standards. All are available at **www.booksforlifefoundation.com**.

With careful planning and the guts to stay the course despite rejection, you can become a successful published author or poet. By being attentive to **Mark's Ten Steps To Publication**, a roadmap of sorts based on my experiences, you can savor a moment you will never forget—holding a copy of your published book for all the world to see.

With this in mind, let's unfold the map, consider several useful tips that have proven worthy, and begin the journey so you too can shout to the world: "I am published."

Mark Shaw

A man is known by the company his mind keeps.

THOMAS BAILY ALDERICH

Step #1
Analyze The Publishing Industry
To Gain Confidence

Why Writing?

Let's begin with inspiration. Please repeat after me: **I Will Be Published! Once again—I Will Be Published!**

Thank you. Keep this promise in mind while reading *Book Report*. And remember—**authors and poets are the most important people in the publishing world. Without them, publishers don't exist.**

"Being published" assumes many forms. They include binding several copies of a personal memoir or journal entries for family and friends, writing a magazine or newspaper article, penning a short story or essay for publication in magazines or writer's journals, writing a short article to be published on an Internet site or the company newsletter, crafting a poem to be included in a magazine or anthology collection, writing several poems for inclusion in a poetry book or chapbook, or completing a fiction or non-fiction manuscript that will be self-published or released by a traditional publisher.

This said, whether you have created a book idea, a few sentences, a paragraph or two scribbled on a torn sheet of paper, a chapter outlining characters, partial text ripe for a short story, essay, or magazine article, half of a non-fiction book revealing that Neil Armstrong did *not* walk on the moon, the first draft of the great American novel, or several pages of poetry—**STOP**. Before proceeding, enter the real world of publishing.

To confirm that the quest to become a published author or poet is a priority, ask a basic question: What is your motive for writing? The answer is critical, since the journey generates a wide range of emotions including elation, loneliness, excitement, and frustration.

There are many possible motives for writing. Some people write to prove they can with no desire to have others read their work. Many write with profit in mind even though the creative arts are not about earning huge sums of money. Others want to deliver an important historical message through poetry or non-fiction while still others wish to write a work of fiction to provide escape or entertainment.

Whatever the motivation, the literary profession is based on a **special relationship—the writer and his or her words**. On paper, or a computer screen, you will create word after word producing stanzas, sentences and paragraphs, pages, and ultimately, a book. Along the way you may encounter writer's block, tear up pages, threaten to throw your computer into the nearest dumpster, attempt to kick the loyal dog, and hate the fact you ever decided to write.

Each individual's experience varies, but writing is not for the meek. It's no surprise that many authors and poets become alcoholics, junkies, or lunatics. "The mind is a precious thing," the saying goes, "so don't disturb it." But you *will* disturb it, and it *will* disturb you. When problems surface, you may feel that ANYTHING is better than facing a keyboard or writing another word.

Despite these obstacles, if you accept the challenge to write professionally, then a logical strategy is imperative. **To maximize the odds of becoming published, collect information about the publishing industry, improve your writing skills, learn how to professionally submit material, and conduct research to discover literary agents or publishers who are most likely to represent or publish particular genres of work.** Completion of these tasks won't guarantee a published book, but the chances of it occurring will be increased a hundred-fold.

Book Store Research

Whether you can define the book genre you contemplate, have no clue as to subject matter, or have already written several stanzas, a chapbook, short story, chapters, or a manuscript, **understanding the publishing world is critical**. By examining the current state of affairs in the publishing industry, you can learn much about whether your book idea is commercially viable. If it is not, then the evolution of new ideas, or a different slant to an idea already conceived, may be warranted.

A common error committed by many aspiring authors and poets is to complete a manuscript or collection of poetry while possessing little knowledge of the inner workings of the publishing industry. Writing for publication without researching the literary marketplace is akin to listing a home before assessing its market value. Lack of information decreases the chances of selling the house just as lack of expertise about the publishing industry hinders the potential to be traditionally published by a company that will cover all costs of releasing a book.

Laborious reading or extensive research isn't required to begin a sojourn into the publishing world. Instead, visit a large bookstore or an independent outlet. This scouting mission is guaranteed to enlighten, since bookstores are packed with written works published in many forms and through many means, often involving writer ingenuity and alternative publishing strategies.

Upon entering the bookstore, note the rectangular table or tables positioned within twenty-five feet of the door. Multiple books are stacked on them, carefully positioned to attract attention.

Welcome to the "head tables"—sometimes called the "front-of-store tables." They features books released by the crème de la crème of the publishing industry such as Simon and Schuster, Random House, Doubleday, Penguin, HarperCollins, Warner, Bantam, Knopf, Delacorte, William Morrow, Hyperion, Little Brown, Dutton, and St. Martin's. These companies and others who have hit the jackpot with a book invest promotion and marketing funds so their books will receive maximum exposure. Because the books are chosen by the bookstore buyers and not by publishers (who nevertheless pay for the space), there may be successful books from smaller publishers mixed in.

Studying the head tables (in some stores they are marked "Bestsellers," "New Hardcover," or "New Paperback,"), permits you to determine what genre of books are being marketed at different times of year, what authors are writing them, and what publishing companies have released them. This provides an overall understanding of the machinations of the publishing industry.

The "head tables" may or may not include works of poetry. If not, glance around the bookstore for the area where best selling poetry is displayed. Note the names of notable publishers and make a mental note of what type of poetry is being published by each publisher.

Publishing Industry Overview

While circling the head tables or the area where best selling poetry books are displayed, note the ambience of the bookstore—the whispering of customers discussing which book to purchase while reading snippets from jacket covers or the first pages of the text. At the store's café, people read, flip through magazines, write in notebooks, or type away at a laptop as the aroma of cappuccino drifts through the air.

Remember that those meandering around the store are potential customers for *your* book. They are the very people who may pay as much as $29.95 for a hardback edition. If enough of them can be convinced it is a must-read, a bestseller results.

Pick-up the books on the head tables, feel their texture, and note the colors, the graphics or photographs, and the style of print. During one visit, the table might reveal such books as *The Purpose-Driven Life* by Rick Warren, a special book that is a must-read for everyone, *The DaVinci Code* by Dan Brown, Mitch Albom's *The Five People You Meet In Heaven*, Alice Sebold's *The Lovely Bones*, and Nicholas Sparks' *Nights In Rodanthe*. Poetry headliners might include *Circles On The Water* by Marge Piercy, Walt Whitman's *Leaves of Grass*, and the *Collected Poems of W. B. Yeats*. A popular book for those interested in poetry is Edward Hirsch's *How To Read A Poem and Fall In Love With Poetry*.

Many of these authors are the generals in the current army of contemporary books. Most of the well-known fiction writers could write a book about the disappearance of a lamppost and sell 500,000 copies. They enjoy a following of loyal fans awaiting their next book with heart-stopping anticipation.

While glancing at the books on the head tables, check the titles to reveal which is fiction or non-fiction. It will approximate two to one, fiction to non-fiction, but the ratio varies from week to week. Celebrated authors corner the fiction market, but non-fiction books such as *Tuesdays With Morrie* provide inspiration since sports personality Mitch Albom was a virtual unknown before this book was published. No one could have predicted that it would be on the *New York Times* bestseller list for more than *300* weeks and counting.

Before departing the head tables, open a few books. Read the inside jacket cover text, the author biography, and the back cover text. On the second or third page, the name and location of the publishing company is provided. If poetry is your specialty, do the same with books written by prominent poets.

When glancing at the books, become familiar with the major players in the publishing industry, especially those who may be involved in a specific genre. With this in mind, scribble a note or two listing publishers that have published the type of book envisioned. As the writing process continues, add to the list. When the time arrives to seek publication, the list will be helpful.

To learn more about the team who collaborated to publish a book similar to one under consideration, check the "Acknowledgments" page. Besides the publishing company and the author, the team may include the writer's agent and an editor or editors who championed the book. Note these names for future reference.

Notice the titles and subtitles on the book covers. Jot a few down, since the title is as important to marketing the book as the words written within. Publishers develop ulcers worrying about titles guaranteed to *hook* the reader.

Book Genres

Within a few minutes, you have learned more about the publishing process than you realize. **Since there are few courses teaching the basics of real world publishing, self-education is a necessity.**

Being informed is crucial. Doing so will help with creation of the type of book publishers must add to their list for fear of missing a bestseller.

Further your learning process by walking through the bookstore to view the enormous number of book subjects available. This may trigger book ideas or reveal that a book has already been written on the very subject being contemplated.

Book categories abound and vary somewhat from store to store. They include: Self-Improvement, Cooking, Relationships, Wine and Spirits, Diseases, Addiction/Recovery, Diet, Woman's Health, Teen Series, Beauty and Grooming, Humor, Biography, Games, Sports, World History, Metaphysics, Travel, and Military History. There are also sections marked Music, Study Aids, Religion, Language, Philosophy, Fiction/Literature, Juveniles, Architecture, Art, Science Fiction, Mythology, Personal Finance, Computers, and more.

Surveys vary, but become aware of publishing trends when considering a book idea. Most industry experts agree children's books, published in hardcover and trade paperback, occupy the top two or three spots on the pecking order. Romance novels follow. They usually account for nearly one-half of the mass-market paperbacks (smaller and less expensive than trade paperbacks and hardcovers) purchased each year. Non-fiction books, biographies, autobiographies, self-help, inspiration, and so forth are among the best sellers, with fiction (general trade paperback and hardcover, general fiction, mass-market paperback, and mystery, mass-market paperback) completing the list. To gain a current understanding of which books are selling, consult bestseller lists in various publications.

If you are interested in children's books or poetry, concentrate on these sections while roaming the bookstores. Children's books enthusiasts will discover that companies like Simon and Schuster feature divisions specializing in books for young readers. Children's books enjoy a long shelf life whether they are picture books, books specifically for babies and toddlers, young readers, middle readers, or young adult readers.

Travel books and cookbooks may be potential publications for the budding author. Everyone loves a travel book to aid vacation or business plans. Hundreds of cookbooks are published each year. As with any category researched, pay close attention to current books on the store bookshelves.

Religious books are a popular venue for first-time writers. There is a huge market for religious novels and inspirational books. To date, Rick Warren's *The Purpose-Driven Life*, a book that can literary change your life, has sold more than six million copies.

Poetry lovers should pay attention to imprints of major publishers focusing on poetry releases. Picador, a division of St. Martin's, published *The World As A Lie*, a collection by James Dickey, Penguin released Walt Whitman's *Leaves of Grass*, and Scribner *The Collected Poems of W. B. Yeats*.

Thousands of new works of fiction and non-fiction are released every year based on more than half-a-million submissions to publishing companies. The number of poetry submissions is astronomical, as well. **No wonder many would-be authors and poets are intimidated. Don't be.**

While touring the bookstore, remember your mindset is one of an *aspiring author or poet*, not a *customer*. This is a research mission involving investigation. Plan to spend an afternoon or even a full day or two browsing the shelves. Consider what is being written, how the books look and feel, their length, and how they are presented. **Each book has its own self-contained marketing program designed with one thing in mind: sell the book.**

With this goal in mind, examine the packaging, the cover, and how the author or poet is showcased. Reading the author or poet's biography on the inside back jacket cover will provide insight as to his or her background and their previous publications. Inspiration is garnered from first-time authors and poets who have been published.

The type of writing contemplated—fiction, non-fiction, or poetry will dictate the amount of time you spend in that particular area. Focus on books released in recent years. With so many books published, and so little space, only books that sell remain on the shelves. Many *front-list* books (recent releases) become *backlist* assets that will sell year after year. Others have their fifteen minutes of fame, and are returned to the publisher or banished to the "remainder" bin marked at two bucks a copy.

Nobody can predict exactly what book will become a bestseller. Some books appear to have *bestseller* stamped on them, but many times the so-called experts don't know and are guided by "hunches." Who could have predicted that a number one non-fiction business bestseller would be Spencer Johnson's *Who Moved My Cheese?* Some publishing company editors may have rejected the book assuming it was a booklet about the plight of Wisconsin dairy farmers.

Checking the fiction bestsellers provides a few surprises. There are the predictable names—John Grisham, Tom Clancy, James Patterson, Mary Higgins Clark, and Stephen Coonts. But among the bestsellers is the *Left Behind* collection by Tim LaHaye and Jerry B. Jenkins, little-known authors before their breakthrough books, and *A Girl Named Zippy*, by first-time author Haven Kimmel.

Successful poetry books include those by Billy Collins, Julianna Baggott, and J. Allen Rossner. They have developed a wide following.

Reference Magazines

To learn more about book publishing and outlets for publishing articles or short stories, check the magazine section. To complete the first day's "training" regarding the book business, select publications such as *Publisher's Weekly, The New York Times Sunday Edition, Writer's Digest, The Writer's Handbook, Writer's Journal, Poetry Magazine, Poets and Writers* Magazine, **and** *The Writer.* Just as those immersed in the financial world consult *Forbes* to stay abreast of developments in that field, these publications are a guidepost to what's occurring in the book world.

Other sources of knowledge about the publishing industry are publications by chain bookstores and *Book Sense*, a directive of books recommended by independent outlets. Each provides insight regarding current trends in the publishing industry.

Publisher's Weekly

Publisher's Weekly **is a must read for aspiring authors and poets.** The first half features advertisements for new releases, publishing news detailing sales records, the revolving door shifts of executives from company to company, and the names of authors signed to write new books. These include celebrities who are advanced a million dollars to write about the color of their toothbrush and the epiphanies that surfaced during their rehab. One year, it seemed every issue carried news of yet another body part that actress/author/fitness guru Suzanne Somers could perfect.

Publishing excesses aside, becoming familiar with the names of those in positions of power in the literary industry is important because they are the ones who consider a book for publication. Even if a book concept is rejected, the person rejecting it may rotate to a new literary agency or publishing company and later consider another book written by the same author. This is why it is wise to never write a nasty letter after being rejected. Accept the decision and move on.

The middle pages of *Publisher's Weekly* feature interviews with publishing heavyweights or successful authors. Valuable tips emerge based on their experiences.

Several pages near the back of *Publisher's Weekly* are dedicated to reviews of books being published in the coming months. They are catalogued under the banners of fiction, non-fiction, audio, poetry, and paperback. This section keeps the writer current on the latest news about books being published, while providing insight into reviewers comments regarding their content and potential.

Included with the review section is a column titled, "Poetry Notes." In one issue, the magazine featured information about publications such as *Poetry In Motion From Coast to Coast, Good Poems*, and *Poems For America: 125 Poems That Celebrate the American Experience.*

Another issue of *Publisher's Weekly* was of special interest to aspiring novelists. Under the banner, "First Fiction For Fall," the magazine lists several publications by first-time authors. The list provided ideas as well as inspiration to those who believe the odds of a first-time author securing a publishing commitment are prohibitive.

Spring and fall editions of *Publisher's Weekly* are important for authors and poets. They feature multiple pages listing book titles being released during that season. These pages provide insight into publishers and the types of books each company favors. It also presents a glimpse of the varied subject matter that becomes fodder for publication. Keep in mind that one season's hot topics may be cold by the time a new book on the subject is written.

New York Times

The *New York Times Sunday Edition* supplements *Publisher's Weekly*. **Other newspapers feature book review supplements, but the *New York Times Book Review* is king.** Read it several times to soak up every ounce of knowledge. Advertisements touting books are interesting and valuable, reviews are revealing, and the bestseller list indicates what books people are reading.

One fiction list included two diverse books, *Full Tilt*, by Janet Evanovich, and *Mrs. Dalloway*, by Virginia Woolf, the classic 1925 novel about a day in the life of Clarissa Dalloway.

Heading the non-fiction list was *Catch Me If You Can*, by Frank W. Abagnale, a memoir of life on the lam by a former con man, imposter, and escape artist. Also listed was the surprise hit, *Seabiscuit* by Laura Hillenbrand and *Bias,* by Bernard Goldberg, an account of a former CBS television journalist about how the media distorts the news.

For those interested in business books, the *Times* feature a separate listing in the business section under "Business Bestsellers." Note the variety of book topics. One list included Jack Welch's *Jack, Straight From The Gut,* Spencer Johnson's *Who Moved My Cheese?, Fish!* by Stephen C. Lundin, and *Swimming Across*, Intel co-founder Andrew Grove's memoir.

The *Times* includes two other lists of interest to aspiring authors. They are bestsellers for "Advice, How-To and Miscellaneous," and "Children's Paperback Books." Both are excellent reference sources.

Reading these lists and those in *Publisher's Weekly* provides hope for the beginning writer. **No idea is sacred. It doesn't take a genius to discover a unique concept for a book that can be worthy. Imagination is the key. Never doubt your ability to create an exciting book that can be a bestseller.**

Writer's Digest

Writer's Digest is a required reading for any beginning writer. No reviews or bestseller lists are featured—just pertinent information about writing and writers. The articles are valuable, since many contain tips concerning the craft of writing.

Various articles in *Writer's Digest* have included: *How To Build A Novel Proposal, Inspiration 101, The Insider's Guide to Software For Writer's, 100 Best Book Markets For New Writers, How Not To Be A Paperback Writer,* and *How To Set Your Writing Goals.*

Another feature of *Writer's Digest* is a list of popular reference books for writers. Among them are *Discovering the Writer Within, Grammatically Correct, Fast Fiction, The Writer's Guide to Character Traits, Novel Writing, Get Organized, Get Published, Keys To Great Writing,* and *The Writer's Idea Book.* These books provide information regarding every facet of the writing profession.

Several examples of book text are featured in the magazine as are tips regarding selling manuscripts. There is information about writing workshops conducted by professional authors and advertisements for writing competitions such as the John T. Lupton $25,000 "New Voices In Literature" Awards presented by Books For Life Foundation. The competition rewards aspiring authors for their Book Proposal and Query Letter expertise. Details are available at www.booksforlifefoundation.com.

Certain issues of *Writer's Digest* chronicle the inner-workings of major publishers including HarperCollins, Simon and Schuster, Time Warner, Random House, and Penguin Group USA. These publishers account for more than 75 percent of all books sold. The *Literary Market Place*, available in most libraries, is an excellent reference source supplementing information featured in *Writer's Digest.*

The Writer's Handbook and Writer's Journal

The Writer's Handbook contains essential information for the writer. Besides delivering a competent list of agents and publishers of books and magazine articles, the publication provides insightful articles by noted authors. Among those who have contributed are John Updike, Elmore Leonard, Sue Grafton, Russell Banks, and Stephen King. Much can be learned from their experiences regarding how to become a published author.

A worthy magazine for aspiring authors is *Writer's Journal*. One issue featured an interview with Mitchell Ivers, senior editor at Simon and Schuster. Asked about company philosophy, Ivers stated, "The mid-list [books by established writer's that sell well but not great] is vanishing—especially in the mystery genre. Book stores don't want them and we're cutting way back on them." He added, "[the] exception to that rule is in the romance area."

When asked what type of book he hopes to discover, Ivers said, "Stories of people's lives. I like stories about people who say yes to life when life says no to them. I like books that help people; that last and linger in the reader's minds." Regarding advice for the beginning writer, the senior editor wrote, **"Don't write for the reward: the book contract, fame, money. Write for the love of writing, find value in what you're saying and be passionate about it."**

Poets and Writers Magazine/Poetry Magazine

Poets and Writers Magazine is a prestigious publication packed with useful information for aspiring writers and poets. Founded in 1970 to "foster the development of poets and fiction writers and to promote communication throughout the literary community," the magazine presents vital facts about every aspect of the writing process. Published bi-monthly, one issue featured *8 Editor's Tips On Getting In The Glossies*, as well as sections detailing *News and Trends, The Literary Life*, and *The Practical Writer*. Special notices and advertisements for awards, grants, conferences, and residencies are also included.

Another excellent source of information for poets is *Poetry Magazine*. Checking their Web site at www.poetrymagazine.com provides current information about the poetry-publishing world. The magazine sponsors the Ruth Lilly Poetry Prize, an annual competition awarding a deserving poet, $100,000.

BookExpo America

To expand publishing industry education, consider a trip to the annual BookExpo America convention. Locations have included Chicago, New York City, and Los Angeles. More information is available at www.bookexpoamerica.com.

Colorful booths spanning several halls house the majority of the publishers across the country. Large publishers occupy the largest, most expensive space. Medium sized and smaller publishers, including university presses, are also well represented.

Walking amongst the booths is electrifying. Large placards promoting books by the famous and not so famous drape booth walls. Long lines snake around corners as fans line up to meet, greet, and obtain the autographs of famous authors.

Publishing company representatives mingle with retailers, their authors, poets, the media, and distributors from around the world. An event or one-day admission price permits writers to frolic with those who *are* the publishing industry. During the event at Chicago's McCormick Place, several social events were held to permit those who love books to chat with those who love books. A local book fair was featured so book enthusiasts could locate a rare copy of Steinbeck for a buck-and-a-half.

BookExpo America presents the perfect arena for aspiring authors and poets to meet independent booksellers from around the world. **Even though chain stores rule the industry, there are superb independent outlets.** Knowing the owners and their sales force can prove invaluable, since independents champion first-time authors and poets.

Each BookExpo America registrant is provided a convention guide that is a great resource for any aspiring author or poet. Included are the listings of the exhibitors. Inspect it, discover who is appearing and where, and then visit exhibits, meet people, and note what books are being promoted. Display posters highlight major marketing campaigns being planned.

Most BookExpo America publishing company booths are piled high with catalogs focusing on future releases. Galleys (review copies of soon-to-be-released books) are sometimes available although many publishers attempt to limit these "freebees" to retailers. Studying various writing styles and storytelling variations for future books can be most helpful.

The point of attending BookExpo America is to meet and greet while exchanging business cards. Networking with agents, publishing executives and others immersed in the industry is essential. After the convention, add the names of those met to ever-growing lists compiled in anticipation of submitting material to the marketplace.

If attending BookExpo America is impossible, consider visiting an American Bookseller (sponsor of BookExpo) regional book show. These are great venues to meet smaller and regional publishers.

For those interested in the potential to meet industry professionals at consumer book shows, research such venues as LA Book Fest, NY is Book Country, and the Miami Book Fest. All provide opportunities to soak up the atmosphere of the book business.

The Internet

To supplement knowledge you gained through bookstores, publications, and BookExpo, check the Internet web sites where books are marketed and sold. Look at Amazon.com and Barnes&noble.com in particular. This is another source of bestseller information as well as information regarding how books are being promoted online. It is also a good way to search for other published books that may compete with the book being contemplated.

An excellent source of publishing industry news is the Internet publication, *Publishers Lunch*. Its free daily dose of news regarding "who is buying what from whom" is valuable. *Publishers Lunch* is free of charge at www.publisherslunch.com.

Education is Power

Knowledge regarding the business end of the publishing industry is power for those who dream of writing professionally. Instead of pursuing the dream half-cocked, those who investigate the publishing world can make their dream come true. They bear allegiance to **Mark's Step #1—Analyze The Publishing Industry to Gain Confidence**.

With this understanding, and an understanding of the writing process, it is logical for you to ask, **"How can I become published?"**

There are several alternatives, but the path to being published by a traditional publisher is quite logical. In its simplest form, a writer first generates an idea for a book. Based on an outline, the writer creates at least a partial manuscript that develops the idea, while the poet selects several poems for inclusion in their collection.

Using this material, a Query Letter and Book Proposal is completed. Either through their own efforts or those of a literary agent or entertainment attorney, the Query Letter and/or Book Proposal is submitted to one or more publishers. **If a publisher says the magic word, "Yes," a deal is negotiated.**

The author revises the book in tandem with an editor at the publishing company. A release date is set, usually months or even a year ahead to provide time for editing, book layout, and a marketing and promotion campaign. The completed book is then published amidst a grand celebration.

Getting from point A (idea) to point Z (publication) is a magical mystery tour filled with adventure. Regardless of whether you choose fiction, non-fiction or poetry, the journey begins with a search for what literary material is marketable in the publishing world.

Step #1 Summary

- **Visit chain bookstores or independent outlets to research the book industry.**

- **Check book covers, inside jackets, and Acknowledgments for publisher, author, agent, and editor information.**

- **Compile lists of agents, editors, and publishers that may be interested in your book genre.**

- **Review publishing industry reference publications such as *Publisher's Weekly, New York Times, Writer's Digest, Book*, etc.**

- **Consider attending the annual BookExpo America convention Writer's Program.**

Some books are to be tasted, others to be swallowed, and some few to be chewed and digested.

FRANCIS BACON

Step #2
Write A Story You Are Passionate About— One That Is Marketable

Short Stories, Magazine Articles, Essays

"Damn the torpedoes, full speed ahead" is one way to begin the writing process. But just as a baseball player with dreams of playing in the major leagues begins his quest in the minors, a bit of seasoning is warranted before you plunge into the world of writing for publication.

This seasoning involves writing short stories, essays, magazine or newspaper articles, or poetry for mainstream publications. Doing so teaches the discipline of writing with space and word constraint to produce good beginnings, middles, and ends to stories. For poets, it is the opportunity to test their mettle in a single poem or two.

Another benefit of writing short-form material is the ability to test linguistic skills and begin developing a personal writing style. The process may also help you decide whether to write fiction, non-fiction, or poetry.

Most important, publication of short stories, essays, newspaper articles or poetry provides a showcase for your talent while earning you a publishing credit. The latter will prove helpful when you seek publication for long-form fiction or non-fiction material, or a collection of poetry.

Many celebrated authors began by writing magazine and newspaper articles, and short stories. Among them was Ernest Hemingway. His talent was recognized while he wrote for publications such as *Atlantic Monthly* and *The Toronto Star*.

Several modern day magazines, including *Esquire, GQ, Harper's, Jane, Playboy, Seventeen,* and *Zoetrope,* print short works of fiction. Publications like *Vanity Fair, Atlantic Monthly*, and *Ladies Home Journal,* among others, will consider short works of non-fiction.

One author who gained exposure by writing short stories is Terry McMillan, best selling African-American author of *How Stella Got Her Groove Back*. She began reading literary works by African-

American writers while shelving books at a Port Huron, Michigan library at age sixteen. While majoring in journalism at UC Berkeley, she wrote *The End*, her first short story. When it was published, it provided a springboard for her long-form efforts.

Mary Higgins Clark, author of several best selling mysteries, jump-started her career by writing short stories. The first sold for $100 to *Extension Magazine* after six years and more than forty rejection slips. This modest success stimulated Clark, who wrote *Aspire To The Heavens*, a novel about the life of George Washington. It was a dismal failure, but her second effort, *Where Are The Children*, proved successful. This book paved the way for such bestsellers as *Before I Say Goodbye, Deck The Halls*, and *The Street Where You Live.*

J. K. Rowling, famous for the Harry Potter series, began her career by writing short stories. While attempting to complete two novels, she conceived a "what-if" idea. It focused on a young boy who didn't realize he was a wizard. The skills she had honed writing short stories enabled her to complete *Harry Potter and the Sorcerer's Stone*. It was published a year later to wide acclaim, catapulting Rowling to international fame.

Charles Dickens garnered experience as a newspaper reporter before turning to long-form writing. He then wrote short texts to accompany a series of humorous sport illustrations. Next came *The Pickwick Papers.* It led to *Oliver Twist, Nicholas Nickleby,* the first of Dickens' successful Christmas stories, *A Christmas Carol, A Tale of Two Cities*, and *David Copperfield.*

Poets gain credentials through publication of their poetry in reputable magazines and journals. Publishers scan these publications searching for new talent.

Seasoning for me occurred when I wrote several columns for *USA Today* during the Mike Tyson trial. The credit led to a publishing commitment for *Down For The Count.* To those who scanned my manuscript, I wasn't a novice writer with little credibility, but rather one who had been published in a national newspaper.

If you decide to write short stories, educate yourself about this form of writing. The easiest way is to return to the bookstores and focus on the classics. Look for anthologies of short stories by a variety of famed authors. These will expose you to several examples of good writing. Pay attention as to how the authors formulated the beginning, middle, and end of their stories.

Celebrated author Elmore Leonard stated, "Read and study what the writer is doing. Find a writer you have a rapport with, and study the paragraphing, study the punctuation, study everything." William Zinsser, author of *On Writing Well*, echoes Leonard's comments. He wrote, **"Writing is learned by imitation. If anyone asked me how I learned to write, I'd say I learned by reading the men and women who were doing the kind of writing I wanted to do and trying to figure out how they did it."**

Resource Material For Short Stories, Magazine Articles and Poetry

Marketplace information for short stories or magazine articles is easily obtainable. Several books listing publications accepting unsolicited submissions are released each year, but *Writer's Market* is most inclusive. The cover of one edition promised, "75 Literary Agents, 1000+ All New Publishing Opportunities, 1400 Consumer Magazines, 450+ Trade Magazines, 1100 Book Publishers." There is also *Writer's Market—Online, Children's Writer's and Illustrator's Market, Christian Writer's Market Guide*, and *The Writer's Handbook*.

For the poet, *Poet's Market* is the standard bearer of the poetry-publishing world. From cover to cover, it provides tips on all aspects of the poetry publishing process including potential markets for submission and requirements regarding form and substance.

Submitting written work to the outlets in the proper form is critical. *Writer's Market* and *Poet's Market* provide battle-tested suggestions. Following the guidelines suggested is key, since editors seek professionals who know the rules.

Once you've conceived a short story, magazine article, or poem, compile a list of publications most likely to accept it. There are several with outstanding reputations including *The Paris Review, Rosebud, The Magazine For People Who Enjoy Good Writing, Poets and Writers Magazine, Ploughshares, Stone Soup, The American Scholar,* and *The New Yorker*. Being published by them is an honor. A former editor at Simon and Schuster ordered his underlings to scour such publications scouting for potential writers.

Depending on your area of interest, read the above-mentioned magazines as well as *Vanity Fair, Atlantic Monthly, Harper's, Omni, Rolling Stone, Seventeen, Reader's Digest, PC Computing, Esquire, Gentleman's Quarterly, Cigar, Ms., Oprah, Ladies Home Journal, Washingtonian,* and *Ellery Queen's Mystery Magazine.* Reading good writing helps you develop good writing skills, and ideas for books abound in the pages of top magazines. From an article in *Vanity Fair,* I developed an idea for a book about a teenage computer wizard employed by the government to slay cyberspace terrorists.

Poetry publications of note include *Poets and Writers, Poetry Magazine,* the *Kenyon Review, Glimmer Train, Atlantic Monthly,* and the *Atlanta Review.* Libraries are good sources for these publications.

Be selective when choosing publications for submission of material. It is unprofessional to submit an article to a magazine that does not publish that genre of material. Sending an article on raising Argentine llamas to *Architectural Digest* is embarrassing and signals to the publisher that you have not done your homework.

Newspaper Experience

Writing newspaper articles or columns provides another source of education and exposure for aspiring authors. Writing with word count restrictions forces one to be brief and to the point. Journalists face deadlines, providing a discipline helpful when publishers demand revisions within a certain time frame.

The journalist hones editorial skills and investigative methods that prove worthy when writing long-form. Becoming a competent reporter, columnist, or freelance writer provides credentials that impress publishers, since the sucessful journalist has name recognition, a proven track record, and a readership that may purchase books.

To gain notice for your writings, consider an op-ed column, letters to the editor, or other means to gain publication. Every time your words reach a readership, you add to your writing credential.

One misconception in literary circles is that writing short stories or articles is inferior to writing long-form. There is an expertise to both, but being restricted by a word count may prove more challenging than writing a book the length of *Gone With The Wind.*

Fiction Or Non-Fiction

Whether to write fiction or non-fiction is an important decision for the author with publishing aspirations. If you have inclinations toward both, try both. Write a few chapters, a short story, or an article portraying a true-life event. Then let your imagination flow. Decide which provides more satisfaction, since writing with passion is essential to future success.

The decision to write fiction or non-fiction should not be made without considering an important question: **Is it easier to become a published author by writing in one genre or the other?**

There is no clear consensus as to whether fiction or non-fiction provides a better stepping-stone to a career as an author, but far more works of fiction are presented to literary agents and publishers than non-fiction. **With so much competition, the odds of success for a first-time author of fiction are diminished.** This is because publishers realize it is normally the *author* who is the star since readers return to purchase books by authors whom they have enjoyed before.

Non-fiction may provide more opportunity. First-time authors with a "platform" (expertise in a particular subject) abound, since generally **the *subject matter* is as important as the name of the author on the book cover.** Publishers recognized that the true story focusing on discharge of chemical waste by a large corporation portrayed in *A Civil Action* was the star, not the unknown author, Jonathan Harr. A similar situation occurred following the terrorist attacks on the United States when several books by unknown authors about the Taliban, Osama bin Laden, Afghanistan, and chemical warfare became bestsellers.

As with all rules of thumb, there are exceptions. Non-fiction is a broad genre including how-to and instructional books, biography, inspirational books, humor, and what is known as "narrative non-fiction"—true stories unfolding in much the same storytelling pattern as fiction. Authors of narrative non-fiction can also become superstars with a dedicated readership, as did Jon Krakauer, author of *Into Thin Air* and *Into The Wild*, or Stephen Ambrose, author of *Undaunted Courage*. Editors reviewing narrative non-fiction submissions look for many of the same qualities they seek with fiction—**a compelling story with unforgettable characters written in page-turning style.**

An exception to the author being the star of fiction may occur when the subject matter of the novel focuses on a headline-making topic. During the period following the Washington D.C. area sniper attacks, novels featuring themes about serial killers were popular.

Marie Butler-Knight, the publisher of Alpha Books, an imprint of Penguin Group USA, believes the genre of non-fiction can make all the difference regarding publishing potential. "Generalizations can be dangerous because there are different types of non-fiction," she says. "How-to/informational books are easier to break in with *if* you have subject matter expertise. If you're a generalist author, you better have a subject matter expert as a co-author or you'll have a hard time convincing a publisher to publish you."

Regarding biographies and narrative non-fiction, Butler-Knight disagrees with those who believe the genres are totally story-driven. "In order to succeed, these types of books need to tell compelling stories," she states. "They require the same sort of writing skills as fiction. To a publisher, this sort of work is totally author-driven and every bit as risky as publishing fiction."

The publishing world's view toward fiction and non-fiction is symbolized through the comments of Jane von Mehren, executive editor of Penguin Books. She told *Writer's Digest*, "Non-fiction has become a strong, sophisticated area . . . **In many ways, non-fiction is easier to publish than fiction because it targets a very definable audience, and it's easier to package books and target them to specific readers."** She added, "It's a booming area. **In non-fiction, we look for books that will have a long shelf life, offering solid information and advice useful for years to come.** It really helps when a non-fiction author is already an expert in his or her field, and the book builds on an existing platform."

Von Mehren stated, "**In fiction, we're looking for a breakthrough story that will have a long life in trade paperback . . .** Trade paperback fiction is gaining momentum, with excellent literary titles getting broader exposure . . . An unknown writer can break through with a great story. For an editor, that discovery is still an incomparable thrill."

Whether to attempt to dent the traditional publishing industry with works of fiction or non-fiction is the writer's preference, but John Baker, a fixture at *Publisher's Weekly* for years and a noted expert on the book industry, reveals interesting statistics he learned from a top literary agent. "I'm told that 95% of the material that agents receive is fiction," he said. "And that they sell 5%. Of the 5% of non-fiction that lands on their desk, they sell 95%."

The First Book

Launch of a first book is critical to planning a professional writing career. Combining passion for the subject matter with marketability is a key.

Developing a work of fiction demands that you investigate the marketplace. Your story must provide a unique perspective on a topic that will titillate the reader. **"What if" scenarios are a popular launching pad for aspiring novelists.** They permit creative speculation that can stir a reader's imagination.

One author in favor of this method is John Irving. Creator of such classics as *Hotel New Hampshire, The Cider House Rules*, and *The World According To Garp*, Irving discusses the "What if" scenario in the Acknowledgments section of *The Fourth Hand*, a fascinating tale about a television newscaster whose left hand is eaten by a lion. After stating that it was his wife Janet who asked the compelling question, "What if the donor's widow demands visitation rights with the [donated] hand?" Irving admits, "Every novel I have written has begun with a "What if . . .?

A common thread in successful novels is the inclusion of a love story. It can be between man and woman, man and man, woman and woman, parent and child, human and animal, or patriot and country. Writers are strongly advised to include this element because few novels prove successful if they don't weave a terrific love story into the mix.

A staple for aspiring authors to consider in the non-fiction arena is the biography. Well-researched books chronicling the lives of famous people have launched many a writing career.

If the subject is still alive, permission may be required unless this person is a public figure. Publishers regard "authorized biographies" of living subjects as preferable, but "unauthorized biographies" are commonplace.

Before proceeding with a biography, or any book, consult *Books in Print*, Amazon.com, publisher's websites, and other sources to discover whether a similar book on the same topic has been published. If it has, read a copy to explore storytelling methods and determine how you can differentiate your book from others already on the market.

If a novel or biography on your subject has already been published, don't be deterred from pursuing the subject yourself if you can present a fresh slant on the story. There may be 2000-plus books dealing with the JFK/Oswald assassinations, but none has been written telling the story through the eyes of the famous attorney Melvin Belli. He represented Jack Ruby, Lee Harvey Oswald's assassin. My research has provided strong suspicion that Belli was hired by the underworld to discredit, and in effect, silence Ruby. This became one of the themes for *Code of Silence, Melvin Belli, Jack Ruby, and the Assassination of Lee Harvey Oswald.*

If you are a poet, research the marketplace to learn what poetry is selling and why. Since public taste changes as often as the seasons, poets must stay current. Reading recently released books or chapbooks provides clues as to what is marketable. **Passion for the material you write is paramount, but understanding publishing trends will enhance the opportunity for you to secure the first publishing commitment.**

Book Scope

Many beginning writers with traditional publishing aspirations decide to write a book about a subject too small in scope. One writer told me his book idea about a cyberspace killer stalking fellow players of a video game. The idea was unique, but the stakes weren't high enough to garner interest from agents or publishers. I suggested one of the players be the son of the Secretary of Defense. The twist elevated the story to provide a national scope, one affecting an official of the United States government.

The non-fiction arena provides similar challenges. **Whether your work is a biography, chronicle of an event, or debate of an important issue, the scope must be of significant importance to gain national interest.** Otherwise agents or publishers will pass believing the book audience is limited.

Poetry collections should be wide in scope. The poet with aspirations to be published should ask: "Who is the audience for this book?" Hopefully the audience includes a wide array of readers so an agent or publisher recognizes the work's potential.

Many authors and poets want to write an autobiographical story about special events occurring in their life. There are exceptions, but most often the scope of such a story is too limited to interest a literary agent or publisher. One writer focused his book on a youth summer camp he attended where a tragic death occurred. The story was important to him, but too personal to interest a broad readership. I suggested he write about another topic. When he becomes well established, perhaps the summer camp story will have a greater chance of success.

Assessing the market potential for any book you contemplate is essential. Literary agent Caroline Carney suggests aspiring authors estimate anticipated sales before contacting a literary agent or publisher. "One of the easiest benchmarks," she states, "is to look at the size of the most popular association in your field (or, in the case of fiction, in a field reflecting the enthusiasm of your main character)." Carney further advises writers to visit the library and consult *Bacon's Magazine Directory* to discover the circulation size of the largest magazine catering to their primary reader's particular interest, or to note sales figures listed on paperback reprints of popular titles in a particular genre.

Carney believes the aspiring author must pay attention to guidelines within his or her field of interest. "Those contemplating a sports book," she explains, "should adhere to the old saying, 'the smaller the ball, the higher the sales.'" This means literary agents and/or publishers, based on past sales figures, will be more interested in books about golf, tennis, and baseball than they will about football or basketball.

Collaboration

Many authors increase the likelihood of being published through collaboration. They agree to assist a celebrity or collaborate with a successful author to tell their story.

When considering a book idea, search for a subject you believe the reading audience will be curious about. Doing so resulted in my second book.

For years I had been a friend of, and the lawyer for, noted golf course architect Pete Dye. He and his gifted wife Alice were responsible for creating many innovative golf courses around the world. The courses continued the Scottish tradition by featuring pot bunkers, railroad ties, unruly heather, surly mounds, and small greens producing a phenomenon called "target golf." Among their masterpieces was the TPC course in Jacksonville, Florida, featuring the famed island green, PGA West with bunkers so deep golfers disappeared in them, and Teeth of the Dog, a showcase of Dye's genius in the Dominican Republic where seven breathtaking holes border the Caribbean.

At a nearby course called LaRomana Country Club, inspiration occurred while Pete and I were competing in the Sugar Open, an annual tournament. On the 10th hole, I faced a second shot to a par five. I was certain I could loft the ball onto the green setting up an opportunity for an eagle. I selected a 4-wood only to hear Pete say, "You can't hit the ball on the green from here." Chuckling, I said I could, but he repeated the warning. Pete then proceeded to explain how he had designed the hole and why the easiest and smartest way to play it was to hit a medium-iron down the right fairway to set up a simple third shot. I accepted his advice, and made a birdie, but it occurred to me that Pete's design strategy needed to be recorded. The result was the collaboration; *Bury Me In A Pot Bunker, Golf Through The Eyes of the Game's Most Challenging Course Designer.*

A second collaboration with the Dye family, this time with Alice, resulted in the book, *From Birdies To Bunkers.* Packed with vignettes providing insight into Alice's remarkable amateur golf career, and her success as a pioneer for women's rights, *From Birdies To Bunkers* is inspirational as well as informational.

Collaborations have permitted many successful writers to launch "solo careers." The publishing credit is a key. Collaborating with famed aviator R. A. "Bob" Hoover on his autobiography, *Forever Flying,* provided me with a strong credential when Pocket Books, a division of Simon and Schuster, a major publisher, published the book.

Some writers collaborate on books, whether fiction or non-fiction, with authors who possess a publishing track record. Doing so permits them to piggyback on the author's credentials to gain the all-important first publishing commitment.

Collaboration unfolds under two different circumstances. The first involves participation as a **ghostwriter.** This is a behind-the-scenes writer normally provided no book cover credit, but a sizable paycheck. Many writers earn a decent living as ghostwriters. They prove they can collaborate and write a competent book. This adds to their resumes when they attempt to publish their own work.

Essential to a ghostwriting arrangement, or for that matter collaboration, is timing. When the celebrity is "hot," publishers want to take advantage of the sudden fame. As a ghostwriter, you may face grueling deadlines, but it is important to remember quality is imperative. I turned down a "quickie" biography of Tiger Woods since I did not feel I could write it in a professional manner within a few weeks.

A better alternative to ghostwriting is to collaborate with a celebrity or well-known author, gain a credit, and earn some money. While collaborating with a celebrity, don't forget that you are not writing for yourself, but in the "voice" of the subject. Credibility can be lost if the speech usage does not reflect the celebrity's.

If you decide collaboration with a well-known personality is an option, compile a list of celebrities from the world of entertainment, sports, business, or government service. *People Magazine, Entertainment Weekly, Biography,* and *Premiere* are publications that may provide book ideas.

Before you contact literary agents representing celebrities or the celebrities themselves, be prepared to present a unique angle or slant to the book you contemplate. Consider a memoir or a book about an important issue. For instance, if you know that a certain celebrity has supported the plight of Costa Rican refugees and you believe a book would be worthy, contact them through their agent.

Never be intimidated to approach a celebrity personally or through an agent. At worst, he or she will say no. It's important to be persistent if you believe your idea for the book can succeed. Always be prepared with a fifteen to twenty word pitch, an outline, and a biography listing any writing credentials.

Financial matters regarding collaboration are simple. A fifty-fifty partnership regarding expenses and revenues is realistic, but many collaborating authors receive less. The agreement should be in writing to alleviate misunderstandings in the future. A sample collaboration agreement is presented in the Appendix as a guidepost. You can tailor this agreement to your specific facts and circumstances, or better yet, retain an entertainment attorney familiar with such contracts to assist you.

Beware of celebrities possessing an ego the size of the solar system. Find one who is secure. This ensures that you can write the story and not be inhibited by a subject who changes his or her mind regarding what will be published. The fear of publication can occur after your subject has revealed information never before disclosed. This reluctance to "tell-all" is why most books *about* a celebrity are a better read than those *by* the celebrity.

Book Ideas

Book concepts spring into the mind from all directions. Remember Muhammad Ali's famous quote, "The man who has no imagination has no wings."

Writers must develop strong antennae to avoid missing an idea or event that may provide fodder for a book. Ideas are everywhere (H. L. Menchen wrote, "There are no dull subjects. There are only dull writers."), and success can strike like a lightning bolt out of the blue.

Asked how he decided to write *Ragtime*, E. L. Doctorow stated, "[Inspiration] can be anything. It can be a voice, an image; it can be a deep moment of personal desperation. With *Ragtime*, I was facing the wall of my study in my house in New Rochelle and so I started to write about the wall. Then I wrote about the house that was attached to the wall. It was built in 1906, you see, so I thought about the era . . And one thing led to another and that's the way the book began."

William Faulkner's classic, *The Sound and the Fury* was inspired, he swore, "with a mental picture." The picture, he wrote, "was of the muddy seat of a little girl's drawers in a pear tree, where she could see through a window where her grandmother's funeral was taking place."

Author Simon Garfield provides a good example of someone birthing a unique idea. His book, *Mauve,* is the history of the purplish color invented by English teenager William Perkin in 1856. Another is the writings of Richard Hamblyn. His book, *The Invention of Clouds,* surveys the landscape with a passionate tone.

Best selling author James Patterson (*Along Came A Spider, Kiss The Girls*), a former advertising executive at J. Walter Thompson, uses a creative pattern. He told *Writer's Digest*, "I have a big folder of ideas and when it comes time for me to write a new book, I'll pull it out and go over everything that's in there." Patterson then picks two or three ideas from the folder and writes them down. "Then I write a page or two on each to begin to see if there is a story I like," he says.

In addition to an "idea folder," I keep a small green notebook in my pocket. It contains a "book idea" page, and pages listing books in progress. When an idea pops into my head, I write it down. In August of 2001, I was consumed with a "what if" idea regarding an invasion of the United States. I noted it in my notebook. A month later, much to my sorrow, the terrorist attacks at the World Trade Center and the Pentagon occurred. The "what if" had become reality.

Some ideas take longer to develop than others. I met the legendary San Francisco attorney Melvin Belli in the mid-1980s. He was a swashbuckling character right out of a romance novel—the Ernest Hemingway of the legal profession. Even though we lost contact after I left California, I was fascinated with "The King of Torts" and his role in defending Lee Harvey Oswald's killer, Jack Ruby. The idea to write about Mr. Belli and the Ruby case ruminated for fifteen years, but finally the time was right.

The search-for-the-truth path to non-fiction presents many great opportunities for the writer. The book can be investigative featuring little known, fresh facts about a subject. Other non-fiction areas of interest might be "How-To" books, inspirational material, straight interview books, and satirical material poking fun at politicians or sports figures.

Novelists, such as nine-year-old Sam Spahn, author of *Krill-Guy, The Adventures of an Invincible Penguin*, discover ideas from true stories, personal experiences, or the "what if" scenarios. Although personal experiences may fuel your inspiration, remember to give your story a universal twist so others can relate to it. A useful reference is *Novel Ideas*, penned by Barbara Shoup and Margaret Love Denman. The book features information about the creative process and the thoughts and ideas of twenty-four prominent authors.

For young writers, *Writing For Children & Teenagers* by Lee Wyndham is a useful reference book. The book promises to "tackle the special problems of writing for the young, and of writing for the look 'n' listen age."

For aspiring poets, the world is the classroom. The "idea book" mentioned is a must since there is inspiration everywhere. Poets must grab ideas and phrases as they float by.

Person

Books can be written in first, second, or third person. When you are deciding which writing tool to employ, the question is whether you will be the participant in the story (first person – "I ran down the street after the dump truck"), an observer (third person – "Alfred directed the motion picture based on the best selling book."), or speak directly to the reader (second person – "You should never try this at home."). Using more than one person can be confusing, particularly in fiction or narrative non-fiction.

There should be unity to your presentation. Utilizing a mix of first, second, and third person is most common in instructional writing as employed in this book. **Since writing a book is like having a conversation with the reader even though you are not present**, decide how best to "address the reader" with the message being conveyed.

If you write in first person, you must portray the actions of subordinate characters through the voice of the main character. Third person permits you to describe the action as the characters interact. Second person is good for advising or instructing the reader directly, as if you are speaking intimately, one to one.

Celebrity memoirs are normally written in first person. Biographies and books chronicling events or issues generally employ third person.

Positive and negative factors affect the "person" chosen. Writing novels in first person lets you spin a tale and display a distinctive voice similar to that utilized by well-recognized author Elmore Leonard. Employing this method is often suggested for seasoned writers, since weaving the story through the main character is challenging.

Writing in third person allows you to write "about" characters, an event, or an issue. Many authors of non-fiction are inclined to choose this method.

The choice of a person for writing poetry is only restricted by your imagination. Deciding on a particular person dictates word usage, but you are free to spill your words on the page as you choose. Once again a distinctive voice is the key.

Built-In Promotion

Writing poetry, short stories, magazine articles, or a book linked with a memorable event provides a built-in promotional angle. An example might be releasing a book about landing on the moon in 2009, the 40th anniversary of Neil Armstrong's remarkable achievement.

Providing a promotional angle increases your chances of being published. Instead of having to create a marketing strategy, the publisher is presented with a ready-made publicity campaign. This in keeping with **Mark's Step #2—Write A Story You Are Passionate About—One That Is Marketable.**

A reference book titled *The Timetable of History, A Horizontal Linkage of People and Events* is helpful to any aspiring author. The book, written by Bernard Grum, presents information about history-making events in chronological order. It offers useful information under such headings as History/Politics, Literature/ Theater, Religion/Philosophy, Visual Arts, Music, Science/Technology, and Daily Life.

Reading *The Timetable of History* or similar publications may trigger book ideas. Those who decide to pursue writing non-fiction as a career should consult the latest edition on a regular basis.

Two of my books, *The Perfect Yankee* (released during the 40th anniversary of Don Larsen's World Series perfect game), and *Nicklaus, A Biography* (published on the 25th anniversary of Jack's greatest year), received additional media coverage by being linked with an event. *Testament To Courage*, the memoir of Holocaust victim Cecelia Rexin, was released on the Day of the Holocaust.

In future years, books chronicling the tragic events of September 11, 2001, will be released on various anniversary dates. They will include tributes to those who lost their lives in the attacks on the World Trade Center, the Pentagon, and airliners, portrayals of New York City police and fire department heroes, and biographies of President George W. Bush, Osama bin Laden, Rudy Giuliani and other historical figures.

Literary agent Susan Gleason warns that publishers may be leery of "event oriented" books believing that once the event has passed, interest in the book will wane. But many of these books have proven worthy, providing a strong shelf life long after the event.

Motivation and Writing Credentials

Before choosing a book topic, ask yourself a critical question: **Why am I the one person in the world to write this book?** The answer is relevant whether you are contemplating a novel, writing non-fiction solo, or considering collaboration and ghostwriting opportunities.

Being qualified to write a book is linked with motivation. Literary agents and publishers are curious about why you believe you can provide a fresh voice or unique information. You must convince the agent or publisher of your passion for the material and that you possess the credentials to write a book that will succeed.

Motivation appears in many forms. James Baldwin (*Go Tell It On The Mountain*) stated, "[The subject] must be something that irritates you and won't let you go. That's the anguish of it. Do this book, or die. You have to go through that. Talent is insignificant. I know a lot of talented ruins. Beyond talent lie all the usual words: discipline, love, luck, but most of all, endurance."

Prospective agents and publishers will assess whether you possess the endurance Baldwin mentions to complete a book. Many aspire to write a novel, a work of non-fiction, or a collection of poetry, but many fail since they cannot sustain momentum through the rigors of the writing process. Publishers want those who are "finishers," writers who will fight the fight to complete a book on schedule.

Agents and publishers seek authors possessing proper credentials (a platform). Credibility is the issue. A history professor will be more likely to write a credible Civil War epic than will a heart surgeon. And an investigative reporter for the *New York Times* is more qualified to write about the Iraqi war than the owner of a health food store in Topeka.

With this in mind, review your credentials and consider a subject that will impress an agent or publisher. While submitting the manuscript chronicling the Mike Tyson trial, publishers were reminded that I was a former criminal defense attorney; head of the media committee assigned to oversee coverage of Tyson's trial, had been a legal analyst for major networks, and had written several columns for *USA Today*. Answering the question as to why I was the one person in the world to write a historical book about Tyson and the trial was easy.

An aspiring novelist client faced a significant challenge since he had not been published. He was a business lawyer and intended to use this credential in his Query Letter to agents and publishers. After some probing, I learned he was born in Nova Scotia. He also told me he was an amateur astrologist and a stamp collector. More important, he stated the novel he had written was based on a nightmare incident he experienced while playing an Internet video game. His Book Proposal and Query Letter incorporated these unique characteristics into the text. He had been transformed from being a business lawyer into a writer with a fascinating background and experience with his chosen genre, one intriguing to any agent or publisher.

An example of writing about an experience involves the book, *A Trial By Jury*. D. Graham Burnett, a Princeton historian of science, was the jury foreman for a murder trial in New York City. Though his expertise had not been seeded in the law, experience as a juror permitted him to be an authority. In the tone of *Twelve Angry Men*, the great film directed by Sydney Lumet, *A Trial by Jury* is a compelling book.

John Grisham used his credential as an attorney to advantage while writing his first novel, *A Time To Kill*. Deciding it was important to chronicle a case disturbing to him, Grisham began to write. With his wife as editor, he completed the novel and promoted the book himself. Selling it out of the trunk of his automobile, Grisham was determined to succeed. The book was a modest success, but it led to *The Firm,* an international bestseller later produced as a film. A multitude of bestsellers followed, but none would have been published if Grisham had not possessed the credibilityof having been an attorney with a talent for storytelling.

Stephen Coonts, author of multiple *New York Times* bestsellers, was an Ensign in the United States Navy. After receiving his flight wings in 1969, he served aboard the *USS Enterprise* during the final few months of the Vietnam War. This was followed with two years as a flight instructor aboard the *USS Nimitz*.

The result of Coonts' love for aviation and recollections of his days as a Naval aviator provided a publisher with sufficient credentials to interest them in his first novel, *Flight of the Intruder*. *Final Flight, The Minotaur*, and *Under Siege* followed, rocketing Coonts to international acclaim.

The renowned author Tom Clancy earned his credentials through old-fashioned hard work. When the Maryland-based insurance broker heard the story of a Russian frigate attempting to defect to Sweden, he was mesmerized. Though he possessed no background as a naval or intelligence officer, or writing experience, he researched the subject and began to write a novel. The result was *The Hunt For Red October*, a spellbinding thriller. Future bestsellers *Patriot Games* and *Clear and Present Danger* followed causing Clancy to become a frequent guest aboard jets, submarines, and destroyers.

Being qualified to write a story or a collection of poetry provides confidence, an essential characteristic for any aspiring author. Knowing your subject matter will help you to press ahead on those days when your brain refuses to cooperate and the page is empty.

Above all, agents and editors at publishing companies seek qualified writers with the imagination to create a fresh idea resulting in a book that will entertain or inform like none before it. Your challenge is to provide that concept, one causing the agent or editor to throw their hands in the air and shout, "Yes!" When that occurs, you will hear the magic words, "We will publish your book."

Copyright

To ensure no one steals your book concept, copyright the material. This is essential even if you believe it will never be seen by anyone but Aunt Myrtle.

First consider copyrighting your material when you have a satisfactory draft of your book. Book Proposals and Query Letters may also be copyrighted.

A copyright protects literary work under United States law for the life of the author or poet plus seventy years. Copyrighting material is easy. **For details, consult the Library of Congress web site.** The necessary documents can be downloaded.

Proper authentication of the literary material is required. After a few questions are answered, the completed document and a copy of the literary material, accompanied by a filing fee, are mailed to the address provided. Within weeks, a letter is forwarded designating a copyright number. File this document in a safe deposit box.

A terrific reference source regarding copyright is *Kirsch's Guide To The Book Contract*, by attorney Jonathan Kirsch. In simple language, he explains why you should protect your writings.

When a book is traditionally published, the copyright continues in the name of the author even though the publishing company obtained specified rights to publish it. **The book will be assigned an ISBN (International Standard Book Number) to distinguish it.** Internationally recognized, this ten-digit number (1st digit—country of origin, 2nd digit—publisher designation, 3rd set of digits—title of book, last digit—self-check) identifies the book for purposes of commerce and supply chains. **If you self-publish, you can obtain, for a fee, an ISBN number at www.bowker.com.** Once it is issued, you should register the number with *Books In Print* to insure the book information is available to major retailers, librarians, and independent booksellers across the country. Book titles can be registered at www.bowkerlink.com.

A barcode used by bookstores and other retailers to record sales and price will be printed on the book. Most popular is the 10-digit ISBN. Other barcodes may be printed on the cover or jacket, including UPC and EAN numbers. A traditional publisher will handle this for you.

There is one barcode per book. More information can be obtained at the Bowker web site.

Protecting your writings is essential. You have worked hard to conceive a terrific book idea, one that is marketable. Now you are ready to make certain the writing is the very best it can be.

Step #2 Summary

- Hone writing skills by penning short stories, magazine articles, newspaper articles, essays, short poems, etc.

- Review *Writer's Market* and *Poet's Market* to learn valuable information.

- Read prestigious magazines to understand the literary marketplace.

- Consider whether fiction, non-fiction, or poetry is more marketable for you.

- Research the genre and category of the book being contemplated to discover similar books.

- Provide a wide scope for your book to attract a broad potential audience.

- Consider collaboration with your first book.

- Decide whether to write in first, second, or third person.

- Choose a book subject with a built-in promotion.

- Ask yourself—why am I the one person in the world best qualified to write this book?

- Copyright your material for protection.

Checklist To Evaluate
The Merit of a Book Concept

Yes/No	Questions
_____	1. Is the subject matter of the book unique?
_____	2. Are you passionate about writing this book?
_____	3. Can you describe your book concept in fifteen words or less, preferably less?
_____	4. Is there broad readership for the book?
_____	5. Why are you the one person in the world who should write this book?
_____	6. Is there a built-in audience for the book?
_____	7. Do you have a unique slant on a subject already covered in a book?
_____	8. Is the book promotable?
_____	9. Is a celebrity name attached as a collaborator, or as the writer of the Foreword or Introduction?
_____	10. Can you name ten successful books similar to yours?
_____	11. Is your book better than similar successful ones?
_____	12. Does the book cover a timely subject?
_____	13. Can you link the release of the book to an anniversary of an event of note to aid promotion?
_____	14. Is the book about a famous subject?
_____	15. Do you have a unique credential or "platform" from which to write the book?
_____	16. Do you have a competent game plan to promote the book?
_____	17. Can you convince a New York-based agent or publisher your book will sell more than 15,000 copies or more?
_____	18. Does your book provide the answer to a question or solve a problem?

(Agents and Publishers seek books providing solutions.)

Tip—Answers to these questions permits you to evaluate the potential success of your initial book. Be objective, and if your concept doesn't appear to be meritorious, consider another book topic. Perhaps the initial one will become a future book once you are established as a published author.

Mark Shaw

There is no such thing as a moral or an immoral book. Books are well written or badly written, that is all.

OSCAR WILDE

Step #3
Your Passport To Publication
Is Good Writing

The Writing Process

There is nothing more personal than writing. Thoughts originating in the deep recesses of the intellect are unique. When these ideas are reduced to writing, they become a direct reflection of one's spiritual and intellectual being.

Those who choose to write professionally must do so with passion and a sense of responsibility since their words will affect the reader's mindset. Thoughts and ideas expressed verbally flutter through the air like multi-colored butterflies and seldom are accurately recalled. A famous psychologist once stated that people don't comprehend the substance of spoken words unless they are repeated six or seven times. Written words expressing thoughts and ideas are more likely to be recalled since readers choose quiet time to enjoy the very essence of published works. **Authors and poets have the opportunity, in a day and age when people don't listen, to inspire, inform, challenge, and entertain whether they write fiction, non-fiction, or a collection of poetry.**

For those choosing to pursue a writing career at an early age, the battle plan is clear: keep an open mind and absorb everything life has to offer. For suggestions on how to be more creative, read *Pencil Dancing, New Ways To Free Your Creative Spirit* by Mari Messer.

Formal education is available through writing classes, books on writing, seminars, and college courses. Search for competent instructors with traditional publishing credits or outstanding academic skills.

To bolster the ability to write with sufficient knowledge, the aspiring writer must garner a sense of history, of what occurred to alter the course of mankind and why. Course study in psychology, philosophy, history, and classical literature provides a solid foundation.

Extensive travel is the comrade of good writers. Spanning the globe opens the door to a rich heritage. Sojourns to Greece, Egypt,

Italy, England, France, and many other countries are valuable. Asked his advice for young writers, William Faulkner stated, "Travel and read."

While visiting foreign countries, learn about the people, the history of the country, and the customs. Working in a foreign country provides a wealth of knowledge. Don't shy away from what might be considered taboo employment. Faulkner wrote, "The best job ever offered to me was to become a landlord in a brothel."

Writing workshops, seminars, and writers' conferences are meat and potatoes if writing professionally is your goal. This is the perfect environment in which to gather valuable tips and nuances from those who have achieved the goal of being published. Many such events are publicized in independent, creative-arts oriented newspapers such as *The Village Voice*.

If you decide later in life that writing is a profession of choice, the alternatives differ. Workshops, seminars, and conferences are valuable tools for learning, but a crash course on writing professionally is a prerequisite if you have not exercised this skill in many years.

Having no formal training, I relied on others to assist me when I began to write *Down For The Count*, the book investigating the Mike Tyson trial. Colleagues with backgrounds in literature and English perused the manuscript as well. I did the best I could with what I knew at the time.

Education is essential to learning the craft of writing, but those who proclaim that someone with no formal literary training cannot succeed should recall the background of no less a "scholar" than William Shakespeare. While he was schooled in Greek and Latin literature, rhetoric, and Christian ethics, there is no evidence that the Bard was ever taught the art of writing. History indicates he left school at age fifteen, never pursued further formal education, and was not considered a learned man. This did not prohibit him from writing what many experts consider to be the most extraordinary body of works in the history of literature.

Poet Walt Whitman further proves that formal training is not linked to literary success. His formal education ended at age eleven.

Unlike other writers of his time who enjoyed structured, classical educations at private schools, Whitman learned about writing in the local library. He then joined a newspaper, *The New York Mirror,* where he wrote his first article in 1834. Less than two decades later, after dabbling in short-story fiction, Whitman wrote the classic, *Leaves of Grass.*

Regardless of the success enjoyed by authors such as Shakespeare and Whitman, my path toward becoming an author would have been less cumbersome had I spent more time learning the craft. At the time, my sole intent was to have book after book published to earn a living and avoid traveling far from home. This was a goal since I had become the stepfather of four young children, including triplet boys, at the ripe age of forty-four. Writing professionally was the link to spending quality time with the kids as they grew up.

If you are the "I just decided to take up writing and I want to be published" type as I was, then become an avid reader and practice writing. In his book *On Writing*, famed author Stephen King stated, **"If you want to be a writer, you must do two things above all others—read a lot and write a lot."** Best selling romance writer Nora Roberts echoes King's sentiments. She began her career as a stay-at-home mother who wrote ideas in a notebook during a snowstorm in 1979. Pleased with her efforts, she continued to write. The result was her first published work, *Irish Thoroughbred.* Since then she has written several bestsellers, all because, as she says, "I don't believe in waiting for inspiration. It's my job to sit down . . . and write."

Whether you are interested in writing fiction or non-fiction, you should read both. Read the classics—Hemingway, Joyce, Dickens, and Steinbeck. Poets can learn from Whitman, Frost, Edgar Allen Poe, and Edna St. Vincent Millay. Each of these great writers admits their education about writing was influenced by the books they read. Asked what authors he enjoyed, Hemingway listed more than thirty-four before confessing that to list them all "would take a day to remember." Among them were Mark Twain, Bach, Tolstoy, Dostoevsky, Chekhov, Kipling, Shakespeare, and Dante. Hemingway admitted he also gained education from artists and composers. "I learned as much from painters about how to write," he stated, "as from writers . . . I should think that what one learns from composers and from the study of harmony and counterpoint would be obvious."

Competent authors are superb storytellers. While reading the classics, note how the canonized authors weave a story. Whether the choice is fiction or non-fiction, the story must be clear, have a good beginning, middle, and end, and never be boring. Reading well-written books helps you realize how others have accomplished the feat. In *On Writing*, Stephen King states:

> Good writing . . . teaches the learning writer about style, graceful narration, plot development, the creation of believable characters, and truth-telling. A novel like *Grapes of Wrath* may fill a new writer with feelings of despair and good, old-fashioned jealousy—I'll never be able to write anything that good, not if I live to be a thousand—but such feelings can also serve as a spur, goading the writer to work harder and aim higher. **Being swept away by a combination of great story and great writing . . . is a part of every writer's necessary formation.** You cannot hope to sweep someone else away by the force of your writing until it has been done to you.

In *Bird by Bird*, by Anne Lamott, the author presents an interesting strategy regarding fiction storytelling. Lamott quotes Alice Adams from a lecture about short story writing. The excerpt reads:

> [Alice] said that sometimes she uses a formula when writing a short story which goes ABDCE, for Action, Background, Development, Climax, and Ending. You begin with action that is compelling enough to draw us in, make us want to know more. Background is where you let us see and know who these people are, how they've come to be together, what was going on before the opening of the story. Then you develop these people, so that we learn what they care most care about. The plot – the drama, the actions, the tension – will grow out of that. You move them along until everything comes together in the climax, after which things are different for the main characters, different in some real way. And then there is the ending: what is our sense of who these people are now, what they are left with, what happened, and what did it mean.

Fiction writers can learn from Scott Turow, author of several bestsellers, including *Presumed Innocent*. An excerpt reads:

> The atomized life of the restaurant spins on about us. At separate tables, couples talk; the late-shift workers dine alone; the waitresses pour coffee. And here sits Rusty Sabich, thirty-nine years old, full of lifelong burdens and workaday fatigue. I tell my son to drink his milk. I nibble at my burger. Three feet away is the woman whom I have said I've loved for nearly twenty years, making her best efforts to ignore me.

Besides being a terrific storyteller, character description was Jack Kerouac's specialty. An excerpt of *On The Road* reads:

> He was a gray, nondescript-looking fellow you wouldn't notice on the street, unless you looked closer and saw his mad, bony skull with its strange youthfulness – a Kansas minister with exotic, phenomenal fires and mysteries. He had studied medicine in Vienna; had studied anthropology, read everything; and now he was settling to his life's work, which was the study of things themselves in the streets of life and the night.

In *Balzac and the Little Chinese Seamstress*, author Dai Sijie sweeps the reader into his novel portraying life during China's Cultural Revolution. An excerpt reads:

> The room served as shop, workplace, and dining room all at once. The floorboards were grimy and streaked with yellow-and-black gobs of dried spittle left by clients. You could tell they were not washed down daily. There were hangers with finished garments suspended on a string across the middle of the room. The corners were piled high with bolts of material and folded clothes, which were under siege from an army of ants.

Providing a good beginning, middle, and end to a story by doing so with each paragraph provides excellent storytelling. In *Down and Out*

In London and Paris, George Orwell presents a worthy example. The excerpt reads:

> The Jew delivered the cocaine the same day, and promptly vanished. And meanwhile, as was not surprising after the fuss Roucolle had made, the affair had been noised all over the quarter. The very next morning the hotel was raided and searched by the police.

In the non-fiction bestseller, *Seabiscuit*, author Laura Hillenbrand captures the reader's attention by providing visual and dramatic scenes propelling the reader into the middle of the action. An excerpt reads:

> A minute later the field bent around the far turn and rushed at the grandstand. There was one horse in front and pouring it on. His silks were red. It was Seabiscuit. The crowd roared. Pollard [the jockey] and Seabiscuit glided down the lane all by themselves, reaching the wire in track-record-equaling time. Kayak was right behind them. It was Pollard's first win since 1938.

Journals and Idea Books

Learning the craft of writing is a continuing process. One of the best means to hone the craft is by writing in a journal or diary. It promotes discipline while providing a chronology of your life.

Author John Fowles (*The French Lieutenant's Woman*) stated, "I am a great believer in diaries, if only in the sense that bar exercises are good for ballet dancers; it's often through personal diaries that the novelist discovers his true bent." This comment is applicable for non-fiction writers as well.

One exercise to consider requires writing in a journal each day for a week. Content and length are optional, but the goal is to complete the task. Then cast aside the journal for a few days before reading it. If you're satisfied with the text, and the process involved, then you have the potential to write professionally. If you hate what you wrote, and the discipline of having to write each day, then consider basketry, modern art, or some other means of expending creative energy.

Another useful exercise is to organize a folder containing observations about others. Good writers are people watchers. Whether you do so in a park, at sports events, or at a bus stop, chronicle your thoughts and observations. Vivid description and words evoking emotion are the earmarks of the good writer. To enhance this skill, study speech patterns, how people move, what habits they possess, and face and body features. Make lists of these characteristics; then add other elements. A fat notebook I often refer to includes pages listing names (Avon Privette, Paris Wolfe, Tootie Witmer, Audrey Wink, Holly Furfer, Bobby April, David Duck), smells (bug spray, moth balls, fresh strawberry pie, chemical fertilizer), descriptions (salty, speckled, overripe, furry), hair style (butch, raggedy, ponytail, mousy), and body parts (webbed feet, spindly toes, stubby arms, firm butt, limp face, spidery fingers, slumping posture, drooping eyes, artificial eyes, whiskey nose, parched lips, dead legs). Another list includes weather descriptions (gray drizzle, sideways rain, Oklahoma wind) and sky descriptions (primrose, veined with dry lightning, streaky blue).

In another section of my "help" book, one added to on a daily basis, I list "useful phrases." Included is soft laughter, hushed giggle, black scuff marks, pocket change, replied indifferently, fork patrol, pigeon toed, steady gaze, shimmered in the moonlight, and crumpled pompadour.

Before beginning the writing process, consult your lists and permit words and ideas to fill your brain with creativity. Clever words and phrases spice up the text, providing the reader with the all-important asset that E. B. White emphasizes: **visualization**. Learned author John Cheever endorsed White's viewpoint when he stated, "The books you really love give the sense, when you first open them, of having been there. It is a creation, almost like a chamber in the memory. Places that one has never been to, things that one has never seen or heard, but their fitness is so sound that you've been there somehow."

Having gained the essential skills necessary to write well, the aspiring author or poet is in pursuit of a realistic goal: being published. A good book idea plus an excellent strategy plus hard work permits this goal to be realized.

Word Usage

While reading, note the author or poet's word choice. There are those who love the vocabulary and appreciate hundred dollar words that claim, "I'm a literate son-of-a-gun with a graduate degree in Webster's." But language must never be vague, elusive, or downright inaccessible. A story loses much of its flow and meaning if the reader spends too much time opening a dictionary. Phrases like "revelatory episodes," "epigrammatic prose," and "diorama of American plenty" will confuse and dismay 95 percent of the population.

Throughout my tenure as an author, readers have provided feedback indicating that my books are "easily read." Little highbrow language exists in my books because I purposely exclude words preventing the flow of the language. I want to make them stop and think or enjoy the text, not be impressed with my use of big words.

Doing so is essential if you want to reach a broad readership, because **writing is personal, not only for the *writer*, but for the reader.** As the writer, you are conveying information regarding a story intended to captivate the reader. You want your words to leap off the page and infiltrate the reader's brain to entice, excite, entertain, or make them stop and think. When readers purchase a book, it will be successful if they ask, "Who is this author or poet and what is he or she trying to show [not tell] me?"

Punctuation Usage

No matter how good the book, magazine, or article idea may be, punctuation errors diminish the chances of becoming published. No literary agent, editor at a publishing company, or editor at a magazine or newspaper has the time to wade through punctuation flaws. Noting them produces an instant feeling that the writer is unprofessional.

Glaring errors such as locating a period or comma outside quotation marks in a sentence are commonplace and embarrassing. Ninety-nine times out of a hundred, the period or comma will be positioned inside the final quotation mark.

A common error occurs when writers don't realize that all numbers up to a hundred are written out. Also—no numerical number ever begins a sentence.

Proper use of hyphens, semi-colons, colons, and commas is a must for aspiring authors and poets. Be aware of the rule regarding when to capitalize the first letter of a word following a colon.

Writers should italicize the names of films, books, screenplays, operas, plays, and magazines. Quotation marks are permitted for book chapters, poems, articles, songs, and short stories. Underlining any of the above is not necessary for emphasis.

Learning basic rules ensures that writing mistakes will not prevent literary agents or publishers from casting aside submitted material due to blatant errors. The authors and poet's best friend is a competent editor or a grammar book complete with punctuation tips such as *The Chicago Manual of Style, Associated Press Stylebook,* or *Grammar Report*, a Books For Life Foundaton publication. To assist you with basic information regarding proper writing skills, a Writing Skills Checklist is provided following this chapter.

<u>Professional Advice</u>

Above all, heed **Mark's Step #3—Your Passport To Publication Is Good Writing**. Modern day study guides for the aspiring writer abound. If you are a beginning writer, consult a basic book on style, grammar, and punctuation to guide your efforts. There are few hard and fast rules regarding these areas, but standards and guidelines exist to assist your understanding regarding how to write according to publishing industry standards.

Once you have learned the basics, consider two books to aid you as you become more proficient at writing.

The *Chicago Manual of Style* is a dense book not vacation reading. Set aside ample time so you can focus on its contents. A better idea is to consult the book in spurts, take notes, and then refer to it again and again like a close friend who tells the truth.

Publishers prefer that authors and poets adhere to the rules presented in this publication, but *Elements of Style*, by William Strunk Jr. and E. B. White, is ninety-five pages long, the perfect length for obtaining good, solid information about writing. Spending less than ten dollars for the book is one of the best investments an aspiring author or poet can make.

Professor Strunk published the classic for his students in 1919. It soon became known as the "little book that could." Over the years,

White, most famous for writing *Charlotte's Web,* has revised it for modernization purposes, but the gem features Strunk's brilliant mind probing the depths of writing and what is proper and correct. Under titles such as "Elementary Rules of Usage," "Elementary Rules of Composition," "A Few Matters of Form," and "Words and Expressions Commonly Misused," the Cornell professor provides simple, clear, and brilliant guidelines. Among the jewels are warnings against overuse of adverbs and adjectives, advocacy of active voice and positive words, and rules for positioning pronouns. *Elements of Style* explains the whys and wherefores so even a dunderhead can understand. I recommend putting the book under your pillow while you sleep with the hope that the knowledge will seep into your brain.

While the first four sections of the book are a must-read, E. B. White added Book V titled, "An Approach To Style." He writes, "Up to this point, the book has been concerned with what is correct, or acceptable, in the use of English. In this final chapter, we approach style in its broader meaning: style in the sense of what is distinguished and distinguishing. Here we leave solid ground. Who can confidently say what ignites a certain combination of words, causing them to explode in the mind?"

Regardless of the caveat, White's suggestions *are* on solid ground. Sections include: "Placing yourself in the background," "Write in a way that comes naturally," "Work from a suitable design," and "Write with nouns and verbs, not with adverbs and adjectives." White discusses the need to revise and rewrite, not to overwrite, and not to overstate.

After discovering Strunk and White's book and consulting the *Chicago Manuel of Style,* I was pleased to note that much of what they suggested had somehow been incorporated into my writing style. This stemmed from reading what other *good writers* had written . . . and perhaps some *bad writers'* work as well since I learned to discern the gibberish many believed necessary to tell their stories.

Absorbing the lessons outlined in the "little book" provides a basis for developing writing skills. Each author or poet chooses a storytelling method, but proper usage of language guarantees that errors won't signal lack of talent. Editors at publishing companies dismiss a manuscript or collection of poetry if there are misspellings and grammatical errors, but they also pay close attention to word usage.

Learning good writing skills at an early age will benefit aspiring authors and poets. Parents interested in supplemental materials to improve children's writing skills may consider the Shurley English method. More information is available at www.shurley.com.

Clarity

In *On Writing Well*, author William Zinsser states, "Good writing has an aliveness that keeps the reader reading from one paragraph to the next, and it's not a question of gimmicks to 'personalize' the author. It's a question of using the English language in a way that will achieve the greatest clarity and strength."

Fiction writers must ask themselves several questions regarding clarity. Is the story time-oriented so the reader understands the time frame being presented? Are the characters well defined and do they act in a manner consistent with the background provided? Is there a believable backdrop for the story, one that is vivid? Have I written a clever dramatic story with a ticking clock to add suspense?

Non-fiction writers face a comparable question—will a story that is quite clear to the writer be as clear to the reader? Will the reader understand the message being conveyed by the text? This applies to poets as well.

Author John Updike provided a guidepost regarding clarity. He wrote, "When I write, I aim in my mind not toward New York, but toward a vague spot a little to the east of Kansas. I think of the books on library shelves, without their jackets, years old, and a countryish teenaged boy finding them speak to him." Author Zinsser suggests, "Clutter is the disease of American writing. We are a society strangling in unnecessary words, circular constructions, pompous frills, and meaningless jargon."

As the writing process continues, writers must be certain they have told the story they intend to tell, and with accuracy. Many times we read what our brain *wants* to read instead of what *is* on the page. In a final draft of this book, I credited Robert Frost with writing *Leaves of Grass*. I knew better, but had Frost on the brain. When an editor pointed out the mistake, I was embarrassed.

One method of determining clarity while proofreading for errors is to read the material aloud. By inspecting and hearing

each word, meaning becomes clearer and mistakes are revealed that would otherwise have been overlooked.

Writing Skills

Information about how to write and writing style are referenced in many books including *Elements of Style* by professors Strunk and White. White was correct when he wrote that no one understands why a certain group of words carefully joined produce magic on the sheet of paper for one author while resulting in gobbledygook for another. Each writer's composition of words will differ according to his or her skill and experience.

In his book, *On Writing*, Stephen King offered a simple explanation for what he believes is important when considering writing style. He wrote, "Book buyers want a good story to take with them on the airplane, something that will first fascinate them, then pull them in and keep them turning the pages." Mystery writer Tony Hillerman (*Hunting Badger*) told *Writer's Digest*, "I feel my first priority as a writer is to entertain the audience."

Never forget every book is an adventure—Write it like one. This is true whether you are creating a tortoise and hare story, a book about the inner workings of the latest computer, a chronicle of the evolution of Red Lobster stores as an American success story, a biography of the gifted poet Etheridge Knight, or a collection of poetry about why birds fly south for the winter.

Author James Patterson espouses a unique perspective of writing. In *The Writer's Handbook*, he states, "In the beginning, I really worried a lot about sentences in my books. But at some point . . . I stopped writing sentences and started writing stories. And that's the advice I give to new writers. Sentences are really hard to write. Stories flow. If you've got an idea, the story will flow. Once you have the story down you can go back and polish it for the next ten years."

No one doubts that clear, concise storytelling featuring language that *shows,* but does not *tell,* is paramount to success. Some writers sprinkle flowery language throughout their manuscripts. Others write like Hemingway and produce some sentences that are never-ending. Regardless, the finest writers, whether they are writing fiction, non-fiction, or poetry, are brief and visual, two great talents gained through experience. Being visual means to flavor your writing with the five senses—sight, smell, touch, taste, and hearing—so the reader consumes and is consumed with the text.

Professor Strunk wrote in *The Elements of Style*, "If those who have studied the art of writing are in accord on any one point, it is this: the surest way to arouse and hold the reader's attention is by being specific, definite, and concrete. The greatest writers—Homer, Dante, Shakespeare—are effective because they deal in particulars and report the details that matter. Their words call up pictures." Strunk added, "Vigorous writing is concise. A sentence should contain no unnecessary words, a paragraph no unnecessary sentences, for the same reason that a drawing should have no unnecessary lines and a machine no unnecessary parts."

Author Nora Roberts believes visualization means proper selection and description of characters whether the book is fiction or non-fiction. She told *Writer's Digest,* "Your characters have to jump off the page. They have to appeal to the reader in some way . . . They need to be appealing, humorous and human."

Literary agent Julia Castiglia echoes Roberts' words in *Writer's Digest*, "What we really look for are books that are well written, with a certain zing to them that climbs off the page and wraps itself around our brains, that so entrance and seduce us that we just can't say no."

Word Choice

The requirement that the writer *show* the reader and not *tell* cannot be over-emphasized. Word choice is key. Mark Twain wrote, "The difference between the right word and the nearly right word is the same as that between lightning and lightning bug."

To improve a story, use active words portraying concrete images instead of abstractions: avoid crutch-words ending in "ly;" avoid "not" and "no;" use active verbs like "clawed," "swatted," and "pawed," instead of linking verbs like "is" and "was;" avoid overuse of gerunds (verbs used as nouns by adding "ing"); and use stronger nouns instead of adjectives. Regarding the need for active verbs, author William Zinsser wrote, "Verbs are the most important of all your tools. They push the sentence forward and give it momentum. Active verbs push hard; passive verbs tug fitfully."

Avoid words such as "a little," "very," "kind of," "pretty much" or "really," qualifying other words. They are often unnecessary and make your writing sound trite.

Concise word usage translates to paragraph length. Reader attention span is short, so use of a few sentences separates the text and keeps the flow of the story at a steady pace. Long paragraphs are bulky and can bog down the reader. Avoid them.

Strong word usage is essential at the beginning of a chapter, or a verse. Words completing a chapter or a verse must tantalize and urge the reader onward.

Adverbs and Adjectives

Stephen King's book, *On Writing*, provides several important tips. One suggests a writing mantra to be repeated again and again.

King said, "The adverb is not your friend." He believes if the word chosen cannot stand on its own, replace it with one that does.

Word choice signals the distinctive voice writers convey in conversation with the reader. How they manipulate certain words into the story dictates the tone of that voice. William Zinsser states, "Bear in mind, when you're choosing words and stringing them together, how they sound. This may seem absurd: readers read with their eyes. But in fact they hear what they are reading far more than you realize. Therefore such matters as rhythm and alliteration are vital to every sentence." Zinsser adds, "Develop one voice that readers will recognize when they hear it on the page, a voice that's enjoyable not only in its musical line but its avoidance of sounds that would cheapen its tone: breeziness and condescension and clichés."

Never one to discount the advice of an author like Stephen King who has sold more books than there are people in China, an "adverb hunt" was commenced during the final edit of my book *Miscarriage of Justice*. To this end, we scoured the manuscript and eliminated 95 percent of the adverbs.

The "word surgery" performed regarding use of adverbs in the book was successful, and the patient lived. Some adverbs can be helpful, but removing the malignant language improved the book considerably.

While editing, we also concentrated on "word brevity," eliminating words not advancing the story. Any time we saw "they were," "they are," "there is," "it is," or "it was," we crossed them out along with dreaded clichés.

Many authors develop an affinity for one word. Mine is "that." I love the word, but often it is not required. During editing of this book, I attempted to eliminate as many "thats" as possible. I'm sure I could delete others, but at least I have spared readers many of my unnecessary, pet words. Be careful though: non-use of a word where it is required can be as bad as overusing it.

Brevity is essential. Without exception, less is better. When Ernest Hemingway was chided for the short length of his classic *Old Man and the Sea*, he answered critics by saying, "[It] could have been over a thousand pages long and had every character in the village in it . . .That is done excellently and well by other writers . . . So I have tried to do something else. First I have tried to eliminate everything unnecessary to convey experience to the reader so that after he or she has read something it will become part of his or her experience and seem actually to have happened. This is very hard to do and I worked at it very hard."

Author Zinsser echoes Hemingway's thoughts. He states,

[The] secret of good writing is to strip every sentence to its cleanest components. Every word that serves no function, every long word that could be a short word, every adverb that carries the same meaning that's already in the verb, every passive construction that leaves the reader confused as to who is doing what— these are the thousand and one adulterants that weaken the strength of a sentence.

Historians recall that brevity was a key to Abraham Lincoln's speeches. During his Second Inaugural Address, he utilized just 701 words. Five hundred five of them were of one syllable; 122 contained two.

To realize that short books are jewels of the writing profession, recall such classics as *The Great Gatsby, The Red Badge of Courage, Turn of the Screw,* and *A Lost Lady. Tuesdays With Morrie* is another. A helpful book for those who love to use run-on sentences is *The Dictionary of Concise Writing: 10,000 Alternatives to Wordy Phrases* by Robert Harwell Fiske.

Run-on sentences permit readers little time to breathe. Early in my career, every paragraph seemed to feature the dreaded run-on. Only by weeding them out, splitting up thoughts, and focusing on being concise have I become a better writer.

Style of writing is an individual matter. It is important to know the standard rules for writing, but many successful authors have broken the rules. Lori Foster, a noted romance author, wrote in *Writer's Digest*, "What really sells your book is your individual voice, not the rules that you obey." Elaborating, she stated, "Just about everyone has heard the dozens and dozens of rules listed as a criteria for getting published in romance. They include: no hopping from one character to another's head, one point of view per scene, no exotic settings, and no athletes or television personalities. In truth, there are very few definite rules."

Truman Capote's thoughts on rules are right on point. He said, "Writing has laws of perspective, of light and shade, just as painting does, or music. If you are born knowing them, fine. If not, learn them. Then rearrange the rules to suit yourself."

Keys To The Writing Process

If you decide to write an entire manuscript or collection of poetry before completing a Query Letter and/or Book Proposal, remember one important rule: Once you start, don't stop. The main reason most people intending to write a book never do is because they encounter a stumbling block regarding word choice, punctuation, or grammar usage. Before they know it, the creative juices turn sour.

Author and literary writing guru Natalie Goldberg speaks to this in her book *Writing Down The Bones*. She believes initial thoughts "capture the oddities of your mind." She writes, "First thoughts have tremendous energy. It is the way the mind flashes on something." Author Goldberg provides a list of exercises in her book to inspire writers toward creative thinking.

Author John Steinbeck (*The Grapes of Wrath*) spoke to the importance of completing what you begin. He stated, "Write freely and as rapidly as possible and throw the whole thing on paper. Never correct or rewrite until the whole thing is down. Rewrite in process is usually found to be an excuse for not going on. It also interferes with flow and rhythm which can only come from a kind of unconscious association with the material."

In a 1947 letter to Jack Kerouac, writer Neal Cassady, upon whom Kerouac based the character Dean Moriarty in *On The Road*, wrote in a letter to Kerouac:

> I have always held that when one writes, one should forget all rules, literary styles, and other such pretentions as large words, lordly clauses and other phrases as such . . . Reather, I think one should write, as nearly as possible, as if he where the first person on earth and was humbly and sincerely putting on paper that which he saw and experienced and loved and lost; what his passing thoughts were and his sorrows and desires. . .

Actor Sean Connery, playing the part of fictional author William Forester in *Finding Forrester*, addressed the subject in an interesting manner. He stated, "You write the first draft with your heart. You re-write with your head."

Instead of worrying about mistakes or lapses in the text, plow ahead. There will be time later to fill in the blanks or correct errors. To aid your efforts regarding manuscript form, a Manuscript Techniques list follows this chapter.

Writing Regimen

There is no definitive answer to how much text a writer should complete each day. Stephen King states in his book *On Writing*, "I like to get ten pages a day, which amounts to 2,000 words. That's 180,000 words over a three-month span, a goodish length for a book."

Esteemed author John Updike (*The Power and the Glory*) writes 1,000 words a day, six days a week. This process has resulted in more than fifty books, two of which have earned Pulitzer Prizes.

Ernest Hemingway, who never began writing unless twenty sharpened pencils were close at hand, described his daily routine by stating:

> I write every morning as soon after first light as possible. There is no one to disturb you and it is cool or cold and you come to your work and warm as you write. You read what you

have written and, as you always stop when you know what is going to happen next, you go on from there. You write until you come to a place where you still have your juice and know what will happen next and you stop and try to live through until the next day when you hit it again. You have started at six in the morning, say, and may go on until noon or be through before that. When you stop you are as empty, and at the same time never empty but filling, as when you have made love to someone you love.

Poet Maya Angelou's regimen is classic. "I have a hotel room in every town I've ever lived in," she stated. " . . . I leave my home at six, and try to be at work by 6:30. To write, I lie across the bed, so that [my] elbow is absolutely encrusted at the end . . . I stay until 12:30 or 1:30 in the afternoon, and then I go home and try to breathe."

Tom Wolfe (*A Man In Full, The Right Stuff*) sets page goals. He stated, "I set myself a quota—ten pages a day, triple-spaced, which means about eighteen hundred words. If I can finish that up in three hours, I'm through for the day."

Many writers believe they deserve a magnum of champagne in celebration if they can write four to six pages a day. Others write less, some more. It all depends, but never let anything prohibit progress toward the appointed goal. This means the telephone, loved ones, pets, door-to-door salespeople, radio, television, grammar problems, spelling miscues, mosquitoes, or children. All are the writer's enemies since they obstruct completion of the task. My black Labrador's name is Black Sox, but I could name him "Procrastination," since playing ball with him is a tempting diversion to writing.

Block out these enemies, begin to write, then write and write, and write some more. Be sure to "save" the material paragraph by paragraph while working and then save it on a disk when you have completed the day's task so computer "crashes" won't eliminate your text. Mother Nature is another enemy of the writer and her electrical storms are computer killers.

When words are dashing out of the brain, there is exhilaration beyond comprehension. While the juices are flowing, the fingers can't work fast enough. The rush is better than any chemical "high."

Every writer discovers a time and place to write, but my regimen is quite consistent. Being a morning person, I write from just after 5:00

a.m. until 7:30 or so. Breaking up the writing period is a quick break to share Rice Krispies with Black Sox.

Some days, I am tempted to read my composed material to Black Sox a la John Steinbeck. He wrote, "I've always tried out my material on my dogs first. You know, with Angel, he sits there and listens and I get the feeling he understands everything. But with Charley, I always felt he was just waiting to get a word in edgewise. Years ago, when my red setter chewed up the manuscript of *Of Mice and Men*, I said at the time that the dog must have been an excellent literary critic."

Once breakfast is completed, I walk outside, take a few deep breaths, and then return to the writing table until eleven o'clock. By then, my brain is empty.

Afternoons are set aside for research and a wretched occupation: editing. Most weeks I write every day except for Saturday when I attempt to break par against a great group of buddies at the local golf course. Even then, I carry five-by-seven note cards in case an inspiring thought or observation leaps into my mind.

A proposed regimen is as follows: The writer decides on Sunday to complete the first fifty pages of a manuscript. He or she writes ten pages on Monday and Tuesday, and ten more each on Wednesday, Thursday, and Friday. This night is reserved for celebration, Saturday for recovering from the Friday night hangover, and Sunday for the Sabbath. Poets can adapt a similar regimen for their work.

By not touching the manuscript, the writer will have a fresh perspective on Monday. Best selling author Truman Capote (*In Cold Blood*) was a proponent of this method. After describing himself as a "horizontal author [who] can't think unless I'm lying down," he stated, "when the yellow draft is finished, I put the manuscript away for a while, a week, a month, sometimes longer. When I take it out again, I read it as coldly as possible, then read it to a friend or two, and decide what changes I want to make."

Revisions

When people ask what I do, I tell them that I am a "re-writer," not a writer. This emphasizes how much time is spent revising text.

The process of rewriting is complex. Pulitzer Prize winning author Elie Wiesel stated, "Writing is not like painting, where you add. It is not what you put on the canvas that the reader sees. Writing is more like a sculpture where you remove; you eliminate in order to make the work visible. There is a difference between a book of two hundred pages from the very beginning, and a book of two hundred pages, which is the result of an original eight hundred pages. The six hundred pages are there. Only you don't see them."

When you are in the revision stage, as opposed to when you are rushing through a first draft to complete it start to finish, speed is the enemy of quality. To be sure the work is the finest it can be, take your time. Columnist James Kilpatrick wrote, **"Edit your copy, then edit it again; then edit it once more.** This is the hand-rubbing process. No rough sandpapering can replace it." William Zinsser stresses the importance of revisions. He concludes, **"Rewriting is the essence of writing well; it's where the game is won or lost."**

Every time text is revised, it improves. Many times writers return to words they've written and are amazed at the flow and clarity. Other times the material embarrasses them. How I wish I could re-write many of the first books I had published using the skills learned over the years. Nearly every published author or poet I know feels this way.

Revising material is a constant process. In *On Writing Well*, William Zinsser proclaims, "Writing improves in direct ratio to the number of things we can keep out of it that shouldn't be there. Examine every word you put on paper. You'll find a surprising number that don't serve any purpose." He adds, "Most first drafts can be cut by 50% without losing any information or the author's voice."

Laurie Rosen, editor of thirty-seven bestsellers, advises novelists to follow ten basic steps while considering revisions. Among the ones she listed in *Writer's Digest* are: Revise toward a marketable length (Average novel length is between 60,000 and 100,000 words. Manuscripts exceeding 100,000 words are a tough sell), torque the power of your scenes (emphasize the purpose of the action), tease the reader forward into the next chapter, give your antagonist some depth, and dramatize, dramatize, dramatize."

Some authors or poets set page counts or deadlines for completion of revised drafts. Meeting them is an excellent form of discipline. **Setting reasonable deadlines is suggested.** No writer should create or edit when the brain is weary.

Critique

When an acceptable draft is completed, let others review it. It doesn't matter if your reviewer is a spouse, a relative, or a friend down the street.

Writers need a variety of people to provide <u>objective</u> opinions. Being removed from the material, reviewers can spot flaws and misinformation, and correct mistakes. They may even suggest an alternative means of telling a story.

The key is locating people not afraid to say what they think. Then, when criticism is leveled, swallow your ego and be receptive. While writing one book, a longtime friend who was an English major in college reviewed the manuscript. I cringed while perusing her comments since every page was saturated with red ink. On one page, she circled two paragraphs free of error and printed beside it, "Did you write this?" Her questioning my ability made my face turn red in anger, but I knew in some ways it was an off-hand compliment. At least I took it that way. When the book was completed, I knew I had become a better writer because of her stern comments.

Good writing requires dedication and perseverance since words are the writer's communication with the world. Only through hard work will the message be strong. For aspiring authors and poets attempting to impress literary agents and editors, good writing is their most important calling card.

Step #3 Summary

- Read the classics to understand good writing.

- Keep an "idea book" of word usage.

- Don't overwhelm the reader with "high brow" language.

- Read *Elements of Style*—then re-read it. Keep a list of language "Do's" and "Don'ts."

- Read self-help books on proper use of punctuation.

- Discover a writing regimen that works for you.

- Remember, good writing is clear and concise.

- When you start writing a manuscript or collection of poetry, don't stop until your first draft is completed.

- Rewrite and edit. Every time a re-write occurs, the text is better.

- Solicit objective critique of your writings.

- Remember—there may not be a "right" word to use, but there is a "best" word.

Writing Tips Checklist

- Purchase and read grammar and punctuation books including *Elements of Style* by Professors Strunk and White.

- Use strong, active words. Nouns and verbs are preferred.

- Avoid overuse of adverbs and adjectives. Look for nouns and verbs that stand on their own.

- Eliminate clichés.

- Be brief. Avoid run-on sentences.

- Avoid superlatives. Don't exaggerate. Let facts speak for themselves.

- Use strong verbs that move the story forward.

- Don't overuse obscure words to impress.

- Avoid weak words such as probably, maybe, something, anything, awhile, several, lots, get, a lot, almost, perhaps, and so forth.

- Construct clear, concise sentences. Don't use too many "ands."

- Attempt to use positive words and avoid "not."

- Don't use "etc." or abbreviations.

- Write out the numbers one to ninety-nine and numbers beginning sentences.

- Avoid exclamation marks unless called for in dialogue.

- Remember the general rule that quotation marks are positioned outside periods and commas.

- Use single quotes for a quote within a quote.

- Avoid phrases such as "It is interesting that," or "I really believe that."

- Italicize book titles, CDs, films, operas, and plays; quotation marks are   acceptable for poems, short stories, articles, songs, and book chapters.

Manuscript Techniques
Format Do's and Don'ts

Do use 8 ½ x 11—20 unlined bond paper.

Do use black type.

Do use Times New Roman print.

Do type on one side of the paper.

Do use a one-inch margin on the left side of the paper.

Don't worry about the right margin. Leave it undefined.

Don't staple the pages together.

Do double-space the lines utilizing 12 point font.

Do average 250 words per page—(twenty-five, sixty character lines).

Don't provide extra spaces between the paragraphs.

Do indent and single-space lengthy quotes or excerpts.

Don't use quotation marks when indenting quotes or excerpts.

Do provide Chapter titles and sub-titles using 18 and 16 point font size respectively.

Do center chapter titles and subtitles.

Don't leave subheadings at end of page.

Don't provide address, telephone number, fax and e-mail information on cover page.

Do include address, telephone number, fax, and e-mail information in Query letter.

Optional—Do type first word of your last name and keyword from title at left margin on each page.

Do type page number in lower right hand corner of page.

Do provide running number of pages.

Do check to make certain no pages are left out.

Don't submit manuscript until it has been edited several times. Perfection is required.

Don't trust your computer to do the work for you—check the dictionary.

Don't type "The End" on the final page of the manuscript.

Do reduce illustrations or photographs to 8 ½ x 11 paper if they exceed that size.

Do print, if at all possible, on a laser printer.

Poetry Submissions

Do use same preparation suggestions as above with the below—mentioned additions.

Don't type more than one poem to a page.

Do single-space the text.

Do leave two spaces between stanzas.

Don't include name, address, and so forth on each page.

Do include above information in Query letter.

Do begin title of poem four-five lines from top of each page.

Do center title of poem.

Do type title of poem in all caps.

Do leave three spaces between title of poem and first line of poem.

The reading of all good books is like conversation with the finest men of past centuries.

RENE DESCARTES

Step #4
There Is No One Right Way To Tell A Story, But There Is A Best Way

The Writer's Persona

At a recent writer's gathering, the question was asked, "Mark, has your ability to become published been a matter of luck, fate, coincidence, karma, good planning, or all of these?"

The answer to the question is simple. Once the first book, *Down For The Count*, was published, I embarked on a designated game plan intended to provide stories of national interest that were marketable.

The word "marketable" was the key. **Too many aspiring authors and poets do not research the literary marketplace to learn whether their book concept is worthy.** Instead, they forge ahead to write a book with little chance of garnering a traditional publisher or finding success through traditional self-publishing. They would be wise to plan their attack on the publishing world by investigating what type of book can be written that will result in a publishing commitment. Like me, they can then build on the first book with a second one, and so forth.

Information regarding deals being made by publishing companies is readily available. One source is Publisher's Marketplace, an offshoot of Publisher's Lunch. For a reasonable fee, daily updates regarding book commitments are available at www.publishersmarketplace.com. By studying these deals, aspiring authors may stay current concerning what book concepts are selling and to whom. The listing of literary agents who have sold the books to publishers is also beneficial.

I chose the non-fiction biographical arena since it appeared to be the easiest entry to building a career in the publishing world based on my credentials. Each book contained information about a particular subject I believed worthy. Along the way, I have experimented with writing fiction and poetry. This learning process continues with the belief that I will be published in these arenas in the future.

Book topics differed since subjects were chosen based on three criteria: a passion for the material, chronicling an event or person with an historical theme, and the likelihood a traditional publisher would be interested in the book. Some book ideas were rejected because they did not meet these criteria; others were discarded when there was no publisher interest.

Since I am the ultimate pack rat who never throws anything away, I keep Book Proposals or manuscripts in a safe place. One never knows when a change in the publishing climate will occur and one of the book ideas that was rejected will be in favor.

Several advantages to being an author were attractive. Never a fashion plate, I appreciated the fact that people expected most authors to be colorblind and wear hand-me-downs from Goodwill. This attracted legendary author George Bernard Shaw, a distant kin. He stated, "My main reason for adopting literature as a profession was that, as the author is never seen by his clients; he need not dress respectfully."

An author or poet schedules his or her own hours—no nine to five requirement. Most important, "creative" people can be "strange." If they dribble their food, slosh beer around in their mouth before swallowing, or drive a purple Volkswagen bus with tinted windows, society excuses the behavior. As a creative person, writers can change their mind as often as the television weatherman.

Above all, the opportunity to tell stories that could make people stop and think was the main attraction for me. I also realized that there is considerable satisfaction to a process where you begin with no written words, just an idea, and then, through hard work and perseverance, end up holding a manuscript, and later, a published book in your hands. **Realizing your story will be read by many others makes all the tough days sitting in front of a computer worthwhile.**

Authors and poets vary regarding the satisfaction they enjoy when their books are published, but I consider them to be "children" that have been scattered across the universe. Books are extensions of the human mind and the power of the written word must never be underestimated.

Storytelling

Author's experiences regarding storytelling abound. **Creativity is a key, but so is organization.** It is crucial since any story, fiction, non-fiction, or even poetry, should progress in an organized manner.

The story doesn't have to be told chronologically, but it must have a logical progression. Otherwise, the reader is lost.

Telling stories through the written word requires a different talent from verbal expression. A dear departed friend, Jack Leer, was the finest storyteller I ever knew. He could stand in front of a group of people, and they would be howling in no time.

Jack's talent did not extend to the written page because he could not write like he spoke. A different expertise was required, and he did not possess the dedication to learn the craft.

Storytelling methods differ as much as the colors of the rainbow. Truman Capote stated, "Since each story presents its own technical problems, obviously one can't generalize about them on a two times two equals four basis. Finding the right form for your story is simply to realize the most *natural* way of telling the story."

Ernest Hemingway, when asked about the talent for writing fiction, said, **"You invent fiction, but what you invent it out of is what counts. True fiction must come from everywhere you've ever known, ever seen, ever felt, ever learned."**

The aspiring author or poet should examine as many books as possible to learn various storytelling methods. Note how each writer has chronicled the story he or she wishes to tell. This is essential whether the story is contained in a magazine or newspaper article, a short story, a Query Letter, a Book Proposal, collection of poetry, or a manuscript.

Down For The Count

Storytelling was a learning experience for me, but speaking to judges and juries when I was a criminal defense lawyer provided a perfect training ground. Arguing the innocence of a client to twelve souls charged with life and death matters required organization of the evidence so the jury heard the story I wanted them to recall when they deliberated. Years of preparing those speeches permitted me to hone my skills as a storyteller.

My education about speaking to juries began with the very first case assigned me when I was a public defender. My client was a young man charged with killing his 300-pound girlfriend from six feet away in front of her children with a shotgun. When I visited James in jail, he told me his defense was that he was trying to shoot over her head to scare her. My job was to defend him according to the facts he provided, and I argued his version to the jury. It only took the jurors ten minutes to convict him of first degree murder, but the final argument was my first experience with storytelling in front of an audience.

As the years passed, I continued to speak to juries honing my storytelling abilities. When I first considered writing a book, I relied on the storytelling methods used in criminal trials.

To tell the stories that became my first book, *Down For The Count*, I began by dramatizing the courtroom as boxer Mike Tyson awaited his fate after a grueling rape trial. The jury returned and the judge announced the guilty verdict. This was featured in the Prologue.

Chapter One, aptly titled, "Guilty" began with a strong sentence. It read, "When Mike Tyson first heard the word 'guilty' spoken by Judge Patricia Gifford, his head cocked to the side as if he had been hit with a thunderous right cross. He whispered, 'Oh, man,' and slumped down in his seat."

Reader's feedback told me I had captured their attention triggering a desire to read further. In *On Writing Well*, author William Zinsser expresses the need to do this better than anyone. He wrote, **"[Your] lead must capture the reader immediately and force him to keep reading. It must cajole him with freshness, or novelty, or paradox, or humor, or surprise, or with an unusual idea, or an interesting fact, or a question. Anything will do, as long as it nudges his curiosity and tugs at his sleeve."**

The vivid portrayal of Tyson's reaction led back in time to the investigation of his crime. Chapter One recounted the circumstances under which the prosecution decided whether to seek an indictment against the former heavyweight-boxing champion of the world. The story then continued in chronological order through the months leading up to the trial. This was most important since much of what happened to Tyson *at* trial was directly due to what occurred *before* trial. This was especially true when his promoter and self-proclaimed mentor Don King hired Washington D.C. highbrow lawyer Vincent Fuller, an attorney with no experience in the criminal courtroom, to defend the accused rapist. This caused Tyson to be defenseless.

Once pre-trial matters were considered, the trial unfolded. Events were chronicled with two goals in mind: to permit readers to judge for themselves if the boxer was guilty and decide whether a black celebrity could gain a fair trial in a Midwestern city, Indianapolis, Indiana, in the early 1990s.

The publication process for *Down For The Count* was a great learning experience regarding the workings of the publishing industry. Like others who dive in with no research, I did not have a clue as to how it operated.

The original title for the book, I'm a bit ashamed to say, was *Beauty and the Beast*. It featured no Prologue. Chapter one began with the incident between Tyson and the alleged rape victim, Desiree Washington. It proceeded in real time.

When a competent draft of the manuscript was completed, I forwarded it to several prospective literary agents whom I had selected from a reference book. One agent responded believing he could sell the book. At his request, I made several revisions.

The agent was so certain he had a best seller on his hands that he conducted an "auction." This involved notifying publishers of his intent to provide them with manuscript pages. Once editors had read them within a twenty-four hour time limit, they would telephone with bids for the rights to the book.

The literary agent requested that I stand next to the telephone to sort through the various offers as the day passed. I did so for eight hours, but he never called. To his amazement, and my chagrin, no one wanted the book. The consensus was that the world knew everything it wanted to know about the Tyson trial.

Reeling from defeat, I tossed the manuscript aside. I still believed in the book, but no one else did. Being a stubborn cuss, and not one to give up, I kept thinking about how I might improve the text to garner a broader audience interest in the social impact of the Tyson case. What drove me was a character trait important to any aspiring author or poet: **perseverance.**

Two months later, I had the idea to include in the text the relationship between the issues involved with the Tyson case and several significant legal events surrounding the trial. They included the Rodney King beating by California police, the Anita Hill-Clarence Thomas Senate hearings, the William Kennedy Smith rape trial in Florida, and the racially motivated Bensonhurst murders in New York City.

Armed with a new title, *Down For The Count*, and a new theme for the book, I completed another round of revisions before the manuscript was submitted. I did not include a Book Proposal or a Query Letter since I had no knowledge of the form.

By revising the storytelling method to reflect how the Tyson trial compared with the legal events surrounding it, I found a publisher. **An open-minded approach to storytelling alternatives had paid off.**

Assisting my quest to discover a marketable concept for the book was a question I asked myself: What provocative thought did I want readers to examine? To be provocative, good non-fiction must leave readers with a question they had not answered before. With *Down For The Count*, I wanted readers to stop and think about whether justice had been served. Providing this theme tantalized the publisher as well.

Bury Me In A Pot Bunker

The challenge in writing *Bury Me In A Pot Bunker,* the book chronicling the life and times of famed golf course designer Pete Dye, dealt with storytelling sequence. I considered several alternatives, but finally chose to open the book with background information about Pete and his gifted wife, Alice. Understanding their roots, and the inspiration guiding their pioneering efforts, grabbed the reader from page one.

Having traced the root of Dye's genius, the book then took the reader on a meandering journey of their greatest courses. Readers learned a side of golf they had never known since there were few books explaining the "how's and why's" behind the design of golf courses. Woven into the text was Pete's sense of humor and his ability to create challenging courses from flat, barren land that any self-respecting cow would avoid.

Spending time with Pete permitted me to capture the essence of his voice. This translated into easily read text that wasn't so technical as to overwhelm the reader.

Impressing publishers with the credential or "platform" to write the book is essential to securing a publishing commitment. To do so, I visited such revered Scottish courses as St. Andrews, Prestwick and Royal Dornach. This provided a sense of golf history and helped me understand and convey how Pete had discovered design concepts from the legendary designers of old.

Having learned from my agent that the Book Proposal route was worthy, I prepared one for *Bury Me In A Pot Bunker*. Mentioning that famed golfer Greg Norman would write the Foreword for the book provided a boost.

The editor who purchased the rights to the book was not a golf fanatic, but someone who loved the history of the game. Tracing Pete and Alice's fascination with that aspect of golf proved to be a winning strategy.

Forever Flying

In the 1970s, I had the opportunity to work with the famous attorney, F. Lee Bailey. He chose me as local counsel for a case involving a diabolical physician suspected of beheading an undercover D.E.A. agent who suspected the doctor of drug dealing. I assisted Lee with the defense and we kept in touch thereafter.

Some twenty years later, Lee's agent telephoned asking if I would be interested in collaborating with the legendary aviator, R. A. "Bob" Hoover, on a book. Lee represented Hoover in connection with FAA attempts to deny him a license to fly in view of his advanced age. I flew to Washington D. C., watched Lee in a Court of Appeals hearing, and met Hoover. Impressed with his background and fighting spirit, I agreed to the collaboration.

Organizing the storytelling order for the book that became *Forever Flying* was difficult. R. A. "Bob" Hoover was a true renaissance man who had been successful with several careers. Besides being a World War II hero shot down by the Germans, a prison camp survivor who stole a German plane and flew to freedom, a terrific experimental pilot who was a finalist along with Chuck Yeager to break the sound barrier, Hoover was the greatest aerobatic pilot who ever lived.

To hook readers, Chapter One featured an encounter between Hoover and the Russian government during a Moscow international air race competition. When the Russians refused to allow him to perform certain aerobatic maneuvers in a new experimental airplane, he did so anyway. Tense moments occurred as embarrassed Russian officials decided whether to arrest Hoover. They didn't, but the episode showed that he was a courageous aviator.

After the Russian incident, the story backtracked to Bob's early days. The book then proceeded in chronological order to include Bob's successful fight with the FAA.

To compare how *Forever Flying* evolves, and the means by which Chuck Yeager's own story unfolds, read his bestseller, *Yeager*. The storytelling method differs, since interspersed with Yeager's recollections are reminiscences quoted from those who knew him well.

When Paul McCarthy, a senior editor at Pocket Books, Simon and Schuster, read the Book Proposal, he was smitten with Hoover's story. An aviation enthusiast, Paul purchased the rights to the book realizing Bob was a hero known to thousands of aviation fans. **This provided two important elements toward securing a publisher: a built-in audience and tremendous opportunities for promotion of the book.**

Literary agent Richard Pine's decision to present the book to Paul McCarthy was based on his personal knowledge of Paul's love for aviation. Writers can learn from Richard's example. When attempting to decide which literary agents or editors would welcome submission of a book idea, homework is required. By specifically targeting the book idea to match with agents or publishers who have been involved with books of the same genre, the chances of securing agency representation or a publisher commitment can be maximized.

The Perfect Yankee

The Perfect Yankee provides an example of discovering little known information others had avoided. While reading Mickey Mantle's bestseller, *My Favorite Year, 1956*, I noted a chapter titled *Perfect*. It chronicled the magical performance on October 8, 1956 by journeyman New York Yankee pitcher Don Larsen. Against the defending champion Brooklyn Dodgers, Larsen pitched the only perfect game in World Series history—no hits, no runs, and no errors.

Convincing the unassuming Larsen to write a book was difficult. For years, he had been reticent to tell his story. Don had even refused accomplished author David Halberstram.

Telling Don Larsen's story required focusing on his incredible achievement. After several fruitless attempts to do so in a chronological manner, I conceived the idea to weave his life around the miracle nine-innings he pitched in the World Series.

Predictably, publishers were dubious. Writing a book about one game didn't register with most. Many passed on the Book Proposal before the same one that had published *Down For The Count* agreed to publish it. **The editor realized the storytelling method was imaginative.**

Richard Ben Cramer's book, *Joe DiMaggio, The Hero's Life*, illustrates an alternative storytelling method. After presenting a Prologue packed with personal memories of the great ballplayer, Cramer tells his story while commentating on the life and times of Joltin' Joe. A unique voice emerges as if Cramer is sitting in the reading room spewing out facts while revealing his insight into their merit. The author is quite effective with this method.

Aspiring writers should remember that rejection of material might be based more on storytelling method than on content. **Being creative is essential. Consider alternative methods and then decide which one will provide readers with a unique perspective of the story you want to tell.**

Testament To Courage

Belief that the world should read Cecelia Rexin's remarkable story of hope and love spurred my interest in the Holocaust memoir of a Christian German woman who loved others more than herself. This memoir became the book, *Testament To Courage*.

Cecelia's story began when she was an aspiring medical student in Berlin. Opposed to Adolph Hitler's Nazi regime, she assisted the underground. Her roommate turned her in, and Cecelia was imprisoned. After three years, she was sent to Ravensbruck, and then to Auschwitz.

While incarcerated, Cecelia kept a journal she sewed into the hems of her dresses. Throughout her stay, she hid pages chronicling the horrors of Nazi brutality. Among the stories was her account of saving the life of a young orphaned Russian girl named Laddie. At great risk, Cecelia enlisted the assistance of two German prison guards. Laddie was taken to a pig farm where she spent the rest of the war. After the war, she and Cecelia met in an emotion-filled moment in a hospital.

My personal interest in Cecelia's story is an example of another important characteristic a successful writer must possess: curiosity. Without a yearning to learn, to explore, to discover, the writer is doomed. Whether it is fiction, non-fiction, or poetry, the aspiring writer must probe for the truth, for the story no one else can tell, or that no one else seems to feel is important enough to document.

No other writer has expressed the need to probe life's experiences better than Frank McCourt. He wrote the bestseller *Angela's Ashes* at age sixty-six. He told *The Writer's Handbook,* **"If you keep your ear cocked, you'll discover treasures of significance."**

Tom Wolfe wrote of his pursuit of a book that became the bestseller, *The Right Stuff.* "This book grew out of ordinary curiosity," he said. "What is it, I wondered, that makes a man willing to sit on top of an enormous Roman candle, such as a Redstone, Atlas, or Titan rocket, and wait for someone to light the fuse?"

With *Testament To Courage*, this mindset triggered a storytelling method that revealed events during World War II while Cecelia Rexin was incarcerated in the concentration camps. My education regarding the events was provided through a thick book titled *The Second World War, A Complete History,* by Gilbert Martin. It documented every aspect of Adolph Hitler's attempt to rule the world. In it, I marked sections coinciding with the dates Cecelia had noted in her journal.

Weaving events throughout the war with the diary proved worthy. Through Cecelia's eyes and snippets of major events as the war progressed, readers are provided with a sense of historical significance.

The editor, fascinated with Cecelia's story, also appreciated the storytelling method. It distinguished *Testament To Courage* from other Holocaust books.

Larry Legend

Chronicling the life and times of NBA superstar Larry Bird's first year as an NBA coach presented several challenges. He surprised everyone by advancing the Indiana Pacers to the NBA Eastern Conference Finals against Michael Jordan and the Chicago Bulls. That year Bird was awarded Coach of the Year honors and inducted into the Hall of Fame.

To broaden the reader base, I wove exciting moments from Bird's career as a Boston Celtic into the story. This added drama to the text while providing background on the French Lick, Indiana native.

After considering several storytelling methods, I decided to write a Prologue to *Larry Legend* that provided a glimpse of Bird's first game as a coach. **The drama of a last-second loss enticed readers before the text previewed Bird's early years growing up in a small**

Indiana town. Mixing these facts provided the reader with a glimpse of the format for the remainder of the book.

To personalize the story, and separate it from other sports biographies, Bird's story unfolded so readers felt like they were sitting on the bench with him. By visualizing his every move, from his tendency to rub the back of his neck or scratch his cheek, to the facial expressions he possessed when players were out of sync, I provided an image of Bird the impatient coach as compared with Bird the great player.

Probing what unique facts readers expect is an important factor in choosing a storytelling method. Ask yourself what you would want to know about your subject if you were reading the book. **Writers should write with the anticipated audience in mind while being true to themselves.**

While writing *Larry Legend*, I kept in mind young readers who might know little about Bird's great NBA career. **Remember to be clear about your subject matter because while you know everything about it, readers may not.**

<u>Miscarriage of Justice</u>

Keeping an open mind regarding the storytelling process resulted in *Miscarriage of Justice, The Jonathan Pollard Story.*

The Pollard case has always been controversial. A Naval Intelligence Service analyst who spied for Israel in the mid-1980s, he received a life sentence after having pled guilty to espionage. The severity of the sentence was shocking to many, since others convicted of the same offense received lighter sentences. Supporters alleged anti-Semitism; others believed he should have been shot.

Through the years, the Pollard case became a political football. Several times it appeared he would be released, but it never occurred.

After interviewing Dr. Morris Pollard, Jonathan's father, on a radio program I hosted, there appeared to be the need for an unbiased book presenting the true facts in the case. This would permit readers to stop, think, and make up their own minds.

Key to telling the Pollard story was capturing the reader's attention by first outlining the dramatics of his spying escapades. These had occurred from his first meeting with an Israeli contact named Colonel Aviem Sella to the moment when Pollard was arrested. Once this was chronicled, the text reverted back to his early years so readers could gain a sense of who Pollard was and why he acted as he did.

The next section dealt with the events leading to Pollard's sentencing. Details of the sentencing of Jonathan's wife Anne provided the reader with a sense of her background and the love affair that blossomed with Jonathan.

Pollard's harsh imprisonment and supporters' efforts to free him were also chronicled. The final section featured an analysis of the spy's case including comparisons with the prison sentences imposed on spies for both allies and enemies of the United States. The title reflected my belief that Pollard's sentence was disproportionate to his crime.

The long and weary road to publishing the Pollard book spanned more than two and a half years. More than 300 drafts of the book were written. Staying the course proved worthy as it did for Ernest Hemingway, who re-wrote the *ending* to *Farewell To Arms thirty-nine* times.

The publisher of *Miscarriage of Justice* was impressed with storytelling presenting the facts devoid of the author's opinion. Too often writers mesh personal feelings with facts, restricting the reader's ability to stop and think.

From Birdies To Bunkers

While writing *Bury Me In A Pot Bunker* with Pete Dye, I promised his wife Alice that if she ever wanted to write her memoir, I would assist her. Finally, Alice gave her okay.

To chronicle Alice's remarkable amateur golf career and her pioneering efforts as a "woman of firsts," I first interviewed her at the Dyes' Florida home. For five days I listened as Alice described golf tournaments she had won, famous golfers she had befriended, her experiences as a golf course designer, and contribution to the game as the first women board member of the PGA of America. Trials and tribulations as wife to Pete provided humorous interludes.

As I transcribed the audiotapes, I began to wonder if Alice's story was a "straight autobiography." These normally begin with the subject's birth and lead through life experiences. Since Alice's story was so unique, I decided to approach her with the idea of telling the story through short "vignettes" akin to the storytelling method used in several successful books including *Harvey Penick's Little Red Book*.

The literary agent representing the book liked the idea and so did Alice. Soon I had woven together enough vignettes for the sample chapter section of the Book Proposal. The book was titled, *From Birdies To Bunkers, Golf Wit and Wisdom.*

Utilizing a similar storytelling method to the best selling Penick book impressed an editor at HarperCollins. Varying from the norm secured a publisher for the book.

Code Of Silence

The journey to tell the story, *Code of Silence, Melvin Belli, Jack Ruby, and the Assassination of Lee Harvey Oswald* is exciting.

The idea for a biography of one of the greatest attorneys who ever lived (Belli died in 1996) evolved from a friendship I enjoyed with the San Francisco legend in the mid-1980s. A swashbuckling character out of a Damon Runyan novel, Belli was labeled "The King of Torts" by *Life Magazine* due to his pioneering efforts in the field of personal injury law.

While Belli represented such celebrities as Errol Flynn, Mae West, Muhammad Ali, the Rolling Stones, and Jim and Tammy Faye Baker, his most famous client was Jack Ruby. Since more than two thousand books have been written about the events surrounding the JFK/Oswald assassinations, my inclination to write a biography touching on assassination conspiracy theories was met with skepticism. This didn't deter my interest because no one had ever written a book about the tragic events in Dallas in 1963 through the eyes of Belli, Jack Ruby's attorney.

Initial drafts centered on weaving the Ruby trial through the lives of Belli and Ruby. Two colleagues who read the material found it to be confusing. Based on their observations, I altered course and the book opens with a Prologue detailing Belli's appearance in the Ruby case. The book then features a brief biography of Ruby before detailing the life and times of Belli. The trial is then presented followed by information questioning whether Belli was hired by underworld associates to discredit, and in effect, silence Oswald's killer.

This structure provided a clear-cut order to the events transpiring in the 1960s followed by new facts that have surfaced. Readers will be able to consider those facts and then decide for themselves whether Belli was an integral part of the most famous cover-up in American history.

Key to the storytelling process with *Code Of Silence,* like that while writing *Larry Legend,* was discovering what information I believed the reader would most be interested in. Focusing on the Jack Ruby case provided a better way to reach the audience than by beginning the book chronicling Belli's life.

The Patsy and No Peace For The Wicked

These two novels present multiple challenges regarding the storytelling process. Each is based on a true story, providing ample opportunities to mix fact with fiction.

The Patsy, based on my representation of a fifteen-year old boy charged with murder, is intended to portray the underbelly of the criminal court system. To convey thoughts regarding the injustice perceived in the boy's case, a character named Jake Lessing was created. He is a disgraced former *Los Angeles Times* investigative reporter whose credentials included winning the coveted Pulitzer Prize. Banished to the Midwest, he attempts to rekindle a dying career at a mid-sized newspaper. **Choosing Jake to tell the story seemed the most natural way to provide the reader with a roadmap to the rest of the action in the story.**

Through Jake's eyes, the boy's story unfolds as we learn why Jake's past demons threaten to cloud his perception of justice. The Prologue sets up the story. It begins with a dream sequence where Jake is sitting in front of a parole board. Readers are catapulted into Jake's world and his belief that past wrongdoings will result in his imprisonment. This theme plays out as readers learn of the vicious crimes that caused the young boy to be charged with murder. The story is then told in chronological order with new facts about Jake being presented as he decides whether to stay on the sidelines or attempt to save the young boy from execution. Drama builds as Jake and his love-interest, a fellow reporter, race against a ticking clock to learn why a dirty cop, a corrupted prosecutor, and a wayward judge conspire to cover-up the truth.

Several versions of the manuscript were discarded before deciding to weave Jake's story in with the boy's plight. This provides the perfect forum for commentary regarding the inequities of the judicial system.

Use of the "ticking clock" storytelling theme is a proven path to good fiction. The race against time permits the writer to grab readers and keep their attention as the drama builds. While writing, think of the best books, and the best films ever read or seen on the big screen. Many, if not most, build suspense so the reader or viewer is right alongside the main characters as they fight to save themselves from doom.

No Peace For The Wicked is based on the true story of two mentally handicapped men convicted and imprisoned for a murder they could not have committed. **To entice the reader, the book opens with a Prologue chronicling the release from jail of Ike, one of the unfortunate men. The first chapter then describes the moral dilemma facing the book's main character, Luther Parsons, a disgruntled defense attorney.** Upset with his practice, his marriage, and life in general, he escapes to Arizona to start anew.

Despite the perfect weather and a fresh attitude, Luther is burdened by drinking problems. He sits in his BMW ready to dive into the bottle when a former associate telephones regarding the injustice inflicted on the mentally handicapped men. Luther resists the temptation to drink, and returns to his hometown bent on investigating why the two men were imprisoned.

By focusing on the plight of the lawyer, the book hooks readers into wondering what caused the attorney to flee in the first place. Later readers will learn that Luther's negligence caused an innocent man to be executed.

The storytelling venue used in *No Peace For The Wicked* was necessary since the actual case was settled before trial. While much of the text is based on a true story, it was necessary to initially focus on Luther and not the mentally handicapped men so the story could unfold through a fictional account of a trial portrayed near the end of the book.

Storytelling and Works of Poetry

Being a novice poet, I have not attempted to become published in this arena, but there is hope in the future. As I write poetry, I am reminded of the need for terrific storytelling capabilities, since space is a limitation authors of long form fiction and non-fiction do not face.

Poets must convey their message with fury and pace. Word choice is crucial, for they must say what they mean quickly and with great clarity. With only a few stanzas to complete this task, organization and constant reminding that the poem must inspire, explain, or entertain within a few lines, is essential.

Poets I have assisted explain that while the words flow when an idea is ripe, they must be disciplined. While some would become ill at the idea of an outline, others find that organization of the material is a lifesaver. This is quite true when the idea to be conveyed is complex. Returning to the outline permits one to regain the continuity necessary to tell the complete story in concise form.

Poets possess this talent, one they have earned through hard work and sacrifice. Poetry may be the most difficult of all writing genres since the constraints prohibit excessive use of the language. **Get in, get to it, and get out, is the poet's credo.**

Reading successful poetry is a must for any aspiring poet. Watch the techniques, the word usage, the ability to tell a story with clarity, the craft of weaving the message so when the poem is completed, readers say, "Wow, that moved me," or "Wow, what a wordsmith this poet is."

No greater poet ever lived than Walt Whitman. When one reads *Leaves of Grass*, the words are so crisp, clean and meaningful that the reader feels he is standing beside the poet as he created his writing magic.

Poetry may tell a story, simply create a mood, or express an opinion. Whatever the intention, poets should make certain the message is clear. Titles representative of the theme of a collection of poetry are important since they preview that message. When choosing titles, be a creative wordsmith to ensure that readers will recall the distinctive aspect of the poetry.

Learning From Others

To repeat Mark's Step #4, There Is No One Right Way To Tell A Story, But There Is A Best Way. It may be elusive, but a dedicated writer can discover a formula unlocking clarity, brevity, and writing so visual it leaps off the page.

The best advice is to read a wide array of books and pay attention to the methods employed by best selling authors. Study *In Cold Blood*, Truman Capote's masterpiece, and the writings of Kerouac, Hemingway, and Joyce, among others. **Keeping an open mind regarding the storytelling process produces clever text that titillates the reader.**

Fiction writers should also read *Presumed Innocent* by Scott Turow. A lawyer and author, he is a creative storyteller who knows how to entertain. John Grisham's books also contain wonderful examples of storytelling. His trademark is weaving a story with very little "fat" to it. Some critics have disdained this method, but who can argue with an author with such an impressive list of best sellers.

Poets should consider *Collected Poems* by W. B. Yeats. Christian book authors are advised to read the *Left Behind* series. Children's book enthusiasts must read J.K. Rowling's *Harry Potter* series. Her storytelling ability opened her readership to millions of adults.

A Civil Action, Jonathan Harr's book about the evolution of environmental lawsuits in the Boston area, illustrates an effective method of organizing non-fiction. If the genre is biography, read David McCullough's *Truman, Theodore Rex* by Edmund Morris, *Lindbergh* by Scott Berg or *DiMaggio* by Richard Ben Cramer.

Each story, whether it is fiction, non-fiction, or poetry presents variables as to how it may be told. If the story is true, facts are presented and the reader is asked to digest those facts, and learn from them.

If the story is fiction, consider Susan Sontag's thoughts that, **"A novel worth reading is an education of the heart.** It enlarges your sense of what human nature is, of what happens in the world. It's a creator of inwardness." Regarding the challenge to write with that passion, Ernest Hemingway said, "For the true writer, each book should be a new beginning where he tries for something that is beyond attainment. **He should always try for something that has never been done or that others have tried and failed."**

Above all, authors and poets are storytellers even if the story is not readily apparent, as in some poems. **Books can entertain and inform, but perhaps their most important role is to make people stop and think, to consider, or reconsider an issue. An author or poet has the ability to change minds and influence individuals reading his or her works. What can be more important than that?**

Step #4 Summary

- Remember—good stories contain a compelling beginning, middle, and end.

- Research storytelling techniques to provide alternatives.

- Choose a storytelling sequence that immediately captures the attention of the reader.

- When considering storytelling alternatives, ask the question—what is the message I am conveying?

- Great stories are well-paced and keep readers asking for more.

- Poets must remember word space limitations require judicious use of the language.

- There is no one *right* way to tell a story, but there is a *best* way.

A book must be an ice ax to break the frozen sea within us.

ALDOUS HUXLEY

Step #5
Preparing An Outline Is
A Blueprint For Success

Outline Elements

A common mistake aspiring authors and poets commit is to begin writing before they prepare an outline. **Whether the genre is long fiction, non-fiction, short stories, magazine articles, or poetry, a roadmap of some sort is essential to guide the efforts.** Working without an outline is akin to a builder starting construction without blueprints.

Many fiction and poetry writers swear that preparation of an outline inhibits the creative process. They insist the story flows best if they have no preconceived idea where creative thoughts will lead. This process can be effective for seasoned writers, but beginners should consider preparing at least a "mental outline," if not a written one, to guide organization of the text.

An outline doesn't have to be formal. I scribbled the outline for this book (chapter headings) on folded sheets of torn paper while awaiting the arrival of a playwright in Mill Valley, California. Within a few minutes, the backbone of the book was created. Since then, revisions have been made to embellish the text, but the outline has never varied.

An outline should be well defined. **Meat from the bones of the outline—manuscript text—will flow more freely when you have an established direction.** This requires a clear understanding of the message to be conveyed based upon the story. Accomplishing this goal will take time and considerable thought.

Jeffrey Deaver, author of the best-selling *Bone Collector*, is an advocate of outlines. "I sit down with a very rough concept of the story," he stated, "and then over the next eight months, I do a very elaborate outline . . . That's my full-time job doing the outline for six or seven days, eight to ten hours a day."

Once the outline is completed, Deaver permits it to settle similar ". . . to the ritual with baking a cake." "You let things solidify," he explains, "and then you go back and look at it."

Outline forms vary, but the standard practice is to utilize chapter headings with abbreviated text describing the chapter content. The chapter headings will become chapter titles when the book is completed. They provide readers a guide to the text.

The outline will dictate the means by which the story unfolds whether in chronological order or through other storytelling alternatives. Never forget the reader demands entertainment, excitement, and information unavailable anywhere else. The last thing you can afford is to be boring, confusing, or predictable.

The Prologue, if there is one, or the first chapter, if there is not, must be strong enough to hook the reader. When considering storytelling alternatives, determine the most compelling moments within your anticipated text. They may occur in the initial stages of the story, in the middle, or toward the end. This text should be the lead-off man, so to speak, the foot soldier to set up the remainder of the book. Potential purchasers may turn to the Prologue and/or Chapter One to check the beginning of the story. If they're hooked, the book is sold.

Teasing readers with an episode of the story without revealing the entire mix of events or characters has proven successful for many authors. To determine if that style will suffice for you, test it. Consider providing just enough information to hook the reader. Once the material is fashioned, begin the story in chronological order and move forward. Flashbacks are said to be the work of the lazy man, but millions of authors have utilized this mechanism.

Creative revision of the outline, again and again, will produce a solid foundation upon which a successful novel or work of non-fiction can be built. Patience and hard work pays off.

Like fiction writers, many poets view preparation of an outline as akin to blasphemy. They say the words simply flow, and the creative process would be blocked if they took the time to outline their intended message. If this is the case, then there is no need to labor over the blueprint for the poem. But many poets also swear that by jotting down a few thoughts about the intended poem, they can organize their thoughts to better stay on course.

Research

Gritty research precedes preparation of a competent outline. This involves entering the world of the library and/or the Internet. The former is still the staple. The latter is beneficial though research undertaken in cyberspace should be scrutinized, since much of the information is faulty.

This became apparent to me while I was writing the book, *Miscarriage of Justice*. On several web sites and in articles discovered through various search engines, miscellaneous material about Pollard was available. When it was cross-referenced, however, contradictions appeared. The saving grace was reading books on the subject and speaking with individuals who possessed firsthand information.

Being accurate is essential to works of non-fiction, but a fiction writer must be accurate regarding background material. Credibility is the issue. An aspiring author can't afford to locate an Apache Indian in the Sedona area of Arizona only to discover it was the Hopis and the Navajos instead of the Apaches who settled there.

Consider quotes contained in reference material with caution. What someone said is only accurate if the source quoting the reference quoted them correctly. Much misinformation has stockpiled based on one person's misquote being quoted as if it was gospel. To determine accuracy, question, be curious, and tape record interviews with the person being quoted. **Truth is a wayward child, especially when authors and members of the media are consumed with the trend toward "Infotainment," a questionable blend of news and entertainment.**

Readers notice errors. After my book, *Bury Me In A Pot Bunker* was published, a golf historian in Vancouver wrote a three-page letter questioning certain text. To my chagrin, several of his comments were worthy. I added them to a list of typographical errors in anticipation of a second printing. When mistakes are noted, the author or poet's duty is clear. Admit the mistakes, thank the reader, and make the corrections.

Interviewing

Interviews supplementing research are an art form. Several superb books discuss the subject. There is even a college course titled, "How to Interview."

The key to successful interviewing is the ability to listen. Those who do often gather information others miss. Remember the *Bible* quotation, "Be quick to listen, slow to speak, and slow to anger."

Observe selected interviewers on television and note a common error. They have a set of questions in mind, often sequenced by number. No matter what the interviewee says, the interviewer asks the next question without following up or deviating from the predetermined order.

The savvy interviewer listens and varies the question order according to the response from the interviewee. The interviewer may return to the question list, but only after a thorough discussion of facts disclosed by the previous answer.

By varying the questions, an interviewer keeps the interviewee off guard. More important, good listening impresses interviewees, providing a bond of trust that often results in the interviewee disclosing facts they may have otherwise withheld.

To gain a sense of the art of interviewing, note the tactics implemented by Ted Koppel, Charlie Rose, Oprah Winfrey, and Larry King. The latter is a master of the follow-up question, since he listens carefully to answers being provided by a guest. King leans toward the person indicating a genuine interest in the interviewee.

Author John Irving (*Cider House Rules*) believes listening is essential to the writing process. He stated, "A writer is a vehicle. I feel the story I am writing existed before I existed. I am just the slob who finds it, and rather clumsily tries to do it . . . **As a writer, I do more listening than talking.** W.H. Auden called the first act of writing, 'noticing.'"

Jack Kerouac spoke of the ability to listen when detailing the essentials of prose. He stated, **"Be submissive to everything. Open. Listening."**

Tape-record interviews whenever possible. Taking notes is important, but tapes ensure accuracy. Tapes are undisputed evidence of the conversation if you are questioned later regarding book quotes.

Finalizing the Outline

Your initial outline may not be the final one. As the process continues, the outline may change several times as you consider different storytelling options.

Beginning writers ask if the outline should be two pages or two hundred. There is no stock answer, since each outline differs according to the writer's preference and the material. **Some writers**

only require chapter headings to guide them; others several
paragraphs of key points to remember. Discover what works for
you, keeping in mind **Mark's Step #5—Preparing An Outline Is A
Blueprint For Success.**

Within each chapter, include catch phrases that will trigger creative
thinking when the writing process begins. As the days pass, you may
add or delete material, but unless you completely alter your chosen
storytelling method, the overall structure of the book should not
change dramatically. **Watch the flow of the material and note
whether each chapter feeds off the preceding one.**

Never be afraid to mix the material around like a good Greek
salad. To gain a clear understanding of the essence of the outline, read
it aloud. If continuity is a problem, set the outline aside for a day or
so. When you read it again, you will have a fresh perspective.

The chapter headings and snippets of anticipated text for the
outline of Book I of my book, *Code Of Silence* were a result of
numerous re-writes. **After more than *one hundred* drafts, part of
the outline read as follows:**

Prologue

> Frank Ragano meeting with James Hoffa—July,
> 1963. Discussion of JFK assassination by
> Hoffa—order from Hoffa to Ragano that
> mobsters Santo Traficante and Carlos Marcello
> oversee plot to kill JFK. Ragano informing
> Traficante and Marcello of Hoffa order. Ragano
> mention of lawyer Melvin Belli to Traficante.

Book I

Chapter 1— Preliminaries

> Opening of Ruby trial—Dallas—March, 1964.
> Descriptions of Belli and Ruby. Information on
> Dallas and trial judge. Discord with Kennedys
> by labor and mob. Belli participation in Trial of
> the Century.

Chapter 2— Ruby's Lawyer

Belli famous cases—San Quentin convict, artificial leg trial, breast disfigurement, fattest man in the world, Willie Mays v. San Francisco Giants trial. Description of Belli offices.

Chapter 3— Young Belli

Belli background, Sonora to San Francisco. Years at Berkeley, world traveler.

Chapter 4— Ruby's Lawyer

Belli's famous cases—fireman, Horace Fong, Belli flamboyance, fascination with fashion. Belli relationship with actor Errol Flynn. Adventures in Europe. Belli the ladies man. Belli's first marriage. Belli and the media.

The outline for my work of fiction, *No Peace For The Wicked* was a work-in-progress for almost a year. **The book was based on a true story so the challenge was to pace the text so the characters hooked readers. This was essential, since the story was character driven.**

When the outline was completed, a portion of it read:

Prologue

Ike Fellows' release from jail. He is hounded by an out-of-control cop determined to send him back to prison. Ike slithers through the streets intent on making it home safely.

Book I
Chapter 1— Call For Help

Embattled attorney Luther Parsons receives call from friend Sonny in Arizona. Must decide whether to return to Ohio or continue his sabbatical from legal woes and personal problems.

Chapter 2— Ike's Journey

Background re Ike—disclosure of Elephant Man's disease, absence of education, family history, trouble with the law.

Chapter 3—The Lawyer

Background re Luther Parsons, family, law school, rise to prominence as a defense lawyer. Hint of trouble with a case that may lead to disbarment proceedings.

Preparing an outline for a poem or a collection of poetry requires imagination and thought. Like an artist who has a message in his mind, the poet must be creative, innovative, and precise regarding the words that fill a verse. A client of mine decided drafting an outline made sense because she was concerned her thoughts would ramble and lose their potency. Her outline was written in pencil on the back of an envelope. For the poem, *A Day To Remember*, she wrote:

Where have I come from?

Where do I want to be?

Why that is important to me.

How I will stay the course?

How I will be remembered?

Why I care.

When finalizing the outline, be succinct, clear, and the outline will serve you in times of writing turmoil. Referring to it when the story begins to meander is a lifeline to writing success.

Step #5 Summary

- The outline is the blue print of the mind.

- Writing without an outline inhibits the writing process.

- When researching facts, check the validity of the source.

- Interviewing is an art—be a good listener.

- Continually check the outline during the writing process to make certain you are on track.

What is a book? Everything or nothing. The eye that sees it is all.

RALPH WALDO EMERSON

Mark Shaw   109

Step #6
Traditional Publishing Is A Writer's Best Friend

Publishing Alternatives

Those with aspirations to become a published author or poet must define the word "published," since **there are publishers *and then there are publishers.***

Publishing alternatives include: Traditional Self-Publishing, Co-Venture or Cooperative Publishing, Print-On-Demand Publishing, Vanity Publishing, Subsidy Publishing (traditional and Internet), E-book Publishing, and Traditional Publishing through national/international companies, regional/small presses, or university presses. For the first-time writer, each possesses advantages and disadvantages.

Writers intent on building a publishing career should consider each publishing alternative in light of their goals and the industry perception of each publishing venue. A strategy that has proven most successful is to exhaust the potential to be traditionally published before self-publishing. This excludes other alternatives including, above all else, subsidized publication.

Traditional Publishing

Many authors and poets choose subsidy presses because they do not thoroughly research the options. Some give up, believing no traditional publisher will be interested in their material.

Before committing to any alternative publishing options, seek a traditional publisher. These include large, medium, and small publishers, as well as university presses. These companies pay all costs involved in publishing the book.

There are a number of traditional publishers seeking the next bestseller. Think positively. If you believe your book is worthy and should be accepted for publication by a traditional house, give it a try. If this fails, traditional self-publishing is always possible.

Set your sights high. Author Terry Cole-Whitaker's book, *Every Saint Has A Past, Every Sinner Has A Future* is a must read for those who require a daily pep talk about never giving up. She writes, **"I decided long ago that it is much better to strive for what seems to be the impossible and fall short than strive for the possible and attain it."**

Echoing her thoughts was the revered author William Faulkner. He wrote, "[The writer] must never be satisfied with what he does. It never is as good as it can be done. Always dream and shoot higher than you know you can. Don't bother just to be better than your contemporaries or predecessors. Try to be better than yourself."

This credo is pertinent when you consider what best-selling author Tom Clancy (*The Hunt For Red October, The Bear and the Dragon*) says about the writing process. He told *Writer's Digest*, **"Writing a book is an endurance contest, and war fought against yourself, because writing is beastly work which one would just as soon not do."**

Regardless of your attitude toward the craft, having one book published by traditional means is paramount to launching a career. It can be done. Respected literary agent Richard Pine provided inspiring advice early in my career. When I was upset that several publishers had rejected one of my books, he said, **"Mark, it only takes one to say 'Yes.'"**

An aspiring author or poet must believe, "Yes, I will be published." As stated before, repeat this mantra on a regular basis. Years ago, Penny Marshall, the *Laverne and Shirley* television star turned motion picture producer/director, was asked what motivated her. She swore every morning she walked into the bathroom, looked at her image in the mirror, and said, "Today I will produce my film. Today I will produce my film." This type of never-give-up attitude applies to publishing. Those who believe in themselves become published authors whether their books are releases by the "big boys" (Simon and Schuster, Random House, Doubleday or one of their imprints), and so forth, or successful small presses continuing to publish terrific books. More about small presses can be discovered at the *Poets and Writers Magazine* web site or through www.cbsd.com/pubs.cfm the site for Consortium Book Sales and Distribution.

Traditional publishing has several advantages, but one is most significant: The publisher normally pays the author an "advance" so it can publish the book. The amount (usually half up front—half upon acceptance of the manuscript) is based on the number of books the publisher anticipates selling. Using sophisticated data, the company determines the number, calculates the sum the author would earn under the proposed royalty agreement, and then offers a percentage of the total. Advances range from a small amount to a million-plus. Regardless of the advance, remember that the publisher believes in the potential of the book to the extent they are willing to fund printing and editing costs, disperse upfront money, and permit sharing of royalties instead of asking for money. This is significant since industry statistics confirm publishers earn a profit on fewer than 10 percent of the books they release.

Authors and poets earn revenue from the sale of each copy of the book. The royalty may be based on the retail price or the publisher's net income (wholesale price). In today's marketplace, garnering a percentage of the retail price is rare, since publishers provide the retailer with at least a 40 percent discount. More likely, the royalty will be based on the "invoice price," a term referring to the price indicated on the publisher's invoice to wholesalers (distributors) and retailers (sales outlets).

This figure subtracts the discount from the retail price. Any royalty paid will be based on the "net copies" of the book sold. This refers to the total copies invoiced less those returned to the publisher. Since retailers have the right to return books they cannot sell, the publisher will keep a reserve account (revenues withheld from the author or poet) to cover the anticipated returns.

Typical royalty schedules call for the author and poet to be provided revenue percentages based on increments of books sold. Each agreement will differ, but a standard split could call for the author to garner a 10 percent royalty on the first 10,000 books sold, 12½ percent on the next 5,000 sold, and 15 percent thereafter on the sale of hardcover books. Successful authors who have sold mega-books command percentages escalating to 50 percent and beyond with advances in the multi-million dollar range.

Royalties for the trade paperback edition of a book will vary, but the percentage is less based on a lower retail price. Seven-and-one-half percent is reasonable.

Authors and poets wonder whether it is advantageous to consider a traditional publisher since the royalty amount is low as compared with traditional self-publishing where the writer keeps all of the revenue.

This is a matter of choice, but don't forget that with self-publishing you will have a financial outlay of funds to finance the publication of the book. With a traditional publisher, you do not since they cover all of the costs.

Another question that may be faced by authors and poets is whether to accept a trade paperback publishing offer when they seek a hardcover release. A literary agent or entertainment attorney specializing in the literary field can offer advice. Being published in hardcover is prestigious, but trade paperback can provide the launch for a career.

To a budding author or poet, securing a publishing deal with a traditional publisher, big, medium, or small, is cause for celebration. Drink, eat, and be merry for a week.

Securing a publishing commitment, regardless of the advance amount (the advance for the first *Chicken Soup* book was $1,000), or lack thereof, is important to building a career. It provides credibility. **The first publication can lead to a second, since you are "publishable."**

Author and poet interaction with publishing house editors varies according to the size of the publisher. At a smaller "house," the editor may be responsible for one book or as many as three. This scenario permits them to spend considerable time with the author or poet on everything from final editing to promotion.

Editors at medium-sized or large publishers may not have this luxury, since their job responsibility dictates interaction with several authors or poets. Many times the first-time author or poet is relegated to dealing with an assistant to the editor. Sustaining a good relationship with the editor and his or her assistant is vital to the success of the book.

Never forget that while some editors may not be great writers, they possess terrific instincts. Listen to them, learn from them, and respect them, for they are the foot soldiers regulating the flow of material into the publishing industry.

Self-Publishing

Traditional Self-Publishing dictates that authors write the book, design and lay out the pages, design and prepare the book cover or jacket, contact a printer and bookbinder, and pay to have the book printed and bound. Using a commercial layout program such as Pagemaker or Quark ensures a professional appearance for your book. Since keeping the "cost per book" to a minimum is important, obtain several printing and binding quotes. Printing a book of approximately two hundred pages for less than five dollars a copy is possible if sufficient copies are ordered.

On the day your book is delivered, celebrate since you have accomplished a goal others covet. You can give or sell the book to family, friends, and colleagues—whomever you want. You retain any revenue, since no agent or publisher receives a percentage.

When you self-publish, print as many as you wish, whenever you wish. You can sell them at flea markets, on a table in your front lawn, or at book signings organized at bookstores and other outlets.

If you choose Traditional Self-Publishing, you are the writer, editor, promoter, marketer, warehouser, and bookkeeper for your book. If it succeeds, it is because of your efforts. To gain a better understanding of a game plan for self-promotion, consult *The Self-Publishing Manual, How To Write, Print & Sell Your Own Book* by Dan Poynter, *How To Publish, Promote, and Sell Your Own Book* by Robert L. Holt, or *The Complete Guide to Self-Publishing* by Tom and Marilyn Ross. Author Poynter's website at www.parapublishing.com provides extensive information about the self-publishing process. He also hosts compelling seminars around the world.

Since you will not benefit from advice and counsel offered by a publishing company while finalizing your manuscript for self-publication, hire an accomplished line editor to review the manuscript. Doing so will strengthen the writing style and prevent careless grammatical and spelling errors infiltrating the text. Every word written is a reflection of your writing ability, and you want the book to be first rate and professional.

Many self-published authors who do not hire a line editor are embarrassed when their book is released. Careless mistakes ruin good writing.

Remember there are line editors and *then there are line editors*. Request edited works of fiction, non-fiction, or poetry to ensure credibility. Choose an editor with experience in the particular genre that you have chosen.

To help locate other reputable printers, visit www.parapublishing.com. Information is presented under Book

Printing At The Best Price. Before submitting orders, writers should request sample copies of printed material to ensure quality. Keep in mind that the printer and the bookbinder are often the same company. If this is the case with the printer you are contemplating, request a sample of a bound book that is similar to yours (hardcover or paperback). Be sure to get in writing their policy of replacing substandard or damaged copies.

To aid your self-publishing efforts, read the *Writer's Digest* publication, *Publishing Success, The Writer's Survival Guide to Self-Publishing and E-Publishing.* Articles include "8 Steps To A Good Book" (Learn about the eight most common reasons self-published books fail), "Get Your Book On The Shelf" (find out who the middlemen are, how books get into stores and how you can get your book in stores), "Get Booked On Oprah," "Tips From The Pros" (eight successful self-published authors share their stories), and "Words From The Wise" (nine successful e-authors discuss the advantages and disadvantages of e-publishing). Included is a complete listing of publishing companies with specifics about each.

Key to any author or poet's efforts is securing a distribution pipeline so the book can be exposed in bookstores and libraries. Beware of any distribution companies demanding payment in advance for their expenses. If they agree to represent the book, they should assume the risk based on a percentage of the revenue garnered from the sale of the book.

One author discovered a chain store in his area willing to stock a few copies of his book on consignment. To his delight, the store agreed to charge a 30 percent fee, well below standard. Independent bookstores will stock self-published books on a similar basis.

Besides bookstores, you may consider non-traditional outlets. Depending on the genre of your book and its anticipated target audience, you can locate outlets where potential customers will congregate. For instance, *Let The Good Times Roll*, a music anthology book I co-authored, is being marketed through music outlets including nightclubs, bars, and museums. Many of my books have also sold well in a men's clothing store.

Don't forget the Internet as a distribution outlet. Amazon.com is an excellent way to reach both broad and specialized audiences. Their Advantage program encourages self-published authors to expose their books on the website. Other Internet sites, including Barnes and Noble, are also available.

Most authors or poets who self-publish establish their personal website to promote themselves and their book. If you do so, make certain it looks professional. Sloppy websites with cheap graphics will inhibit your reputation as a budding writer instead of enhancing it.

If you decide to sell your book on your website, consider PayPal, the "poor man's credit card" account. Information is available at their website and start-up costs can be kept to a minimum.

Entering your book in reputable competitions, such as those sponsored by *Writer's Digest* or prestigious poetry magazines, is advisable. You never know who will read your works and decide, "Hey, this is a writer I want to know." A list of selected competitions is available in *Poets and Writers Magazine*.

When marketing and promoting your book, consider spending funds to hire a public relations company to represent it. This adds a professional edge to your efforts and provides access to media you may be unable to reach otherwise.

Editor Amy Pierpont believes self-publishing can be a definite asset. In *The Writer*, a recommended publication for aspiring authors, she stated, **"Publishers are always looking for talented writers, and when we find they're already self-published, it is often an added plus because the author comes with a built-in audience."**

Success stories abound among traditional self-published authors and poets who write less for monetary gain and more due to an important story they want to tell. Among them is Costa Mesa, California housewife Laura Doyle. She and her husband self-published a book titled, *The Surrendered Wife*. It detailed how women could transform their marriages into intimate, passionate unions.

To their surprise, the book became a hit on Amazon.com. Scouts at Simon and Schuster learned of the success and offered a contract. The book was a *New York Times* bestseller.

Gordon Miller achieved success by self-publishing. His book, *Quit Your Day Job Often and Get Big Raises* triggered a contract with Doubleday for a second book, *The Career Coach: Winning Strategies for Getting Ahead in Today's Job Market*. "Self-publishing can be a terrific experience!" he swears. "Align everything about the book to your target market. Most of all, have fun with it."

Miller believes self-publishing has earned a brand new reputation. "There is no question that self-publishing has gained more respect," he states, "primarily because there are so many stories of self-published books going on to be national bestsellers."

To aid writers, a snapshot of the self-publishing process follows this chapter. Those who decide to traditionally self-publish wear a badge of courage for their efforts.

Co-Ventures

Many publishing companies are interested in co-ventures. This occurs when an author or poet agrees to finance the hard costs (printing) of the book. For their part, the publishing company advances the remainder of the costs for distribution and, perhaps promotion. Depending on the investment of each party, an agreement is reached regarding future revenues. Each recoups its costs, with the split then fifty-fifty. Every deal varies so the advice of an agent or entertainment attorney is suggested.

Writers seeking co-ventures should focus on mid-sized or smaller independent publishers. Research will reveal publishing companies that may welcome such an arrangement. **Remember that a co-venture is not a subsidy publishing arrangement but a partnership. Beware of being hoodwinked into paying for all of the costs.**

Print-On-Demand

Print-On-Demand publishing is an alternative for the first-time author or poet to consider. Trade paperback-sized books are stored electronically and printed one at a time based on the demand. Turn-around time can be less than forty-eight hours. If a greater quantity is requested, shipment is possible within a week.

Fee-based Print-On-Demand companies are not publishers in the traditional sense. They charge "set-up" fees ranging from ninety-nine dollars to a thousand dollars or more. Some also offer marketing packages and other services. You normally submit your book in electronic form on a computer disk.

Writers receive royalties from the sales of the book. Royalties can range from 20 percent for hardcover books purchased directly from the publishers to 10 percent on those purchased by bookstores, libraries, and the author. This may seem advantageous, but investigate what the fee-based Print-On-Demand publisher can do that you cannot do simply by traditional self-publishing.

The main differences between fee-based Print-On-Demand publishers and traditional self-publishing concerns **control** (when you self-publish, you control all aspects of the book as compared with Print-On-Demand where you choose from the publishing services offered), **book revenue** (traditional self-publishing permits you to keep all book proceeds while Print-On-Demand outlets only provide a royalty), and **book rights** (by traditionally self-publishing, you keep all the rights while some Print-On-Demand outlets require you to contract with them for an extended period of time).

If you are determined to print only a few copies of your book for family and friends with no potential for commercial success, fee-based Print-On-Demand has merit. If you are a public speaker interested in "BOR" (Back of Room) sales, or a businessperson seeking publicity for a specific economic issue, POD can also make sense.

If you do choose a fee-based Print-On-Demand outlet, be certain to hire a line editor with experience in your genre to edit the book. Many POD books are released that include typos and grammatical and punctuation mistakes. Make certain that you have the right to check the final version of the book before it is printed to verify printing quality. When you receive your books, check immediately the printing quality and whether the text includes your revisions. If it does not, return the book to correct the mistakes. Your book is a reflection of you and many are released that prove embarrassing to the writer.

Writers attempting to build a traditional writing career should avoid fee-based Print-On Demand outlets. In the true sense of the words, they are simply subsidy publishers and viewed as such by the traditional publishing industry, bookstores, and libraries. Certain stigmas that attach are described in the next section and reviewers will most likely pass when requested to review the book.

Vanity Presses/Subsidy Presses

Vanity Press is a misunderstood term. Some define it as a company that charges an author for all of the production and marketing costs of their book, but to many, it indicates writers who decide to publish their book for family and friends.

There may be many reasons for doing the latter. A Philadelphia trial lawyer wrote a book chronicling his courtroom adventures. He wanted his children and grandchildren to learn about the justice system during his lifetime. This was worthy and had nothing to do with ego. The accurate term for his effort was self-published.

The term often interchanged with Vanity Press is Subsidy Press. These companies are easy to locate. Vantage Press is the most well known. They accept manuscripts, guide efforts with regard to finalizing proper form and substance for the material and the cover, and then print the book. Editing services and promotional ideas are offered at extra cost.

Similar companies exist on the Internet. **All promise your book will get a look-see from the national chain stores, but the promise doesn't guarantee the book *will be stocked* in those stores.** Most times it will not unless the book stirs enough interest to entice the stores to stock it.

Subsidy Presses have published millions of books. Writers who choose this option have achieved the goal of being published. They are free to sell their books any way they choose, albeit with the press or the publishing company taking its share of the profits. This can range from 25 percent to 50 percent.

As mentioned, a hybrid of subsidy publishers has appeared in recent years. These fee-based Print-On-Demand companies claim to be the author's best friend and some do not demand a share of any book revenues. Nevertheless, organizations that bill themselves as fee-based PODs are in fact subsidy publishers by the very definition of the word "subsidy" since the authors or poets are subsidizing publication. One company, for instance, advertises through mailings "monthly specials" akin to a used car dealer. They also hoodwink the author by making the claim that they will "make [your] book available through more than 25,000 bookstores worldwide." This may be true, but the reality is that few will actually stock the book.

Other Subsidy Press outlets promise that authors will keep the rights to their book. This is acceptable, but the Subsidy Press will receive a hefty portion for each book sold at a price that they determine. Website advertisements alert the author that they have a "variety of options regarding payment percentages." Read the fine print before committing and ask, "What can this subsidy publisher or fee-based POD do that I can't do by traditionally self-publishing where I keep all the revenues?"

If you decide to publish through any outlet that is, in effect, a Subsidy Press, you must have realistic expectations based on the understanding of the advantages and disadvantages of the subsidy press you choose. Some are better than others, but the basic agreement unfolds as follows: The author pays a fee to have a certain number of copies printed. At Vantage Press, 450 copies is the minimum. The company guarantees the book will appear at least once in their *New York Times Book Review* advertisement, and that the book will be distributed through Baker and Taylor, a reputable company. The book will be listed in *Books In Print, Publisher's Trade List Annual*, and the *Vantage Press* catalogue. Book publicity is circulated to local media in the author's area or selected national media through a list the author provides. For this service, the press is entitled to a certain percentage of book revenues.

Vantage Press and other such outlets promise to forward review copies to bookstores and local libraries in the author's area. Major bookstore chains and online book outlets are advised of the publication. If the author schedules book signings, the company will assist with providing books.

Since the Subsidy Press offers such services, many authors and poets wonder why their books do not sell in large quantities. Ninety-nine percent won't because a first-time author or poet has no name recognition, no backing from a nationally known publisher, and no solid marketing and promotional campaign behind them. The national chains and independent stores are reluctant to stock a book by an unknown. They are too busy promoting books by well-known authors.

Libraries frown on all Subsidy Press books. They have limited budgets and are influenced by the bestseller lists. Authors and poets may contact them, but the chances of libraries purchasing the book are slim.

Above all, remember that any Subsidy Press earns most of their money by *charging authors to print the books and for other services, not by selling the books*. Before committing, request a list of best selling books published by the Subsidy Press under consideration.

Understanding their operation can prevent a naive author or poet from being suckered by promises the Subsidy Press can't deliver.

A distinct disadvantage to Subsidy Presses is the stigma attached to it. Many fine books have been published, but there is the perception among traditional publishers, libraries, and the public that a subsidy book is an ego trip not to be taken seriously. Those who publish with Subsidy Presses are marked as rank amateurs who could not be otherwise published. Right or wrong, this is the perception. **As self-publishing guru Dan Poynter says, "The name of the subsidy publisher on the spine of the book is a kiss of death."**

When you copyright material, whether it is the book manuscript or a Book Proposal, you may receive a solicitation letter. The opening line may read, "One of our researchers has come across the manuscript you registered with the Library of Congress and has forwarded your name to us as a possible candidate for publication with our company." The second paragraph mentions "problems" authors have in finding a "commercial publisher." It then reads, "Just having your manuscript read by most commercial publishers is difficult and involves long delays."

This type of language can adversely influence those not familiar with the publishing industry. Beware of such information, or any that discourages traditional publishing or traditional self-publishing. It may not be directly misleading, but there are multiple traditional publishing companies that will consider material and contact the author quickly with an opinion.

Poets should be wary of contests promising that the winners will be included in a published book. Oftentimes, everyone submitting poetry is a "winner," since the contests are intended to lure poets into purchasing the books. Such "pre-purchase" agreements are part of the "publishing trap." It also includes subsidy publishers and literary agents who charge in advance for their services.

Other organizations promise to include poetry in an anthology if the poet will pay a certain fee or purchase books. It is important to distinguish those publishers from the legitimate ones. Those preying on a poet's excitement that he or she will be a "published poet" don't care about how many books are sold, only how many fees they can collect. Avoid such publications for there is a stigma attached to them.

Subsidy publishers rely on the desperation of aspiring authors and poets who believe there is no other way to be published. As stated, beware of the "publishing trap" and consider alternatives before being sucked in by a subsidy publisher, an unprofessional literary agent, or "pre-purchase" poetry book publishers. Investigate before committing.

Internet Publishing

Internet publishing provides a vast array of publishing opportunities similar to standard Subsidy Presses. For a cost, the Internet provider will publish a book as professional as those released by the major publishing companies.

Costs differ for hardcover and paperback editions. Additional fees are charged for editing, cover layout, and other services. Some of the publishers provide free books for author or poet use; some do not. Most retain a hefty percentage of sales revenue. Be wary of promises made that a book will be forwarded to bookstores or other outlets. Many of these companies, like standard Subsidy Presses, earn their revenue from providing author services and not by selling books.

Regardless of the publishing method, authors and poets should not agree to a contract clause binding them for more than a year. Flexibility to accept an offer from a traditional publisher is important.

Contacting Literary Agents and Publishers

If, after considering the options of submitting your book idea to traditional publishers or traditionally self-publishing, you decide on the former, contact literary agents for potential representation.

Locating publishers is simple—gaining their attention is more difficult. While various publications list publishers and contact names, an author or poet submitting material faces long odds. Estimates vary, but publishers confirm they receive thousands upon thousands of manuscripts, Book Proposals, and Query Letters each *week*.

Noah Lukeman, a New York-based literary agent and author of *The First Five Pages: A Writer's Guide To Staying Out of the Rejection Pile*, told *Poets and Writers Magazine*, "To begin with, [writers] *will* need to find an agent. Querying publishers directly is a mistake. If you try, you'll find that the majority of them will simply return your query letter and instruct you to find an agent."

As suggested by Lukeman, **the better and more professional way an author or poet can submit material is through a literary agent or entertainment attorney.** In his book, *Kirsch's Guide To The Book Contract,* author Jonathan Kirsch writes, **"An agent may play a great many roles in the life and work of an author—advisor, cheerleader, confidante, mentor, editor, and more. But an agent is, above all, a salesperson. He tries to find as many potential buyers as possible for the author's work, and seeks to extract the best price available from the interested buyer."**

Knowledge regarding the agency process comes from reading various books such as *Writer's Market* and *The Guide To Literary Agents.* One front cover states that the book will reveal, "500+ Agents Who Sell What You Write, 550 Agencies, 550 Phone Numbers, 200+ e-mail addresses and web sites, 100+ Subject Categories, 100+ Conferences." Other source material includes the *Literary Market Place, Member List, Association of Author's Representatives,* and *Novel and Short Story Writer's Market. Writer's Digest* provides listings of established agents as well.

For information regarding the submission of poetry, consult *Poet's Market.* It reveals submission guidelines, contact names, and other important information. A list of chapbook publishers (release of small volumes of poetry) is included as are the names of reference books helpful to the aspiring poet. *Poets and Writers Magazine* also is a good source for the name of literary agents who will represent poets.

A good source for information about children's books is the Children's Book Council. Information regarding publishing opportunities, trends, and specific data concerning submission of material is available at www.cbcbooks.org. Also reference *Children's Writer's and Illustrator's Market,* an annual publication of *Writer's Digest Books.* Another is *Children's Book Market, The Writer's Sourcebook,* a publication of the Institute of Children's Literature.

Aspiring children's book writers are encouraged to research membership in the Society of Children's Books Writers and Illustrators. Chapters are located in nearly every state and around the world. More information about this prestigious organization can be learned at www.scbwi.org.

Literary Agency Information

The Guide To Literary Agents **is an important reference source for an aspiring author or poet. Read it from cover to cover.** Included with each agency listing (see Appendix for sample Literary Agency and Publisher listings) are addresses, telephone numbers, fax numbers, e-mail addresses, and contact names. Most listings tell how long the agency has been in business and how many clients it represents.

The listing is informative as to the type of material the agency specializes in—fiction, non-fiction, poetry, and so forth. Under "Represents," the agency includes the specific types of books they represent. For instance, one literary agency lists more than a hundred categories including cookbooks, gay and lesbian issues, New Age/metaphysics, action/adventure, romance, science fiction, money/finance, and women's studies.

Important to note is the "How To Contact" section. Here the literary agency provides an explanation as to the rules and regulations for presentation of material. For one company, it reads, "Query [letter] with outline plus three sample chapters. Reports in one week on queries. One month on manuscripts."

Toward the bottom of the agency listing is the phrase, "Recent Sales." This category lists how many books the agency sold during the previous year. It provides an indication of their prowess in the industry, since they not only list the books, but the publishers who bought them. If such companies as Random House, Doubleday, St. Martins, Warner Books, and Simon and Schuster are listed, then the literary agency is a real player, one with contacts throughout the industry.

The Association of Author's Representatives web site (www.aar-online.org) is a terrific source for information about how to secure an agent (a search page denotes agents for literary, dramatic, adult, and children's books – agents are then listed by website address providing a way to check their credentials and submission guidelines) and the basis of an agent/author relationship. The site also presents a list of questions to ask a literary agent who expresses an interest in representing you.

Another helpful website is www.literaryagents.org. This site provides information regarding agents and the type of material they are seeking. There are also tips presented concerning proven methods to secure representation by reputable agents.

Agent contacts can also be secured by checking the publishing deals listed in the newsletter published at www.publisherslunch.com. Each announcement normally contains the name of the agent who sold the book and their website address.

Literary Agency Fees

To understand the business acumen of selected agencies, check the section in *The Guide To Literary Agents* titled, "Terms." This explains the percentage the agency will commission from any revenues the author or poet receives. For one agency, it reads, "Agent receives 15 percent commission on domestic sales, 20 percent on foreign sales. Offer written contracts, which can be canceled after thirty days." This refers to an agreement between the author and the agency for representation that may be cancelled by either party.

While fifteen percent may seem like a big bite, and it is, the number is standard in the publishing industry. Representing yourself deflects any fee, but having a literary agent supporting you and providing advice is essential to building a career. I rationalize the agency fee by saying, "85% of something is better than 100% of nothing."

Most publishing companies would rather deal with a literary agent than with the author or poet who is the creative genius that wrote the book. When business matters occur, editors at publishing companies prefer to discuss them with the agent. He or she will assist the author or poet if a conflict occurs between them and the publisher. Having an agent act as a buffer can prevent hard feelings.

One reminder about literary agents—never forget that they work for you, not vice-versa. If you feel the agent isn't acting in your best interest, let him or her know. Good communication is essential to a long-term relationship, since agents represent many other clients. When agents are upset, it is usually more about them than it is about you. Exercise patience and understanding.

Remember that top literary agents have an on-going working relationship with the same publishing company editors. When conflict occurs, don't hesitate to question the agent about decisions being made. The agent must act in your best interest. If this does not occur, you should part company.

Contacting literary agents by telephone or e-mail after representation has been finalized is proper, but do so with consideration. Agents earn revenue by selling books and do not have time to chat on the telephone or through Internet instant message. Agents should not be considered counselors, therapists, or even editors. They can enhance a career, guide it, and provide support, but their main job is to sell as many books as possible.

Understand that telephone calls are often not returned. If literary agents have news to report, they will contact you. Otherwise leave them alone, especially on hectic Mondays, getaway Fridays, or during August when New York literary agents and editors flock to the Hamptons for sun and surf.

Choose a literary agent with a vision for a lasting career. Before selecting one, discuss long-term goals and the type of material of interest. Planning book two while book one is being readied for publication is essential for fiction, non-fiction, or poetry. Work with your agent to form a team that plans ahead in accordance with trends in the marketplace and book subjects that will be timely.

Book ideas originate with the author and the poet, not from the agent. One poet requested a meeting with an agent so he could learn of ideas for alternative poetry books. I explained that researching the marketplace was his job.

To help you understand the author/poet/agent relationship, a sample agency agreement is featured in the Appendix of this book. Also featured are tips regarding the agent and publisher listings featured in *Writer's Market*.

Securing a literary agent is terrific, but you must continue to be a cheerleader for your book. Check in with the agent on a frequent basis. Remind them your book is the best one ever written and request updates on publisher progress. Most agents represent many books and it is a must to keep yours on the front burner.

Literary Agency Warnings

As stated before, a word of caution is warranted for the uninitiated. **If a literary agent or agency requests that you pay *them* a fee for**

representation in addition to, or as an alternative to a percentage, run like hell.

Well-established literary agencies never charge an upfront fee. Be wary if an agent or agency requests a "reading fee" or "an evaluation fee." Recouping reasonable expenses for copying and mailing is proper, but make certain there is a cap on the amount spent without your written authorization. If there are questions regarding the conduct of a literary agent, contact the Association of Author's Representatives. Legitimate literary agents are members and subject to the AAR Canon of Ethics.

Hiring one literary agent to represent your works is appropriate, but some agents or agencies are better at handling particular types of books than others. Searching the AAR listings guarantees that you are contacting literary agents who will be most interested in your genre of writing.

Literary agent contracts can be written or verbal. When entering into a written agreement, beware of hidden clauses binding you to the agent for a lengthy period. Attempt to work on a project-by-project basis. If the relationship doesn't work, the agreement can be terminated.

Literary Agent Research

A most common question among aspiring authors and poets is: "How can I find a literary agent that will be interested in my book?"

A prelude to this question is whether you need a literary agent at all. If you intend to publish your works for a regional magazine, a literary journal, or independent presses, you probably don't. But if you decide that submission to the larger publishing world is worthy, an agent is essential since most of the prestigious companies will not accept unrepresented books.

To discover the right agent for your book, strategy is a key. When you decide on the exact book you want to write, check literary agency listings to determine which ones represent that genre. **List the "usual suspects" in a notebook and then visit the nearest bookstore.**

Just as the initial visit discussed in Chapter One provided education about the workings of the book industry, this one will narrow the field of potential agents to be contacted. It requires checking the Acknowledgments pages of books similar to the one under consideration to discover if any of the names you have collected from *The Guide To Literary Agents,* or another publication, coincides with those listed in the Acknowledgments. Also note agents listed on the AAR website and at www.literaryagents.org.

This exercise lets you formulate a list of top agents who are candidates to handle the type of book you contemplate. As previously mentioned, the Acknowledgments may also provide the names of editors at the publishing company who collaborated with the author.

A tip for unpublished authors and poets suggests seeking what has become known as an "early-career agent." This means that although all budding writers would love to have John Grisham or Mary Higgins Clark's agent represent them, this is unlikely and probably a mistake since they are too busy representing their big guns.

The alternative is to seek agents who have been representing writers for a year or two and are hungry to move up the ladder in the literary agent world. One of the best sources to discover these agents is in *Publisher's Weekly* magazine where John Baker and other staff members chronicle publishing industry news in the "Hot Deals" column. Examining the news provides up-to-date information. Pay special attention to the announcement that a literary agency has hired new agents. These are likely candidates to be interested in your material as long as it falls into a category they intend to represent. Literary agency websites are most helpful to learn agent specialties.

Organizing a list of agents and publishers who should be interested in your book narrows the field for submission. A separate Rolodex listing of those names is warranted. When you are ready to submit your Query Letter and Book Proposal, the list will serve as a guide. Contacting those individuals will cut the odds, since you will know that these agents or publishers have shown interest in the type of book you are considering. Otherwise, you waste time and effort submitting material to agents who will have no interest.

Don't be afraid to use non-traditional means of contacting literary agents and/or publishers. Anyone can scan the "help-books" and discover names, but if you are dedicated to being published, you will not only hone in on the "usual suspects" interested in the contemplated book, but use friendships, acquaintances, or the bartender down the street to advantage. **Remember that any agency will consider Book Proposals and/or manuscripts in the following order: those submitted by clients and former clients, those**

referred to the agency by other agents or clients, and those arriving unsolicited.

If you know someone who has been represented by an agent, ask for a referral. Don't be afraid to approach published authors or poets since the worst that can occur is for them to say "no."

Meeting literary agents at writers' conferences or conventions is a terrific way to begin a relationship. Resist the temptation to overwhelm the agent with ideas for several books. Simply make the acquaintance and then follow up with a letter or telephone call at a later date.

To attract attention to your Book Proposal and Query Letter, be clever. On the packages I sent out while seeking representation for *Down For The Count*, I imprinted the cover with a red stamped outline of two dogs barking. I hoped an animal lover at the agency might place my material on the top of the pile.

Remember that most agents and publishers are not receptive to receiving a completed manuscript. Instead they welcome a Query Letter and a Book Proposal. Some make it clear that if a manuscript is submitted, it will be deposited in the nearest receptacle.

A reminder—the fiction writer should have a completed manuscript ready for submission at the time their Book Proposal and Query Letter are submitted to agents, since they are less interested in works-in-progress. Remember to indicate a readiness to forward the manuscript upon request.

Literary agents are looking for new writers. They make their money by selling books and are on the lookout for terrific book ideas. As noted agent Kimberly Cameron told *Writer's Digest*, "I am always optimistic every day that I am going to discover a wonderful voice."

Entertainment Attorneys

If you decide to hire an attorney instead of a literary agent, or in addition to an agent, use caution: **there are entertainment lawyers and *then there are entertainment lawyers.*** Many general practitioners and business lawyers have read a book or taken a seminar regarding the entertainment field. They describe themselves as savvy in that arena. Beware of such animals. Check the lawyer's credentials before retaining him or her. Request references and inquire as to their knowledge of the publishing industry.

Publishers relish the opportunity to negotiate with competent attorneys, but those unschooled in the literary world inhibit dealmaking. "The worse thing that can happen," explains Marie Butler-Knight, publisher of Alpha Books, an imprint within Penguin Group USA, "is for the author to be represented by an attorney who isn't knowledgeable about literary contracts."

The Publishing Process

Publishing a book should be an exhilarating experience, but there will be bumps along the way. Adhering to **Mark's Step #6— Traditional Publishing Is A Writer's Best Friend** will help stem the tide of disappointment.

With this in mind, do your homework—the book you believe in deserves it. **Choosing the right literary agent and/or publishing alternative guarantees that you are using a strategy optimizing your opportunities for a career as a published author or poet.**

Step #6 Summary

- Research alternative means of book publishing.

- Beware of Subsidy Publishers or other non-traditional publishers who promise distribution to major bookstores and libraries.

- Poets beware of publishers promising publication if a certain number of books are purchased.

- Instead of subsidy publishers, consider Self-Publishing alternatives.

- When searching for literary agents, check *The Guide To Literary Agents*, *Writer's Market,* and *Poet's Market.*

- Beware of literary agents who request payment in advance for their services.

- Once you have compiled a list of likely agents and publishers, check guidelines to see what form of submission is proper.

Self-Publishing Concepts

Assess the marketplace to be sure your book concept is unique.

Read a competent book on the subject of self-publishing to ensure your understanding of the concepts outlined here.

Complete the manuscript including:
> Prologue and Epilogue, if any
> Copyright page (copyright statement, disclaimers, ISBN, publisher Information)
> Table of Contents
> Acknowledgments Page, if any
> Appendices, if any
> Bibliography, if any
> Index, if any.

Hire a competent line editor to edit the manuscript.

When the manuscript is edited, file for copyright protection from the Library of Congress.

Secure an ISBN number (R.R. Bowker is one source).

Prepare the cover or jacket, including:
> Front cover artwork, if any
> Back cover artwork, if any, text, and barcodes
> Front and back jacket, including artwork, if any, and text
> Inside back cover material, and author photograph, if any.

Investigate alternative printing costs.

Establish storage space for books if you plan to distribute them yourself.

Complete your book printing and binding.

Set release date for publication of book.

Position your book for sale at bookstores, Internet outlets such as Amazon.com, and your website.

Consider contacting independent distributors listed in various industry publications.

List your book in Forthcoming Books and Books In Print.

Read *The Complete Guide To Book Publicity* by Jodee Blanco.

Begin promotion campaign including media exposure, booksignings, and mailings.

Celebrate release of your book with an expensive bottle of champagne.

Begin writing a new book while the current one is being promoted.

All the world knows me in my book, and my book in me.

MICHEL DE MONTAIGNE

Step #7
Market The Query Letter and Book Proposal,
Not The Book

<u>Book Proposals</u>

To maximize the potential to become traditionally published, prepare a professionally written Book Proposal. Why so? New York-based literary agent David Black, discoverer of, among other books, the bestseller, *Tuesdays With Morrie,* states, **"While it's possible that an unknown writer will be discovered by a top literary agent, it's a challenge. The number of books published each year is getting smaller. Make sure you send a proposal of the highest quality, and that it's designed to get respect."**

In *The Insider's Guide to Getting Published,* author John Boswell provides compelling facts regarding Book Proposals. He writes, **"Today fully 90% of all non-fiction books sold to trade publishers [sale to consumers] are acquired on the basis of the proposal alone."**

The percentage of works of fiction sold through Book Proposals is subject to conjecture. Offered the choice of reading a concise, exciting Book Proposal or a 400-page novel submitted by an aspiring author, agents and editors will choose the former. If the Book Proposal material indicates promise, they can contact the writer and request that a manuscript be forwarded to them.

Based on these facts, the aspiring author or poet is encouraged to follow **Mark's Step #7—Market The Query Letter and Book Proposal, Not The Book**.

This said, authors and poets wonder whether they should write the Query Letter or the Book Proposal first. Methods will vary, but I suggest writing the Book Proposal first since you will use portions of the information formulated in the proposal in the Query Letter. Remember that the Query Letter is simply a mini-proposal setting up readers for the extended information about the book contained in the Book Proposal.

The journey toward completing a draft of the proposal begins with understanding what a Book Proposal *is* and what it *is not*. **Above all, the Book Proposal *is* a sales tool.** Within the scope of twenty to thirty pages, less in many cases, the "written pitch" outlines the author or poet's game plan so an agent or editor at a publishing company can consider its merits.

What the Book Proposal is *not* relates to the style of writing. **It should not be promotional, boastful or pompous. A well-conceived Book Proposal doesn't *tell* the reader the book is the greatest one ever written. Instead, the text *shows* them through good writing and interesting facts that the book has merit.**

Being enthused about your book's potential can color your objectivity. Before long, the proposal takes on the aura of a used car salesman attempting to convince Mr. Jones a chartreuse Plymouth has great resale value. Heed the advice of Jack Webb, Sergeant Joe Friday on the television program, *Dragnet*. Confronting a perplexed witness to a crime, Joe would bellow, "Just the facts, ma'am; just the facts."

Literary agent David Black's perception regarding Book Proposals is accurate. He says, **"I can usually tell in 10-30 seconds if the [book] proposal I'm reading is promising, and my instincts are usually correct."**

Ten to thirty seconds—that's not much time. If the writer hasn't hooked readers after they've scanned the cover page, the tagline, and the first few words in the Overview or Synopsis' first paragraph, the book idea is deader than dead.

Agents and editors don't have time to waste. **Either the Book Proposal sparks the immediate brainwave, "Wow, this can be a great book," or the material is headed for the dumpster.**

Sample Book Proposals for fiction, non-fiction, and poetry are presented in the Appendix. Use these proposals as guideposts, noting the proper form. Self-help books vary about the components of the Book Proposal, but the Appendix samples follow a form that has proven successful.

Many writers abhor the idea of writing Query Letters or Book Proposals. The process appears difficult and time-consuming. But with a well-planned strategy, writing the letter and proposal can be completed without actual loss of life. And doing so will pay off. Over the past few years, I have been amused when an author or poet telephones and says, **"You'll never guess what happened. I actually received a letter from an agent or an editor asking to read my manuscript based on the query letter and book proposal."**

Even more satisfying is notice that a writer who composed a Book Proposal using this book as their guidepost has secured a publishing deal. This occurred for Christine Montross, a Brown University medical student whose book about laboratory experiences during her first year was sold by her literary agent at ICM to Penguin Group USA.

Writers like Christine seem amazed at the good fortune, but the response is to be expected. Even when authors or poets receive a rejection letter, most include a compliment regarding the Book Proposal and the offer to consider future book ideas. Plain and simple—forwarding a professionally written Query Letter and Book Proposal gains the attention of literary agents and publishing company editors. Believe it.

Taglines

Any book, whether fiction, non-fiction, or a collection of poetry can be described in ten to fifteen words or less, preferably less. If this is not possible, then the book idea should be discarded, since the Tagline will be an essential part of any Book Proposal.

The Tagline, a.k.a "hook for the book," or "handle," is akin to "pitches" made to motion picture studios by producers and screenwriters attempting to convince executives to produce a film. For *The Perfect Yankee*, the story of Don Larsen's perfect game in the 1956 World Series, the pitch was, "It's *Bull Durham* meets *The Natural* with a touch of *Major League* thrown in." If you are familiar with those films, you know exactly what *The Perfect Yankee* is about.

Examples of great taglines abound. *Pearl Harbor,* the film, gained the connotation, deserved or not, of "Titanic with a love story." Steven Spielberg's motion picture, *A. I. (Artificial Intelligence),* utilized the tagline, "E. T. Grows Up." The film *Rock Star* was dubbed, "The Story of a Wannabe Who Got To Be."

The publishing industry also relies on Taglines to sell and promote books. A book may be described as "It's *Into Thin Air* meets *The Perfect Storm*" or "It's *My Friend Flicka* set in the Colorado Rockies." Comparisons stretch to the author as well. "He writes like John

Grisham," "She can write mysteries like Mary Higgins Clark," and "He's a cross between Hemingway and Woody Allen," are examples.

Perhaps the best illustration of a Tagline for a book that became a bestseller is Grisham's *The Firm*. It read, "It's a book about a recent law school graduate who is offered a job at a law firm that seems too good to be true—and it is." He may have used more than fifteen words, but it works.

Book advertisements such as the ones featured in the Thursday Life Section of *USA Today* provide inspiration for Taglines. Each is designed to convince the public that the specific book is a must read.

Consider this advertisement for the book *Hostage* by author Robert Crais. The Tagline read, "Three fugitives with a desperate plan. Three hostages with a deadly secret. One battle-scarred cop with no way out." For Ross Lamanna's *Acid Test*, the tagline was, "High tech weaponry. Humans beyond humanity. And the world at their mercy." Adding to the lure was the endorsement, "Thrill-a-minute writing . . . like Tom Clancy on speed." *A Love Worth Giving*, by Max Lucado, bore the Tagline, "Love Never Fails (You Just Have To Do It Right)."

For Iyanla Vanzant's *Living Through the Meantime*, the advertisement featured the Tagline, "Leads you step-by-step to a greater understanding of your motivations and your desires, helping you to break the patterns of the past and begin the healing process." A *Los Angeles Times* quote followed stating, "Vanzant is the author people want to hug and thank." Hank Hanegraaff's *The Covering* featured the daunting words, "24/7/365, Protection From Evil."

The advertisement for *Turn Off The Hunger Switch* was clever. It read, "What's Really Keeping The Weight On? Chocolate? Pasta? Chips? Actually, It's All In Your Head. Literally."

The Thursday *USA Today* Book Page provides a bestseller list. Alongside the name of the book, the author, the publishing company, and the price of the book are listed descriptions that reflect the book's Tagline. Written by the *USA Today* editor based on publisher marketing materials, they can be quite creative:

Best selling Books—Fiction/Non-Fiction

Rank of Book/Author	Description	Publisher
1 The DaVinci Code/ Dan Brown Louve	Murder clues left inside Leonardo art at the	Doubleday
2 The South Beach Diet/ Arthur Agatston	Allows dieters to eat food they love	Rodale
3 The Dark Tower V/ Stephen King	Book V in The Dark Tower series	Scribner
4 The Five People You Meet In Heaven/ Mitch Albom	In heaven, life is explained by five people	Hyperion
5 Key of Light/ Nora Roberts	Three women face dangerous quest	Jove
6 New Diet Revolution/ Robert C. Atkins	Kick-start your metabolism to burn more calories	Avon
7 Angels and Demons/ Dan Brown	Organization launches vendetta against the Catholic Church	Pocket
8 The Purpose-Driven Life/ Rick Warren	Subtitle: What on Earth Am I Here For?	Zondervan
9 The Ultimate Weight Solution/ Phillip C. McGraw	The 7 Keys To Weight Loss Freedom	Free Press
10 By the Light of the Moon/ Dean Koontz	Drug could kill or transform	Bantam

Whether the Tagline is five words or fifteen, clarity is essential. Michael Korda, editor in chief at Simon and Schuster, wrote, **"If you** can't describe a book in one or two pithy sentences that would **make my mother want to read it, then of course you can't sell it."** His quote relates to writing whether it is fiction, non-fiction or poetry.

An added benefit to the Book Page in *USA Today* is the listing of new releases. In one issue, three novels, *Backpack*, *Just Like Beauty*, and *Spilling Clarence* were discussed under the banner, "Debut Novels Query Rough, Weird, Touching Terrain." The first paragraph read, "Three quirky debut novels take readers into strange territory: the bohemian subculture of backpackers in Asia, toxic suburbia in the near future, and town dragged into reliving old memories." Each book provides inspiration for aspiring authors since they were "debut novels."

Snippets of imaginative text were provided. For *Backpack*, it read, "I'll be skinny and brown. I'll wear little sarongs and tiny vests, and I'll stand around looking lovely and thinking deep thoughts. Tom will beg me to go back to him but I will have met someone intriguing and devoted, and I will look sorrowfully upon Tom and tell him not to dwell on what might have been."

Taglines for poetry are as varied as the material submitted. **Since most collections of poetry have a common theme, the poet must present a snappy hook providing the reader with a clear indication as to the message being conveyed.** One poet decided he intended to write a chapbook designed to enlighten divorced fathers regarding their responsibilities toward their children. When asked by an editor what the theme of the collection was, he simply answered, "Dads, Don't Be A Dope." Another whose collection featured the "dark side" of religion used the Tagline, "Christ's Underbelly."

Book Titles

Book titles for fiction, non-fiction or poetry must be snappy, concise, and descriptive. Above all, they must pique the reader's curiousity.

With non-fiction, the subject matter is a star and the title will depict a certain person, event, or issue. Titles such as *Ghandi*, *MacArthur*, *Truman*, *Dolly (Dolly Parton)*, *In Cold Blood*, *DiMaggio*, and *Hoffa*, are examples. *One Hundred and One Ways To Invest, Race and Responsibility, A History of National League Ballparks, Suzanne*

Somers' *Eat, Cheat, and Melt Away The Fat,* and *Gay Men In The White House* provide instant recognition regarding subject matter.

For works of fiction, clever word usage provides clues to the book's content. Hemingway's *The Old Man and the Sea,* John Dunning's *The Bookman's Wake,* and Scott Turow's *Presumed Innocent* reflect recognition of the themes presented.

Titles for my publications are the result of extensive consideration. *Down For The Count* described what occurred to boxer Mike Tyson when he was convicted of rape. *Bury Me In A Pot Bunker* might have caused people to think it was a book about death and dying, but it depicted the life and times of golf course designer Pete Dye, famous for golf courses featuring deep pot bunkers.

Forever Flying described the adventures of aviator R. A. "Bob" Hoover. The subtitle, "Fifty Years of High-Flying Adventures, from Barnstorming in Prop-Planes to Dogfighting Germans to Testing Supersonic Jets," added zest.

The Perfect Yankee portrayed Don Larsen's World Series perfect game achievement. *Testament To Courage* described the "angel of mercy" persona of Holocaust survivor Cecelia Rexin. *Larry Legend* chronicled the life of NBA superstar Larry Bird, and *Miscarriage of Justice, The Jonathan Pollard Story* summed up the plight of the most controversial spy in American history.

No Peace For The Wicked reflects the tone for a novel focusing on the wrongful imprisonment of two mentally handicapped men convicted of a murder they did not commit. *The Patsy, A Jake Lessing Novel,* was so titled since an innocent young boy is caught in the web of a corrupt legal system.

Where do titles originate? Inspiration is everywhere, but mine have originated straight from the Good Lord. He awakens me in the middle of the night with the title embedded in my brain. I write the title on note cards I keep by the bed.

A check of the *USA Today* bestseller listing provides a plethora of creative titles. *Who Moved My Cheese?* and *Venus Envy,* the book about Venus Williams and female tennis professionals, are examples of creative titles. Others are *Sacred Sins, The Last Precinct, Wild Justice, Body-For-Life, Earthquake in the Morning, The Red Tent, Four Blondes,* and two personal favorites, *Drowning Ruth* and *The Man Who Mistook His Wife For A Hat.* James Patterson's book, *The*

Lake House, sounds intriguing, especially when readers learn that the main character's name is Ethan Cane.

Titles for collections of poetry must reflect the theme of the poet's intentions. *Sailing Around The Room* by Billy Collins, *Elegy For A Southern Drawl* by Rodney Jones, and *Misery Prefigured* by J. Allen Rosser achieve that goal.

Aspiring authors and poets must create a title so strong it will catch the attention of an agent or publisher. If this is accomplished, it kick-starts a mindset that says, "I must read this material."

Book Proposal Components

If you have decided traditional book publishing is your first choice, determined the book contemplated is marketable, completed the research necessary to ensure accuracy of the text, finalized an outline, written at least three sample chapters, conceived a book title, and described your intended publication in fifteen words or less, you are ready to attempt a first draft of the Book Proposal. It should include:

> Cover page information
>
> A second page featuring a snappy quote that will hook the agent or editor
>
> Contents page, (optional)
>
> Book Tagline (Hook)
>
> Overview (Non-Fiction) or Synopsis (Fiction) of the book concept (Also called Brief Description or Content Summary)
>
> Author Biography
>
> Book Audience
>
> Similar Successful Books
>
> Book Promotion Ideas
>
> Format/Manuscript Status, (optional)

Book-To-Film

Book Outline

Sample Text (two or three sample chapters (dependent on length)

Appendix

Some authors and poets decide to submit only the Query Letter and Sample Chapters, but including the additional information mentioned above guarantees that the writer has provided all of the essentials about their book idea. Take the extra time to prepare material for each section listed. It will pay off.

Examples of Book Proposal formats are featured in the Appendix. Remember: the first page will provide the title, a subtitle if there is one, and your name. The second will present the snappy quote. The third page provides a Proposal Table of Contents. This is optional.

Beginning on the fourth page, with the title of the book at the top, are the components of the Book Proposal. They are: the Tagline followed by the Overview or Synopsis, Author Biography, Book Audience, Similar Successful Books, Promotion Ideas, Format/Manuscript (optional), and Book To Film, if appropriate. The Outline, Sample Text, and Appendix follow these compartments. There is no need to separate the compartments on individual pages—they should flow from page to page.

If the Book Proposal concerns children's books, poetry, essays, or other material that is not long form, the sample material should be representative of that genre. Length is less important than presentation of material showcasing your talent. When mentioning photographs, you should indicate "photographs available on request." Some publishers shy away from books requiring an extensive number of them due to cost factors.

Regardless of the genre of the book, the Book Proposal must be adapted to the material being presented for consideration. Emphasis should be placed on the merits of the book that you believe are most important. Providing the literary agent or editor with concise, well-organized information is a key.

Book Proposal Form

As stated, sample Book Proposals for fiction, non-fiction, and poetry are provided in the Appendix, but **your proposal will be uniquely yours.** Write it in your best, succinct prose in accordance with proper form: easy-to-read typeface, double-spaced, and printed on one side of the page with margins of one inch. Laser-print the text on 8 1/2 x 11 inch white paper (no onion skin). Do not staple it so copies can be made. Many software packages provide the proper format.

Opinions vary among literary agents and publishers, but the basic general format for the Book Proposal is simple. For guidance that will visualize its form, consider purchasing *My Book Proposal*, our foundation software that provides easy-to-use templates outlining the essential elements.

If you do not have the software, I suggest that you open a new computer file and list the various components in continuous order. The cover page will only include your book title in 36 font, the subtitle, if any, in 24 font, and your name in 24 font. A second page will feature a snappy quote from the book designed to capture the attention of the literary agent or publisher. The third page can include a table of contents, and the fourth page will be presented as follows:

Title of Book (18 font – bold)

Note: The components are continuous; each one does not begin on a separate page. The proposal is written in Times-Roman, and it is not stapled so that copies may be made. All except the Tagline and the description section of the Outline is written double-spaced. The entire proposal will be no more than thirty pages. (Except for the headings, the text will be in 12 font.)

Tagline (all headings - 14 font – bold)
> Hook for the book – 15 words or less – show the literary agent or editor what the book or collection of poetry is about. Single-spaced, 12 font.

Synopsis (fiction/poetry) or **Overview** (non-fiction)

Synopsis – plot, characters, beginning, middle, and end, 6-10 pages showing the literary agent or editor what the story is about. (Single-spaced, 12 font, all text below)

Poetry – provide the theme of the poetry collection.

Overview – information provided about the subject, beginning, middle, and end, 6-10 pages showing the literary agent or editor what the book is about

Author Biography

Provide academic credentials, personal information, and publishing credits, if any, but more important, answer this question: Why are you the one person in the world to write this book? Remember, the literary agent or editor wants to know your credentials, your platform, and your expertise to write the book.

Book Audience

Provide information as to who is the target audience for the book. The broader the audience, the better. Remember, 75% of people who purchase books are women.

Similar Successful Books

What successful books or collections of poetry are similar to yours, and most important, why is yours unique or better? If there are none, why will yours be successful?

Promotion Ideas

Why are you and your book promotable, and what unique ideas do you have to promote the book? Remember – literary agents and editors love a built-in audience.

Format/Manuscript Status

Provide reader with storytelling sequence and whether manuscript is completed or will be completed within x months of contract.

Book-To-Film

If you believe your book can become a film, show why by using examples of successful films that feature your subject matter.

Book Outline

Provide chapter headings (14 font) and three to four lines describing the subject matter of each chapter (12 font, single-spaced).

Poetry – provide names of poems and brief description.

Sample Text

Provide one to three chapters (usually the Prologue, if any, and Chapter One and Two) depending on length. The writing should be superb; no grammatical or punctuation mistakes permitted. (Double-spaced, 12 font).

Appendix

Include any pertinent information, (media clippings, photographs, etc.) you believe the literary agent or editor should know to assist promotion and marketing of you or the book.

Quotes

Choosing a unique quote or two for the second page of the Book Proposal is advisable. For the non-fiction book, *Forever Flying*, the quote chosen read, "Ladies and gentleman, let me introduce you to Bob Hoover, the greatest stick and rudder man alive today . . . No, that's wrong, let me introduce you to Bob Hoover, the greatest stick and rudder man who ever lived."—General James Doolittle. For *Code Of Silencei*, I highlighted this quote from gangster Santo Traficante to mob lawyer Frank Ragano: "Whatever you do, don't ask Melvin Belli about Jack Ruby. It's none of your business."

If the work is fiction, consider including a clever quote from the text or one describing the gist of the material. For *No Peace For The Wicked*, a quote by American novelist Mary McCarthy was selected. It read, "An unrectified case of injustice has a terrible way of lingering, restlessly, in the social atmosphere like an unfinished question."

For the book, *Heavy Breathing In Thin Air*, the quote, "I could hardly breathe when I saw Allison since she was a beauty like none before her. My right arm felt numb, and I discovered that my eyeballs attempted to jump out of their sockets as she approached," was used. For *Peace Be With You*, the author chose "Jerome was a sick kid. He never said hello, he dressed in black, and he hated his dog. His only redeeming value was a sense of humor like Woody Allen's."

A clever quote or two piques an agent or editor's interest. They realize the quotes can be used in the marketing campaign for the book.

Overview/Synopsis

Having gained the attention of the agent or editor with the book title and quotes, a non-fiction writer begins drafting the Overview. **Akin to a treatment written for a film, the Overview lays out the story so the reader will understand the flow of the book and the story contained therein.**

One might believe writing a Synopsis (covers the basic plot, characters, and storyline) for a work of fiction would differ from the non-fiction Overview, but
this is not necessarily true. The key is to show the reader a storyline featuring a good beginning, middle, and end. **The Overview or Synopsis is a mini-book, a type of "novella"** *about* **the book.** This will be normally completed in present tense. Few summaries or conclusions are permitted—just fact, fact, fact. **For inspiration, check the inside jacket covers for books similar to yours since the writer has provided a snapshot of the book content akin to an overview or synopsis.**

One proven method is to begin the Overview by stating the name of the book and then writing "tells the story of" followed by a few lines regarding the storyline. For example, *Miscarriage of Justice* tells the story of Jonathan Pollard, the infamous American who spied for Israel in the mid-1980s.

How you describe your story will be a preview of how you will develop your book. The first paragraph or two are the most important. The very strongest material must appear—bang, bang, bang. Author

John Boswell states, "Most editors [I would add, agents] read at only two speeds: slow, when editing a manuscript; and scan, when reading everything else." With the latter in mind, your first paragraph or two must be explosive.

Alternative means of gaining attention from the agent or editor include: a shocking statement, strong visual images, "what-if" scenarios, or pointed questions designed to garner curiosity. Select one guaranteed to titillate readers so they must continue to learn more about the book concept.

In *Your Novel Proposal*, authors Camenson and Cook outlined the elements of a fiction Synopsis. They list, "an opening hook, quick sketches of the main characters, plot high points, the core conflict, and the conclusion." Samples of conflict are presented in the book. Structuring the Synopsis is also discussed.

The length of the Overview or Synopsis will vary. Less is always better, but some stories will stretch to ten pages. Content is most important.

In the Overview for *Forever Flying*, a strong visual image was chosen. The text read, "The sky is his [Bob Hoover's] playground as he twists and turns the bright yellow P-51 Mustang through majestic maneuvers that make the eagles jealous. On the ground, huge throngs of admirers gasp at his daredevil loops and spins and wonder in awe whether the tall, lanky man with the ready smile and swooping handlebar mustache will survive yet another dangerous encounter with death."

The Overview swept readers into the aviation world of R. A. "Bob" Hoover, a World War II hero and aviation icon. The writing was visual, not only concerning Bob's flying escapades, but regarding who he was and how he pushed the envelope despite the stare of death at every turn. This type of description convinced readers they wanted to know more: who is Bob Hoover, why he is so important, and why will people purchase a book chronicling his life?

After readers were hooked, the Overview for *Forever Flying* described Hoover's flying genius. The second paragraph read, "Whether he's performing the 'Cuban-Eight,' 'Sixteen Point Hesitation Rolls,' or the 'Dead-Engine Management Maneuver,' Robert A. 'Bob' Hoover and his vintage plane slice through the clouds like a lightning bolt. When the P-51 dances gingerly to Hoover's

'Tennessee Waltz' aerobatics, you can almost hear the melodic music in the background."

I then addressed Hoover's credibility. The third paragraph read, "Called 'the pilot's pilot,' and the 'greatest pilot I ever saw' by famed aviator Chuck Yeager, fun-loving seventy-four-year-old Bob Hoover is the greatest aerobatic pilot who ever lived. A brave World War II POW who escaped to freedom by stealing a German plane, and a test pilot extraordinaire, the bombastic barnstormer is the giant of his profession, a combination of The Red Baron, Waldo Pepper, and Jimmy Doolittle rolled into one."

The text established Bob Hoover's credentials by feeding the reader vital information spiced with the names of famous people such as Chuck Yeager and General Doolittle. In this paragraph, I included the Tagline that would be part of the verbal pitch my agent would use to sell the book. I'm certain he told the editor who purchased the rights, "Bob Hoover is a combination of The Red Baron, Waldo Pepper, and Jimmy Doolittle rolled into one."

After providing additional facts regarding Hoover's remarkable career (winner of the Distinguished Flying Cross, Purple Heart, Lindbergh Medal), describing several life threatening situations (steering a dead-engine P-80 Shooting Star jet to safety, bailing out of a burning F-84 Thunderjet), and utilizing buzzwords to enhance his status ("embodied the very spirit of the American patriot and emerged as a bona fide American hero"), the Overview for *Forever Flying* backtracked to the early years of Hoover's life. The reader returned to his childhood, flying experiences at age fifteen, his entry into World War II, and his subsequent action as a fighter pilot. The text then described his capture by the Germans when his plane was shot down over the coast of Italy, the torture he endured when he wouldn't reveal Allied secrets and his incarceration in the dreaded Stalag I German prison camp.

As the tale continued, the reader discovered that Hoover stole a German plane and flew to freedom before returning to the United States where he and Chuck Yeager competed to discover who would attempt to break the sound barrier. Hoover's career as a test pilot led to his being crowned the "King of the Air Shows," a tribute to his skill as an aerobatic pilot.

The final paragraph of the Overview provided a frame of reference for Bob Hoover's importance in history. Using modern day sports figures as comparisons, it read, "R.A. 'Bob' Hoover's place in the annals of aviation history is guaranteed. Like Michael Jordan swooping in for a dunk shot from the foul line, Olympic champion Scott Hamilton carving out his gold-medal routine on the ice, or Greg Louganis performing a three-and-a-half double somersault from the pike position, Bob Hoover's incredible artistry with an airplane is an experience never to be forgotten."

The final paragraph is puffy, something normally objectionable. The rest of the Overview is fact, but I needed to provide a standard by which to judge the heroics of Hoover. Comparisons with the sports heroes of that era seemed appropriate.

For those drafting a Synopsis for a work of fiction, similar rules apply. **Paragraphs one and two must be sensational because if they are not, the reader may toss the proposal aside.** The opening paragraph of a Synopsis written by one of my clients was enticing. It read, "Eight-year-old Jason Twinklebean marched into the kitchen. His mother stood by the stove, the smell of turnips sweeping through the air. 'Mom, I just killed the cat,' Jason reported. 'Now there won't be fur on the couch anymore.' 'That's lovely, Jason,' the mother sighed. 'Now go do your homework.'"

The Synopsis for *Moonshine Baby*, Anika Weiss' book, reads in part:

> Rufus Poisson is the Moonshine Baby. He was the boy whose shape the kids outlined in fragments of shell, china and glass on the Bahamian island of Andros in 1972. He is the death row prisoner in Baltimore who, remembering this children's game seventeen years later, decides to drop his appeals and hasten his end.
>
> Ruf's brother Ben, thin-skinned weightlifter, loner, and scholarship student at prestigious Winterbury College in Vermont, stashes his letters from prison away unread for fear that Rufus will drag him down. During orientation Ben meets Lauren Owen, another freshman, who wants to study dance, nothing else. She first fancies him for his provocative value— a black boyfriend, the perfect snub at her family—but will learn that far more than superficial attractions link Ben and her.
>
> Lauren's grandparents still live at Elmshead, the former plantation home where her father Lukas grew up. Unbeknown

to the family, Lukas at seventeen produced the illegitimate heir, Rufus, in a tryst with the black maid Eleanor who wouldn't have the abortion Lukas pressed on her. Instead, she changed her name from Ellie to Nora and smuggled her biracial baby, still invisible inside her, into her marriage to Bruneau Poisson, the oyster canner turned fisherman who took her to live on Andros. On the mailboat headed to the out-island Rufus was born, and nine years later, on the island, Ben.

After Ellie's disappearance Lukas Owen studied to become a mining engineer and forgot her. He married a woman he only half-loved, and they had Lauren who, due to her mother's migraine attacks, spent many days of her childhood at Elmshead. On the old mansion's grounds Lauren's grandmother Viola, haunted by guilt, grew an unorthodox garden of nightshades, plants of the same family as the tobacco that made the Owens rich during slavery. Except she wanted these plants to have a positive effect. So in the grip of early, unrecognized senility she used a potion of jimsonweed to give her granddaughter the feeling she could fly—a pesky delusion in a budding dancer, and one Lauren will beat.

When you complete a draft of the all-important Overview or Synopsis, set it aside for a few days. After retrieving it, read the material out loud, read it to a cat or dog, a lover or spouse, or a tree. Listen to how it sounds. Then revise, revise, revise with one vital consideration in mind: clarity—does it get the message across? Will the literary agent or editor recognize what the book is about? Have you proven that you can tell the story in a few pages and that you are a professional writer who should be taken seriously?

Once these questions are answered, revise again and check grammar and spelling. No material should ever be submitted with "typos." Such mistakes spell doom for the aspiring writer. If an agent or editor has to stumble over misspellings or grammatical errors, they will toss the proposal into the trash. Consult *The Elements of Style*, the *Chicago Manual of Style*, *Grammar Report*, dictionaries, and a thesaurus. Work with determination to make your material perfect.

To ensure that the Overview and the Book Proposal are ready for submission, consider employing a professional line editor. Like wine, a Book Proposal should never be submitted before its time.

A common error aspiring authors or poets make is to believe that one, two or ten drafts of the Overview or Synopsis, or for that matter a manuscript, will suffice. The final draft of the Overview of *Forever Flying* was number eighty-one.

This Overview stretched to six-and-one-half pages, double-spaced. The beginning, middle, and end were solid. The Tagline was provided. Strong buzzwords such as "hero" and "patriot," were included. The only thing missing was a guaranteed ride with Bob Hoover in his P-51! I should have added that.

Author Biography

To provide readers with a sense of why I was the one person in the world to write a book with Bob Hoover, I provided author credentials in the Author Biography section of the Book Proposal. Included were publishing credits for *Down For The Count* and *Bury Me In A Pot Bunker,* as well as *USA Today* writing experience.

The Author Biography should have featured aviation expertise, but my only experience was having flown in an F-4 fighter jet while investigating a story for *ABC's Good Morning America.* That day I sped across the sky at Nelles Air Force Base near Las Vegas. Everything was bearable until the pilot inverted the jet. My stomach disagreed with the maneuver and I vomited all over my cockpit. The puke oozed through an opening and doused the pilot in front of me as a camera captured the images. The day the program aired the segment host David Hartman nearly exploded with laughter.

Since I lacked aviation expertise, the Author Biography pointed out that the collaboration would be enhanced by my involvement because the writing would not be so technical as to prohibit non-aviators from enjoying Bob's adventures. **By stating this fact, a negative was turned into a positive.**

Writers touting works of fiction and poetry should provide information proving their worthiness to write about the selected subject matter. If you have been published, include the names of the publications. Mention any awards you have received, anything to show the literary agent or publisher why you are the one person in the world to write your book.

Credibility is a key. If you have written a mystery based on an unsolved murder in Ireland, mention that you have traveled there to research the facts. Give the literary agent or publisher all the ammunition you can so they realize that you are a writer to be taken seriously.

Book Audience

Publishers considering a Book Proposal will ask one basic question: Who is going to purchase the book? Providing a broad reader base is essential to producing hefty sales.

For *Into Thin Air*, the best selling tale of brave souls who climbed Mount Everest, the potential audience included those who love mountain climbing and a good adventure story. For five-time Tour de France cycling champion Lance Armstrong's best selling book, *It's Not About The Bike,* bicycle road racing fans were a sure bet to read the book. But the publisher also knew Armstrong's inspiring story would captivate those who admired his courageous battle with cancer.

If you have chosen to write fiction, it is essential to identify a broad audience. Harry Potter books attract young readers, but to the publisher's delight, older readers have flocked to the books. Those who write mysteries, children's books, Christian publications, science fiction, sports thrillers, or how-to books will list target audiences so an agent or publisher is certain who the potential reader will be.

Bob Hoover was best known as an aerobatic daredevil, but there was a wide range of potential readership for the book. To specify *Forever Flying*'s audience, the Book Audience section of the Book Proposal read, "*Forever Flying* will not only be an aviation book, but also a heartwarming, inspirational tale about a great aviator and true American patriot. While the book will accurately depict over fifty years of aviation history and contain numerous aviation terms, the text will be written with the general reader in mind." Providing this information clarified that the text would not be technical and that the average knucklehead who knew nothing about aviation would enjoy the book.

Words of wisdom from Matthew Snyder, a book-to-film agent with Creative Artists Agency in Beverly Hills, inspired a line designed to alert an agent or publisher to another aspect of Bob Hoover's story. Matthew said, **"Every good story contains a love story."** With this in mind, the Book Audience section included the words, "Since Bob and Colleen Hoover have been married almost fifty years, *Forever Flying* will feature a great love story."

To assist the range of potential readers for the book, the Book Audience stated, "It is estimated that more than *24,000,000* people attend air show and races in North America. At the Experimental Aircraft Association Annual Flying Championships, *800,000* fans attended. Another *100,000-plus* watched the National Championship of Air Racing at the Reno Air Show and Races."

Having a large "built-in" audience for a book electrifies publishers. If the book is promoted adequately, they know sales can skyrocket. This causes marketing and sales divisions to become excited about the book whether it is fiction or non-fiction.

Fiction writers may want to note a collective group of readers who will be interested in a particular genre. If the book is a work of fiction about the survival of an ancient tribe of Indians in Costa Rica, include information about clubs, associations, and publications interested in this subject.

Author Anika Weiss provides this information in her Book Proposal for the novel *Moonshine Baby*. An excerpt reads:

> *Moonshine Baby* is an operatic, interracial family saga with poignant coincidences and touches of magic.
>
> For readers of a romantic bent, *Moonshine Baby* also tells two love stories. Happening twenty-six years apart, both are charged with the potency of color but in very different ways since the country has moved from anti-miscegenation laws to the careful hyphenations of political correctness.
>
> For readers who care about social issues, *Moonshine Baby* strives to lend a human face to people regarded as untouchables. A novel, with its means of empathy, of stepping not just into another person's shoes, but their mind and skin, might do better justice to showing what it means to schedule a man's death than a philosophical or political argument. Tolstoi put it this way: "The business of art lies just in this,—to make that understood and felt which, in the form of an argument, might be incomprehensible and inaccessible..."
>
> For readers of literary fiction, *Moonshine Baby* counters a currently prevailing simplistic world view that regards good and evil, black and white as easily distinguishable entities. In

vibrant prose this book shows them to be two sides of the same coin.

For readers interested in capital punishment, *Moonshine Baby* addresses the topic at its most thought-provoking by portraying a prisoner who drops his appeals and agrees to his own death. As Governor Ryan's commutation of all death sentences in Illinois proves, the death penalty continues to be a controversial subject, eliciting strong feelings (and actions) among supporters as well as opponents. This novel will attract readers on the fence about the issue as well as those on either side of it.

As previously mentioned, if you are attempting to publish your memoir, remember that while the story may be important to you, family and friends, the scope of the story must be broad enough to convince a traditional publisher that it will sell on a national or, at least, regional level. Many aspiring authors and poets become distressed when their life story isn't of interest to a traditional publisher. They must recognize that if publishers released every memoir submitted regardless of sales limitations, their businesses would fail.

Similar Successful Books

Comparing a book to others that have proven successful adds a positive note to the Book Proposal. Publishers relish comparisons that validate the worthiness of a new book. They also favor books that are "the first to tell a story" within a genre that has proven successful.

With *Forever Flying*, the benchmark for aviation books was *Yeager*, Chuck Yeager's best selling autobiography. Others listed in the Similar Successful Books section of the Book Proposal included Tom Wolfe's *The Right Stuff*, *Loss of Eden*, a biography of Charles and Anne Morrow Lindbergh, and *Men From Earth* by astronaut Buzz Aldren.

Those writing fiction can point to successful books written in a certain genre. For example, if you are a lawyer writing a thriller about the inner workings of a corporate law firm, you will list *The Firm* as an example of a book that discovered a huge audience.

In *Moonshine Baby*, author Anika Weiss provided excellent comparisons for her novel while distinguishing its merit. The section reads:

> Thematically, *Moonshine Baby* resembles such works as Sister Helen Prejean's *Dead Man Walking*, Ernest J. Gaines's *A Lesson Before Dying* and Norman Mailer's *The Executioner's Song*. It shares their concern with the bleak realities of capital punishment and racism, but places them in a more colorful and fabulous universe.
>
> Stylistically, *Moonshine Baby* aspires to the vivid imagination and language of such novels as Arundhati Roy's *The God of Small Things* and Toni Morrison's *Tar Baby*, another tale of race relations set in the Caribbean. As Roy's book enters the minefield of taboo relationships in India, *Moonshine Baby* does the same for American and Western culture where interracial relationships still defy the norm and face enormous prejudice.

When you compare your book with others that have been successful, you must explain why your book is unique and even better. This will stifle any comment that there are too many books being written in a particular genre.

Sources for discovering similar successful books include bookstores, *Publisher's Weekly, Forthcoming Books, Books In Print*, and *Publisher's Trade List Annual*.

Promotion Ideas

To illustrate the potential exposure for *Forever Flying*, a section was added to the Book Proposal titled, "Publications/Associations/Promotion." It noted that magazines such as *Aviation Weekly* covered the industry and that multiple aviation groups familiar with Bob Hoover were scattered around the world.

In the Appendix to the Book Proposal, several articles were included featuring Hoover. The text discussed the enormous respect and hero status Bob enjoyed with fellow airmen.

To further stimulate interest, this section explained that Hoover was intent on promoting the book by scheduling personal appearances when requested. He would be an ambassador for the book, appearing at aviation meetings, air shows, and other gatherings of aviation buffs.

If your work is fiction, you may point out various organizations that are candidates to purchase the book. A mystery set on a submarine or affecting the stealth bomber would be a natural choice for those in the military.

Additional Voices

An important element of the *Forever Flying* Book Proposal was a section titled "Additional Voices To Be Featured In The Book." Bob was famous among aviation buffs, but not well known outside of it so readers of the proposal needed to know that quotes from several well-known individuals would be included. Listed were Neil Armstrong, Arnold Palmer, F. Lee Bailey, radio commentator Paul Harvey, astronauts Jim McDivitt and Wally Schirra, Barry Goldwater, actor Cliff Robertson, and Chuck Yeager. Providing a list of celebrities enhanced the marketability of the book, since these names could be utilized in any publicity and marketing materials.

If a celebrity, well-known expert, or accredited writer in a particular field related to the book has agreed to write the Foreword or an endorsement, this should be noted whether the venue is fiction or non-fiction. Securing praise from a writer who has been successfully published upgrades the potential to secure a publishing commitment.

Many times the endorser will ask the author to draft a sample Foreword or endorsement for review. After an interview to determine the viewpoint toward the book, complete the draft in the voice of the endorser and then forward it to him or her. Writing Forewords for Chuck Yeager, Yogi Berra, Greg Norman, and Nancy Lopez has taught me to understand the value of the endorser's busy schedule. Working with endorsers in a professional manner is the key since they do not have time to waste.

Format/Manuscript Status

Because this was a "as told to" collaboration permitting Bob Hoover to tell his life story, my audience for the Book Proposal (agent or editor) needed to know how the book would unfold. Under

"Format," I wrote, "*Forever Flying* will be Bob Hoover's memoir. The book will be written in first person, but occasionally other voices will be introduced to provide stories and anecdotes about Bob Hoover from those who know him best."

This information was essential since Bob's achievements were so outstanding that I was afraid no one would believe they occurred. Like most brave aviators, he was a very humble man prone to tell a story packed with danger as if it was an every day occurance. When I asked Bob about falling to earth in a burning F-84 Thunderjet, he described the event blandly. I forced him to elaborate and also used the voice of a fellow aviator who knew about the incident to describe the life-threatening danger he faced. This permitted the reader to be in the F-84 cockpit with Bob as the aircraft spiraled toward the desert terrain.

To update the status of the manuscript, I wrote, "Book will be completed within six weeks of contract."

Book To Film

If your book has motion picture or television potential, provide the essential information. This adds another element for the literary agent or publisher to consider, since an additional form of revenue might exist.

Revenue would occur if your book idea is optioned for a film. The deal will be negotiated either through you as the author, your literary agent or entertainment lawyer, or a theatrical agent. Literary agents will charge 15%, theatrical agents 10%, and entertainment lawyer's hourly fees.

For *Moonshine Baby*, Anika Weiss' book about a death row inmate, she provided excellent visualization regarding the book's potential to become a film. It reads:

> Picture a prisoner bowled over in the prison yard by a vision of the moon.
> Picture a boy drawing the island home he misses with colors from his mother's make-up kit.
> Picture young lovers having sex on oriental rugs in search of a flying carpet.

Scenes such as these from *Moonshine Baby* could translate into striking footage. *Moonshine Baby's* visual language and rich settings—from Vermont hills to the hidden blue holes of Andros and Baltimore's gothic downtown prison—create the intoxicating atmospherics a movie needs to enchant us.

The book begins by presenting parallel and sharply contrasting worlds, a juxtaposition of the bright (Caribbean island, college town) and the bleak (Ruf's prison cell) that could be very effective in film.

Biting dialogue, the plot's death row metronome and haunting moments of sex and murder propel the story toward a rising action of revelations by domino effect. The tragedy at the core of *Moonshine Baby* springs from its spirited characters who could inspire powerful screen incarnations. At last, it is these characters' clashing agendas that lead to the inevitable and devastating climax of Rufus's execution. His end is given an unnerving twist: Rufus imagines himself an explorer and the gas chamber a bathysphere used for deep sea exploration. This transformation could be depicted in stunning images.

As highly acclaimed films like *Monster's Ball* or *The Life of David Gale* confirm, the death penalty is a topic filmmakers feel compelled to broach.

Book-to-film production for works of fiction and non-fiction is blossoming. Sylvia Nasar's *A Beautiful Mind* became an Academy Award winning film. *A Civil Action*, Jonathan Harr's work of non-fiction, was an outstanding movie starring John Travolta. Several of John Grisham's novels have been adapted as was John Irving's *Cider House Rules* and *Captain Corelli's Mandolin* starring Nicholas Cage. Films based on Thomas Harris's *Red Dragon*, Robert Ludlum's *The Bourne Identity*, and Janet Fitch's *White Oleander* have excited movie fans. Past motion picture classics based on books have included *High Noon, Cool Hand Luke, The Postman Always Rings Twice, Vertigo, The Thin Red Line, Mutiny on the Bounty, Like Water For Chocolat, Seabiscut, and Catch Me If You Can*.

Film studios and producers often purchase the rights to a book based on the manuscript, but if you believe the book has film potential, you will prepare a "treatment." Akin to the Overview or Synopsis included in the Book Proposal, it sets out in present tense the elements of the story. There is no set length for a treatment. Guidance as to form and substance can be found in many self-help books. A sample book-to-film treatment is included in the Appendix.

A treatment of *Miscariage of Justice, The Jonathan Pollard Story* titled "Ghost of the Sealed Rooms," a reference to Pollard's nickname in Israel, related his story of spying for the Israelis. Providing a dramatic, visual presentation of the scenario for the film caused Twentieth Century Fox Television to option the rights to the book.

To option the rights, the film producer or studio will pay the author an upfront "advance" or "option money." This will permit them exclusive rights to the material for a designated period of time. Further options to extend the time may be included for additional payments.

The author, or his representative, will also negotiate a "back-end" profit participation based on profits when the film is produced and released. Authors are encouraged to negotiate as much "up-front money" as possible, since "creative" profit participation under Hollywood definitions oftentimes produces little revenue.

Book-to-film advances range from one dollar to millions dependent on the interest in the rights. Authors are encouraged to keep option periods to a minimum so there is flexibility if the producer is unable to produce the film. Any author whose book is considered for film should engage a savvy agent or entertainment lawyer to represent their interests.

If you are interested in writing a screenplay based on your book or other material, consider education regarding the writing mechanics and proper form required. Several courses and seminars exist including Robert McKee's Story Structure. For details regarding the form motion picture professionals expect from a screenwriter, check the website, www.finaldraft.com.

Outline

The Outline included in the Book Proposal for *Forever Flying* was succinct. Chapter headings included "Flying Lessons," "Escape From Stalag I," "Dogfighting Over Ohio," "Hole In The Sky," "Forty Minutes of Stark Terror," and "Japanese Masseuse Torture."

A fiction writer client provided an outline with creative chapter headings. They read, "Blind Date Prep," "Wolf-Whistle," "You Ever Heard of Rodeo Sex, Darlin?" "Wormwood Wins The Girl," and "Cyber Coitus Interruptus."

Text listed under each chapter heading provides a thumbnail sketch of the anticipated text whether the book is a work of fiction or non-fiction. Clarity is essential, since the reader must garner in a few short lines an understanding of the author's intentions. Sample outlines are included in the Book Proposal section of the Appendix.

Sample Text

The Book Proposal for long-form works of fiction or non-fiction will include at least one, and perhaps two, sample chapters from the book. **This text showcases the author's talent and must be extraordinary.** The author must revise, revise, and then revise some more until the material is as close to perfection as possible before submission.

For *Forever Flying*, I chose three chapters detailing critical events in Bob Hoover's life. They chronicled his imprisonment and heroics during World War II, an account of little-known facts regarding his participation in the breaking of the sound barrier, and his ascent to fame as the greatest aerobatic pilot in the world.

Fiction writers will include the first two to three chapters (depending on length) showcasing the uniqueness of their story. **Clarity is the key, since the agents and/or publishers will base their initial opinion on an incomplete story.** The hope is that they will be so enthused with the writing and your storytelling ability that they will demand a look-see at the prepared manuscript.

Poetry and children's books authors will provide samples of their work in short-form. Essayists and short story writers will do the same. Again, length is less important than quality.

Sample chapter excerpts for fiction, non-fiction, and poetry are included in the Book Proposal section of the Appendix.

Appendix

Selected photographs of Bob Hoover and several celebrities were included in the Book Proposal Appendix for *Forever Flying*. Among others, there were photographs of Hoover standing with fellow prisoners at the Stalag I German Prison Camp, talking with famed German aircraft designer Willy Messerschmitt, and kneeling with

Chuck Yeager and the crew of the X-1 team responsible for breaking the sound barrier.

Photographs and illustrations will normally not be included with works of fiction, but they can be appropriate with collections of poetry. They enhance the visual nature of the book.

When listing the photographs available, be sure to discuss ownership. Obtaining the right to publish them can be expensive.

Poetry Book Proposals

There are no set rules, but poetry book publishers expect the following from an aspiring poet: **a professionally written Query Letter accompanied by a Book Proposal including a Tagline describing the book in fifteen words or less, a Synopsis of the book of poetry contemplated, information about the poet, details regarding the potential book audience and marketing potential, a list of similar successful books, promotion concepts, an outline, and several sample poems.** Attaching a self-addressed, stamped envelope is required. *Poet's Market* and other publications such as *How To Publish Your Poetry* by Helene Ciaravino list specific requirements for submission.

Poetry submitted should be typed, not handwritten, on fine quality, 8.5 x 11, bond paper. A paper "weight" of more than 24 is suggested. The accompanying materials will be double-spaced, but the poetry is single-spaced with double spaces between the stanzas. If you are writing non-traditional types of poetry such as free form, the layout will differ.

Proper form includes a cover page listing the title of the work, a subtitle, if any, and the name of the poet. A second page can include a few lines from the poetry to catch the eye of the literary agent or publisher. The third page begins with a Tagline specifying the theme of the poetry followed by the Synopsis, Poet Biography, Book Audience, Similar Successful Books, Promotion Concepts, an Outline if there is one, and the Poetry Excerpts. The various compartments follow one another on the pages to provide a flow to the material. An example of a Poetry Book Proposal is featured in the Appendix. It is general in nature and can be modified for alternative forms of poetry.

Most poetry publications are impressed by poems that are not too lengthy. Do not be afraid to be experimental, since uniqueness is a cherished quality. Each poem should be titled for clarity. The pages of the proposal should not be stapled or bound so copies may be made for multiple readers.

Miriam Sagan, a published poet and UCLA instructor, suggested seven tips for aspiring poets she believes are worthy in *Writer's Digest*. They include: "Line breaks should feel natural, not forced, repetition of lines with a similar number of syllables can add to free verse, the opening word of each line should be compelling: use nouns and verbs whenever possible, and ending lines should strive for maximum reader impact."

To enhance publishing opportunities, photographs or illustrations can be helpful. Many poets forward a self-published book along with the suggested new material. This can be helpful to show agents and editors the worthiness of previous work.

E-mailing of poetry Book Proposals is possible, but discouraged since a hard copy of the proposal is much more impressive. See *Poet's Market* for details regarding submissions.

Book Proposals for poetry chapbooks (25-50 pages) compare with those for full-length books of poetry. Potential chapbook publishers and guidelines for submission can be found in *Poet's Market*. Additional publishing alternatives are available in *The Directory of Poetry Publishers*, a Dustbooks publication. They also publish *The Directory of Small Press/Magazine Editors and Publishers*.

Regardless of whether you are submitting a Book Proposal for a full-length book or a chapbook, check publisher guidelines. Failure to do so is a death wish. Poetry publishing expert Jim Walker suggests being aware of suggested "reading periods" when publications indicate they will consider submissions. For a university publication, this may be during the school year or the summer months.

Book Proposal Magic

Whenever possible, the aspiring author or poet should submit a Query Letter and Book Proposal. Length of the proposal will vary, but it will seldom be more than 20-30 pages in length. As stated, a concise proposal of twenty to thirty pages can work to your advantage even when the agency or publisher under consideration requests that only Query Letters be submitted. If the Query Letter is sensational, the concise Book Proposal will gain attention and provide needed information about the book that cannot be specified in a one-page Query Letter.

At a high school seminar on book publishing, I listened as Marie Butler-Knight, publisher of Alpha Books, an imprint of Penguin Group USA, discussed her interest in the following components of a Book Proposal: Topic (a story that is unique and compelling, information or instruction on a hot topic), Approach (a unique twist on a familiar story, a different way of presenting information), Market Size (how many people want this information), Author Expertise (understanding/knowledge of the subject matter, credentials), and Author Writing Ability (a fluid, coherent, readable style, effectively organized). She also mentioned Author Professionalism (willingness to take editorial suggestions and direction, ability to meet deadlines), Profit Potential (what will book cost to publish, what will it sell for, how many can be sold), and Fit For The Imprint (ability to publish this type of book, ability to promote). These are excellent suggestions any writer should pay attention to regardless of whether they are writing fiction, non-fiction, or poetry.

When your Book Proposal and Query Letter are the best they can be, forward them to a literary agent or editor at a publishing company using priority mail, Federal Express, or UPS. This indicates that you are dedicated and serious about the work and separates you from the thousands of others submitting material. Equally important, it provides you with a tracking number to make certain your package arrived.

Multiple books have been written regarding the preparation of Book Proposals. One is *How To Write A Book Proposal* by Michael Larsen. A book titled *1,818 Ways To Write Better and Get Published* by Scott Edelstein is a competent resource as is *Your Novel Proposal*.

A final note regarding Book Proposals—it is imperative that each section stands alone. The writer cannot predict if a literary agent or editor will read from cover to cover or leaf through sections that are of particular interest. They may skip ahead to the Sample Chapter section first to decide if the writing has merit, or glance at the Author Biography or the Similar Successful Books material. With this in mind, write each section as if it were being submitted individually for consideration.

When the Query Letter and Book Proposal are submitted to a literary agency, any one of several people may read it. An assistant may peruse it before the intended agent receives the material. Readers are also employed by agencies. Their sole purpose is to scan Book Proposals to judge their worthiness.

The Query Letter and Book Proposal submitted to a publisher enter a hierarchy differing from company to company. At the top sits the publisher who operates as a quarterback dealing with editorial issues, as well as sales and marketing. Reporting to the publisher is the editor-in-chief to whom all of the editors report. Most publishers require that the editor-in-chief and/or the publisher sign off before a deal is finalized.

Reporting to the editor-in-chief, or the production director among larger publishing companies, is the managing editor. He or she deals with deadlines and coordinates information about the book. Reporting to the editors, or senior editors, are editorial assistants, normally young people new to the business. Any one of these people, or all of them, may read the Book Proposal before a final decision is made.

When a traditional publisher agrees to publish a book based on the Query Letter and Book Proposal, the cycle from idea to publication is complete. The accompanying chart at the end of this chapter provides a simplistic view of this process.

Whether the genre is fiction, non-fiction, or poetry, the Book Proposal, and its partner, the Query Letter, reflects the heart and soul of the book contemplated. By preparing ones that are professionally written, you boost your chances toward the ultimate goal—becoming published.

Step #7 Summary

- Essential Book Proposal components include the Title, Tagline, Author or Poet Biography, Book Audience, Similar Successful Books, Promotion Ideas, Book To Film, Outline, and Sample Chapters or Verses.

- Search *USA Today, Publisher's Weekly,* or the *New York Times* for
  best seller lists for suggested Taglines.

- Research correct Book Proposal form.

- Don't boast about your book in the Book Proposal—show readers why it is outstanding and must be published.

Traditional Book Publishing Chart

Author/Poet
↓
Idea
↓
Fiction   Non-Fiction   Poetry
↓
Book Outline
↓
Manuscript or Collection of Poetry
↓
Query Letter and Book Proposal
↓
Line Editing
|
Book Proposal Components:
Cover Page
Tagline/Overview or Synopsis
Author Biography
Book Audience
Book Promotion
Book-to-Film
Book Outline
Sample Chapters
Appendix
↓
Literary Agent or Book Publisher
↓
Published Book
↓
CELEBRATION!!!!

I have never known any distress that an hour's reading did not relieve.

BARON DE MONTESQUIEU

Step #8
Write A Query Letter Second To None

Query Letters

To gain the interest of literary agents and publishers, you must implement a well-founded strategy. **Since yearly submission numbers approach seven figures, you need to be creative so your book idea gains the attention of the literary agent or publisher under consideration.** This way it won't be thrown in the dreaded "slush" pile to die a slow death.

As stated, checking literary agent and publisher guidelines is the key. Remember: the material you submit is unsolicited; therefore readers will pay little or no attention unless you follow the guidelines.

Literary agents are more accessible than publishers but regardless, you must learn whether the agent or publishing company will accept only Query Letters, Query Letters and a Synopsis, Query Letters, a Synopsis, and two Sample Chapters, Query Letters accompanied by Book Proposals, or perhaps Query Letters accompanied by exhibits describing important aspects of the book. These may include media clippings describing the material being pitched or background on you.

Despite literary agency and publisher guidelines requesting only a Query Letter, few will dismiss a Query Letter accompanied by a 20-30 page Book Proposal. You will decide the best strategy for you, but it is extremely difficult to capture a literary agent or publisher's attention with only a one-page Query Letter. Providing them with additional information about the book in a concise proposal provides your best chance of gaining interest in your book.

Mastering the art of creating Query Letters in accordance with **Mark's Step #8, Write A Query Letter Second-To-None**, is challenging since most writers are not used to this form of writing. Guidance on the proper form and substance is available through many publications such as *Writer's Market.*

Brevity is a key—one page, no more. Literary agents or editors have no interest in leafing through an eight-page letter beginning with announcement of the author's birth and ending with a sentence touting the book as the best ever written. Several good examples of Query

Letters for fiction can be discovered in *Your Novel Proposal* by authors Blythe Camenson and Marshall J. Cook.

Journalists Don Prues and Cindy Laufenberg provide excellent advice regarding the substance of Query Letters. In *Writer's Market*, they state, **"The tone of the writing is important. Create a catchy Query with confidence but devoid of cockiness."**

Remember, the Query Letter is a mini-Book Proposal. In *Your Novel Proposal*, author Cook states, **"In Query letters, I look for calm professionalism. I want to know what the book is, who you are—if that's pertinent—the length and that's about it."**

Authors Camenson and Cook's description of the essential elements of the Query Letter for fiction includes: **"The Hook, The Handle (Novel Theme), a Mini-Synopsis, Your Credentials, Your Credits, What You Are Offering, and The Closing."** Substitute the word Overview for Synopsis and these elements are applicable to non-fiction or poetry letters as well. Much of this information can be excerpted from a draft of the Book Proposal. This is why I suggest writing it first and then using information from the draft to build the foundation for the Query Letter. Writers have informed me that working on Query Letters and Book Proposals assists them with focusing in on their book content and message. Many times, due to the need to be precise with information about the book, they have revised their manuscripts or collection of poetry.

Mention of the book tagline, a "what if" scenario, or a compelling problem requiring a solution work well in the Query Letter's opening paragraph to hook readers. Regarding author or poet credentials, **it is important to explain why you are the one person in the world to write this book.** Include information about the target audience, a built-in audience due to your expertise, and reference the enclosed Book Proposal. Conclude the letter by writing, "Thank you for considering the enclosed Book Proposal. A completed manuscript is available upon request."

Remember to include a self-addressed, stamped envelope for return correspondence. Literary agents and publishers appreciate saving the cost of the postage necessary to return the Query Letter and/or Book Proposal.

Never mention past rejections of material in a Query Letter. You may or may not inform a literary agent or editor of multiple submissions. Most realize that you are doing so to speed up the process.

If you believe your book fits with the current list represented by an agent or published through a publishing company, mention books that are similar. Writing, "I believe *Roots of Evil* will appeal to the same audience as *My Son, The Tyrant*, the book you published last year," will indicate to the publishing company that you have done your homework. A similar line, "*Roots of Evil* weaves a similar story to that of *John, The Mountain Man*, the book you represented in 2002," shows the agent you have checked their listing in *Writer's Market*.

Treat the Query Letter as a prologue to the Book Proposal when they are submitted together. Edit it thoroughly, checking spelling, grammar, and punctuation. Most agents and editors will not consider the Book Proposal if the Query Letter contains multiple mistakes. An editor once told me, **"The Query Letter is your three minutes to sell the book. Don't screw up."**

Laurie Liss, a top agent at New York City's Harvey Klinger Agency who discovered *The Bridges of Madison County*, explains that what she seeks is "a really good, interesting Query Letter . . .What is good to me is if a letter is written really well, is grammatically correct, and lists the agent's name correctly. I need to get the impression that the writer knows what [he or she is] talking about. If you can't write a letter, how are you going to write a book?"

What makes it uninteresting, Liss states, "Is people who write, 'my mother thinks this is the best book she has ever read. I swear my mom is really smart and not biased at all.'" Including photographs apparently doesn't impress Liss. "Pictures make it [Query Letter] really unappealing too. I have never had someone who's given me a picture of themselves who could write."

Liss has other pet peeves as well. "When letters begin, 'You are going to take my book because . . .' I always turn it down. It's almost always subpar. And don't send me a Query Letter saying, 'I am the next Danielle Steel.' My reaction is, no you're not."

Marie Butler-Knight, publisher of Alpha Books, offers this warning. "If you submit the same Query Letter to multiple literary agents or publishers and you customize the contents to each recipient, read each letter carefully before you send it out. Make certain the letter isn't addressed to one agent or publisher but references another agent or publisher in the body of the letter. You'd be amazed at how often this occurs."

The form for a Query Letter is simple. On letter-sized paper, type the date, the name, and the address of the recipient in twelve font, Times-Roman. After the greeting, (Dear Literary Agent or Editor), begin your letter. Since you only have one page to present your book idea, organize it in the following manner:

Fiction	Non-Fiction
First Paragraph - Tagline/Hook or Similar Catchy Text	**First Paragaph - Tagline/Hook or Similar Catchy Text**
Second - Show Me The Story (Plot, Characters, Beginning, Middle, End)	**Second - Book Description (Unique Information, Problem, Solution, etc.)**
Third - Author Platform	**Third -Author Platform**
Fourth - Book Audience/ Similar Sucessful Books/ Similar Books By Agent/Editor	**Fourth – Book Audience Similar Successful Books/ Similar Books by Agent/Editor**
Closing Remarks	**Closing Remarks**

A sample Query Letter regarding *Code Of Silence,* a biography of the famous lawyer who represented Jack Ruby, provides essential information regarding the hook for the book, (use of catchy, well know phrase instead of the tagline), the gist of the text, the source of material, credibility of the author, anticipated promotion, and target audience. It reads:

> Dear Literary Agent,
>   When William Shakespeare said, "The first thing we do is kill all the lawyers," he must have known that the controversial Melvin Belli would drive insurance companies and judges alike batty for more than six decades of the twentieth century.
>   Armed with the grizzliness of Ernest Hemingway, the wit of Will Rogers, and the legal savvy of Clarence Darrow and Edward Bennett Williams, Belli was a courtroom wizard

whose celebrity reached rock star status. Noted attorney Gerry Spence calls Belli, "truly a beacon of light that showed the way."

In *Code Of Silence, Melvin Belli, Jack Ruby, and the Assassination of Lee Harvey Oswald*, the San Francisco barrister's colorful life renders a slice of history from the 1950s through Belli's controversial death in 1996. The Jack Ruby case, Belli's most famous, provides the spine for the book, one that chronicles famous clients such as Errol Flynn, Mae West, Martha Mitchell, Muhammed Ali, The Rolling Stones, Jim and Tammy Faye Baker, the Zodiac Killer, and mobster Mickey Cohen.

Code of Silence will be appreciated by audiences familiar with the "King of Torts," *Life Magazine's* label for him, and those curious about Belli's representation of Ruby, who shot Oswald in the only live broadcast of a murder in television history. For the first time, this case is featured through the eyes of Belli, probing the question as to whether the great lawyer may have been hired by the Mafia to discredit, and in effect, silence Oswald's assassin.

Numerous promotion opportunities for the book exist through the noted Belli Society, ten thousand strong, and media outlets familiar with the Belli legacy. Authorized by his widow, sixth wife Nancy, *Code of Silence* is written in the tradition of the author's twelve published works, including *Miscarriage of Justice, The Jonathan Pollard Story, Down For The Count*, an inside look at the Mike Tyson case, and *Testament To Courage*, a Holocaust memoir. More information about the author, a media analyst for the Mike Tyson, O. J. Simpson, and Kobie Bryant cases, can be learned at www.markshaw.com.

Thank you for consideration of the enclosed book proposal. A completed manuscript is available upon request.

Best,
Mark Shaw

For Anika Weiss' winning entry in the fiction category of the $25,000 John T. Lupton "New Voices In Literature" Awards, she chose the following tagline to open her Query Letter: "Lauren Owen, only child of a Maryland family of former plantation owners, has always wanted a big brother, if only so he would carry the brunt of that bothersome heritage. As it is, she has one. Her brother is black, and lives on death row."

Michael Boxall, the winner in the non-fiction category, utilized a clever strategy in the first line of his Query Letter. It reads, *"Driven by Desire: Sex and the Spread of the New Media* is the first book to trace the rise of the increasingly intimate relationship between sex and the new forms of communications technology."

As stated, the Query Letter for a work of fiction will focus on the plot, the characters, the author's credentials, and the target audience. One written for the novel, *Purple Angel,* reads as follows:

> Dear Literary Agent,
>
> What if Guy Macker, a disgruntled law professor, is forced to defend his pregnant girlfriend for a murder he knows for certain she did not commit?
>
> This scenario sets the stage for *Purple Angel,* a mystery set on the Harvard University campus. Macker's representation of Roxanne Allworth, the vivacious daughter of a Wall Street powerbroker, vaults him into the real world of the criminal justice system. Prosecutors, suspicious of the professor's involvement, investigate his background discovering a past history of mental illness.
>
> When prosecutors threaten to expose Macker and destroy his career, he must decide whether to save Roxanne, pregnant with his child, or leave campus. Determined to fight, he gains an acquittal for her by acknowledging his participation in the murder.
>
> The author is a former criminal defense attorney whose short stories have been featured in several magazines including *Esquire* and *Gentleman's Quarterly.* One of them is the basis for this novel. Promotional opportunities exist due to the author's exposure through the lecture circuit and his appearances on *CNN* as a legal analyst.
>
> The target audience for *Purple Angel* is anyone who loves a good mystery story. Since you represented *Gone Too Far,* a

bestseller by Harry Reasoner, *Purple Angel* should be of interest to you.

Thank you for considering the enclosed Book Proposal. I look forward to hearing from you soon.

Best,
Jerry Bales

Reaction to any Query Letter and accompanying Book Proposal will vary, but remember that it only takes one literary agent or publisher to say "yes." If they do, regardless of a multitude of "no's," your long hours of hard work and perseverance will be worthwhile.

The Poetry Query Letter

Poets attempting to excite literary agents or publishing companies (submitting to publishers is more advisable for poets than fiction or non-fiction writers), regarding their work must write a better-than-best Query Letter. Since there are thousands upon thousands of poetry submissions, poets must write outstanding prose to describe the poetry they have written. Again, the letter should be no more than one page written on 8.5 x 11 inch paper.

Begin the letter with a sentence that will captivate the reader. Use a Tagline (the hook for your book) to pinpoint the theme of the poetry and then provide titillating information designed to make readers say, "I must read the collection of poetry."

Paragraphs two and three of the Query Letter expand upon the theme of the material. Once there is a clear description, offer biographical material that illustrates why, just as with the aspiring author, you are the one best person in the world to write poetry on this theme. Inclusion of publishing credentials is critical as is information on built-in audience for the book. Comparisons to famous poets regarding style and content can be helpful. If you believe your book is similar to one represented by the agency or publisher you are contacting, note the name of the book. This will show the agent or publishing company you have researched their recent books.

As with all writing, clarity, brevity, good word choice, and excellent sentence structure is essential. Any agent or editor questioning the writing ability of a prospective poet will wonder if he or she is a competent wordsmith when writing poetry.

Arrogance must be absent from any competent Query Letter. Lines such as "People say that I am the next Billy Collins or Maya Angelou" will cause instant death to any chances to be published. Be humble while showing the editor that you believe in yourself and possess a fresh voice that must be heard.

Within the letter, provide readers with exact information as to why your poetry is perfect for representation or publication. Once again the goal should be obvious: **you want the agent or editor to say, "I must represent or publish this material or someone else will and it will be a huge success and I will be sorry."**

In the final paragraph of the Query Letter, explain that besides the poetry submitted, there is additional material to be read upon request. Then thank the editor for their consideration and close with something akin to "Yours truly."

Above all, be certain the person you are writing to is still employed at the agency or publishing company. There is nothing more embarrassing than writing a letter to a former employee.

The Query Letter for a collection of poetry titled, *Columbus Was Wrong,* reads as follows:

Dear Literary Agent,

Is the world still round, or were the ancient naysayers correct? Answers to that question and more are explored in a new collection of poetry I have written titled, *Columbus Was Wrong.*

Ten poems are included with this letter. Among them are: Flat or Round, Who's To Say, Christopher Was A Baboon, Not An Explorer, The New World or The Old One, and Gold Blinds Us.

The audience for *Columbus Was Wrong* includes those fascinated with Christopher Columbus, as well as the historical significance of the discovery of America. Similar works regarding whether men walked on the moon, why Charles

Lindbergh did not cross the Atlantic, and how mankind has been hoodwinked into believing global warming threatens our very existence have been published in *Poets Of The Far East, Art Bell's Collection of Serious Poetry, and Dubsdread's Odd Poets of the Twentieth Century.*

The poet's perspective on these issues has been formed from extensive travel throughout the world. During a recent trip to southern Italy, the current collection was created after intensive investigation of Columbus' true mission when he assaulted the new world. The poet believes she is the first to offer through her poetry significant evidence that Columbus' name was actually O'Reilly and that he never set foot on Italian soil.

Thank you for considering the enclosed book proposal. Further samples of the poetry are available upon request.

Thank you.
Best,

Olathobal Moffit

Query letters are the key to unlocking the door of the publishing industry. Cleverly written with an eye toward exciting the reader, they operate as your invitation to those you hope will share your passion for the subject matter of the book. Strong words and visual images optimize your chances that a literary agent or editor will say, "I must read the book proposal," a second step toward gaining a publishing commitment.

Step #8 Summary

- Literary Agents and Publishers will not read manuscripts or extensive poetry collections from an unpublished author or poet.

- Literary Agents or Publishers expect to receive professionally written Query Letters and/or Book Proposals.

- A Query Letter should be concise and targeted to hook the reader on the book concept.

- The essential elements of the query letter are Tagline, Mini-Synopsis or Mini-Overview, Mini-Author Biography, Book Audience, and Promotion Ideas

It is with books as it is with men, a very small number play a great part, the rest are lost in the multitude.

VOLTAIRE

Step # 9
Rejection Is Not Part
Of The Writer's Vocabulary

"Rejectionitis"

Besides a life-size cardboard cutout of Marilyn Monroe, a bookshelf containing the works of Ernest Hemingway, walls peppered with articles and photographs, and a poster of the sleepy Italian Riviera village of Vernazza, my writing studio is speckled with a collection of work-in-progress manuscripts. Whether they will ever be read by anyone other than me and my dog remains to be seen.

These millions of words represent countless hours of writing and re-writing. **There is no substitute for experience. This is especially true of the wordsmith's craft.**

Once you have honed your skills and polished your text to a level of professionalism, you need to test the marketplace. This requires submitting Book Proposals accompanied by a Query Letter to selected literary agents and publishers.

Many writers are reticent to try traditional publishing. An aspiring author on the West Coast studied the craft for eight years. He attended several writers' conferences and workshops. For six months, he worked with a writing group. During that time, he wrote several unfinished manuscripts, one totaling more than 1,500 pages. Despite this accomplishment and the fact that he was a gifted storyteller, he was reluctant to test his material with literary agents or publishers.

The writer suffered from a dreaded disease I call "Rejectionitis." A common illness of many who are afraid to have someone say "no" to their idea or concept, it runs rampant within the world of the writer. Symptoms include long faces, slightly damaged keyboards, and stacks of yellowed paper.

To combat Rejectionitis, writers must develop skin as thick as an armadillo's. They must remember **Mark's Step #9—Take Notice— Rejection Is Not Part Of A Writer's Vocabulary.**

Irwin Shaw (*The Young Lions*) was immune to rejection. He wrote, "Failure is inevitable for the writer. Any writer. I don't care who he is, or how great he is, or what he's written. Sooner or later, he's going to flop and everybody who admired him will try to write him off as a bum." Albert Einstein wrote, **"Great spirits have always encountered violent opposition from mediocre minds."**

This does not mean criticism can be ignored. Don't forget that Ernest Hemingway said of writers, "We are all apprentices in a craft where no one ever becomes a master."

You can avoid criticism and rejection by never submitting work for publication. Your life will be filled with smiles, pretty days, and walks in the park. Nothing you have written will ever be read by the outside world, nothing you have written will produce a laugh or a tear from a reader, and nothing you write will ever make a difference by causing people to stop and think. But you will keep your sanity and the satisfaction of never having been stung by rejection or a bad review.

If you choose to take a risk, know that you will encounter rejection at one time or another. In the publishing industry, it is a way of life. **Pearl Buck, author of the classic, *The Good Earth* and seventy other novels, received a rejection letter regarding submission of a short story to a magazine the very week in 1935 when she was awarded the Nobel Prize for Literature.**

Those who don't try, never succeed. Actor/producer/director/writer Woody Allen believes rejection is an essential part of the human existence. He wrote, "If you're not failing now and again, it means you are playing it safe." An old Japanese proverb states, "Fall seven times, stand up eight."

Believing in yourself and in the Good Lord's plan for you is essential. Lessons learned from Noah can be helpful since he symbolizes what it means to have faith. When God asked him to build the ark to withstand a flood, Noah did not hesitate even though he had never seen rain, lived hundreds of miles from the nearest ocean, and had no way to transport it to the nearest ocean. Regardless, he had faith and trusted God's word. You must do the same if you believe strongly in your book idea, one that is morally right.

Attempts to persuade agents and publishers that my first book, *Down For The Count,* was worthy produced an excess of emotions. Utilizing a "help book," I compiled a list of prospective agents and publishers. I then forwarded the manuscript (I did not know about Book Proposals) to several agents and publishers.

Each day at noon, after completing the writing assignment for the day, I packed the dogs in "Big Blue" (an old Ford truck), and headed to downtown Nashville, Indiana. With a spirited walk, I stepped into the post office and walked to P.O. Box 787. When I noticed a long yellow card requiring a trip to the postal counter, I knew one or more of the manuscripts had been returned. Since there had been no telephone call offering me agent representation or a publishing commitment, I concluded that the material had been rejected.

After retrieving the manuscript from its packing, I glanced at the accompanying letter. To counter disappointment, I immediately placed the manuscript in a new package pre-addressed to another literary agent or publisher. Inside was a fresh Query Letter describing the book. I then mailed the same material to a new source in search of a "yes" instead of a "no."

Maintaining a positive attitude is critical to moving forward. There is nothing we can do about past experiences but learn from them. As I used to tell listeners of my radio program, **"Keep the faith, you never know when there is a miracle right around the corner."**

For me, taking a pre-addressed package to the post office worked the same way. Instead of dwelling on the negative response to the manuscript, I forwarded it to another source in search of success. **This attitude is symbolic of an essential characteristic for writers: never giving up.**

Submission Procedure/Number of Submissions

If you choose to explore the world of traditional publishing, focus on securing a literary agent. From the "usual suspects" list compiled from your research, choose those most likely to have interest. Forward the Query Letter and Book Proposal to them.

If you do not receive a response in three-four weeks, telephone the agency for an update. Be inquisitive, but not intrusive. Explain the reason for the contact and request an update. If none is received after a week, move on. This requires sending another Query Letter and Book Proposal. **Five in circulation at a time maximizes the potential for results.**

If no literary agent responds positively, consider contacting publishers even though many do not permit un-agented submissions. A better idea may be to pursue a new book idea and decide that the previous one may be the second book you publish.

If you decide to contact publishers, peruse the list you have compiled through your research. Forward five submissions to selected editors. Wait three-four weeks and telephone for an update.

Be persistent, but not pushy. Patience is the byword.

A sample Agency-Publisher Submission Record is provided in the Appendix. Keeping good records allows you to track submissions. The listings may also be helpful with future books. Note agents or editors who have rejected material, but requested a look-see at future works.

It is not necessary to do so, but after receiving a rejection letter, consider responding with a note of appreciation for the consideration shown by the agent or editor at the publishing company. When a future submission is made, the agent or editor will remember the common courtesy.

Never Giving Up

When submitted material is not returned, many writers want to scream, "That's not fair." **Instead, remember that the agent or publisher *did not request* submission of the Book Proposal and/or manuscript and have no duty to return it.** Many Book Proposals and/or manuscripts fall into a black hole and never surface. Since you will have protected the material by having it copyrighted, accept your fate and continue the process of securing agency representation or a publisher commitment.

Rejection is a badge of courage. John Grisham contacted many publishers who rejected his book idea. Most thought he was some hayseed from Mississippi who should be ignored.

Jack Canfield and Mark Victor Hansen, the *Chicken Soup* authors, provide inspiration. Thirty-three publishers in New York and another hundred attending the American Book Publishers Association convention decided the first book possessed no merit. Canfield and Hansen licked their wounds, and never gave up. Health Communications, a small Florida-based publisher, believed in the authors and together they have published bestseller after bestseller.

Another author of note who never gave up was John Steinbeck. Born in Salinas, California, he attended Stanford. In 1925, Steinbeck traveled to New York to seek work as a free-lance writer. No one took him seriously, and he returned to California a failure. Undeterred, he began to write short stories. Ten years later, after several attempts to achieve recognition, he published a series of humorous stories about the Monterey *paisanos* titled *Tortilla Flats*. In the next four years, Steinbeck produced the classics *Of Mice and Men* and *The Grapes of Wrath*, among others.

Remember that Babe Ruth held the record for the most home runs during a baseball season until Mark McGuire broke it. The Babe also held the record for most strikeouts. Businessmen all over the globe have founded companies, made millions, hit hard times, filed for bankruptcy, then started again and made millions. **As my father used to say, "Nothing good comes easy."**

Writers' Conferences

To expand your horizons, explore publishing industry alternatives, connect with fellow authors and poets, and find encouragement when rejection has occurred, consider attending writers' conferences. Information about such conferences can be found in *Writer's Digest, Poet's and Writer's* magazine, and other publications. **Listings of various conferences can be discovered through Writers' Conferences and Centers at www.awpwriter.org.**

Networking with industry heavyweights at the conference is of great benefit. Various social functions permit writers to interact with literary notables, including those from the literary field, film, and television. Attendees can sign up for meetings with literary agents and editors from publishing companies and "pitch" a book idea. If author Sylvia Nasar had attended a conference, she would have told the agent or editor, "The idea I have is to write a book about John Nash, the mathematical genius who suffered from schizophrenia and eventually won the Nobel Prize." The literary agent or editor in all likelihood would have requested to see any text she had written since her "pitch" or "Tagline" was superb and indicative of the book that became *A Beautiful Mind.*

Realize that agents and editors are constantly searching for new "stars." They need writers with bestseller potential as much as those writers need them.

When attending a writers' conference, arrive with a definite game plan, since first impressions are critical. Never tell anyone in the publishing world, "Well, I'm not sure what I want to write." **Be**

focused, listen, learn, ask questions, and be attentive. If you have chosen a book idea, be prepared with the fifteen words or less Tagline so you can describe your book. Many people met at conferences will be valued resources as your writing career progresses. Impress them with your ability to answer the question, "What are you working on?" with "I'm currently completing a biography of Albert Einstein," or "I'm writing a novel about the daughter of a famous politican who learns her father was a Nazi sympathizer."

If you have completed a Book Proposal regarding your book idea, be ready to present it to any literary agents or publishers you meet. Be certain it is ready for submission after having been thoroughly reviewed and edited. You only have one shot with agents and publishers so be certain your material is the best it can be.

Attending writers' conferences permits you to soak up the flavor of the publishing industry. The conference provides a crash course in the practical aspects of how you can realize the dream of being published.

If you promise to forward material to a literary agent or editor, follow through. **Building a reputation for being accountable is essential.** Literary agents and editors are looking for responsible, professional writers who can be counted upon. They are not interested in working with disorganized writers who don't keep their word.

Similar accountability will be imperative when you sign a publishing contract. Meeting deadlines is critical for any successful author or poet, since publishers will dictate a timetable for completion of the book. They will set a publishing date and then work backwards. You will be expected to submit material on time. Doing so will create a reputation for dependability imperative in the publishing industry. One of the selling points my literary agent uses while discussing a book idea with an editor is that I have never missed a deadline. This separates me from countless others who have never met one.

Writer's Groups

Many aspiring authors have formed writer's groups. Some have a few members; others more than twenty. They meet once or twice a month to discuss projects of interest, exchange ideas, and provide critique. Encouragement is also a plus since rejection is the aspiring author or poet's middle name.

Members of writer's groups form an enviable bond. Whether the writer is a beginner or a published author, the sharing of thoughts about the writing process and the literary industry is refreshing and quite beneficial.

Beginning a writer's group is easy. Posting signs on university and library bulletin boards or in newsletters will stir interest. Everyone has a story to tell or a book in them, and there are many who welcome the chance to work with others to improve their craft.

Many writers have joined writer's centers. This provides the opportunity to congregate with aspiring authors and poets of all genres. These centers offer classes and seminars helpful in writing fiction, non-fiction, poetry, short stories, and magazine articles.

Many writer's centers and poet's groups offer "open microphone" nights when reading of works is possible. Take advantage of these opportunities to expose your writings to others. Feedback is beneficial and you never know if someone with a valuable contact in the publishing world might be listening.

Bookstore cafes and local coffeehouses are gathering places for writers. Mingle with others who share your passion for books and the publishing process. They may have fresh ideas regarding your book. Learning from others is a great tool for any writer who dreams of saying, "Yes, my new book will be released next month."

As a professional writer, you need to make things happen. Sitting on your duff won't work. Take advantage of opportunities and never be afraid to ask questions of those who have a working knowledge of the publishing industry. Mentoring by experienced writers is a given and your inquiries will be welcomed. Across the world, there are organizations like Books For Life Foundation ready to assist your efforts to become published. **Be proud that you are a writer with publishing aspirations, and never let anyone tell you that you can't succeed.**

Step #9 Summary

- Reaction to creative writing is subjective—don't be offended by criticism.

- Use rejection as inspiration, not a sign of failure.

- Learn from critical feedback, and don't give up.

- Remember, it only takes one traditional publisher to say "yes."

- Use the story of the "Chicken Soup" books as a reminder to persevere.

People say life is the thing, but I prefer reading.

LOGAN PEARSHELL SMITH

Step #10
When Considering A Book Contract, Watch Your Backside

Book Contract Terms – Literary Agencies

When a literary agent offers you a contract, seriously consider having an entertainment attorney review it. This will ensure that you are protected even though most agency agreements feature standard clauses.

These include authorizing the agent to act in your behalf regarding worldwide rights to the book, permitting them to solicit offers for the rights to the book from various publishers, and the right to represent you with your next book. In return for their services, the contract will specify their retention of 15% of your earnings from the book based on any advance offered by the publisher and royalties from domestic sales (20% for foreign).

If possible, be certain to restrict the agent's representation to no more than your current book and the next one. Tying yourself to the agent for an extended period of time may prohibit your switching agents in the future. Also watch the expenses section of the agreement to make certain that you are only being charged for incidental costs (copying, mailings, etc.) for promotion of the book to publishers. If possible, put a cap on the amount that may be spent without your written authority.

As stated before, under no circumstances will you pay the agent for reading fees or to represent you. If he or she demands same, say thank you and move on.

An example of a literary agent agreement is featured in the Appendix. Your agreement may differ, but the sample will permit you to understand a basic contract.

Book Contract Terms – Publishers

The literary rights transferred (the Copyright Act requires any and all transfers to be in writing) from the author or poet to a publisher will vary with each book. **A sample publishing agreement with tips is featured in the Appendix.**

Most publishing contracts contain standard language. Terms are negotiated, but publishers are less likely to be flexible when a first-time author or poet is involved. **Remember that the most important thing is to be published, and if there is no advance and the royalties are minimal, so be it.** You can look forward to earning revenue on a future book.

Rights extended to a publishing company can include the English speaking countries, specific territories, or the world. **If possible, transfer as few rights as possible depending on the advance offered by the publisher.** Domestic rights and foreign rights can be separated or negotiated together. If you do not have an agent, seek advice from an entertainment attorney.

Publishers will normally access literary rights to the hardcover (cloth) edition of the book, paperback rights, e-book rights, audio rights and so forth. **Reserve the motion picture rights if possible.** Owning them, as mentioned earlier, can be worth substantial revenue at a later date, provided the work is appropriate for motion picture adaption. If a film producer expresses interest in those rights, contact an entertainment attorney.

Revisions

Special attention must be paid to the "Revisions" clause of any publishing contract. Working with an editor at the publishing company, you will revise the manuscript in preparation for release.

Each draft will be reviewed, but at some point, the publisher will okay the revisions. If you then decide to revise once again, the "Revisions" clause may dictate that you pay for costs incurred by the publisher to make the changes. To avoid this cost, attempt to negotiate an agreement absent this provision.

For certain types of non-fiction books, the word "revision" may mean something totally different, namely the preparation of a new, revised edition of the book. This would occur after a period of time, assuming that the book contains information that needs to be updated periodically. Including a clause in the contract that guarantees you will be hired to provide updates or make revisions is suggested.

Photographs/ Quotes

Obtaining the rights to book photographs can be expensive. The *AP* (*Associated Press*), *Reuters*, and other outlets such as stock photograph houses charge expensive fees. Many publishers assume the cost, but you should check the "Photographs" provision to make certain you are not responsible.

If photographs are an essential part of the text of the book, you are generally held responsible for securing permissions to use the photographs. The cost of obtaining permission may be included with the advance paid by the publisher. Publishers normally always pay for cover or jacket photographs.

Fees charged for photographs utilized in an "insert" section of the book are not as expensive as those proposed for the front or back jacket covers. If possible you, your agent, or your attorney should attempt to gain the rights to use the photographs for both the hardcover and anticipated paperback editions of the book.

A publishing agreement should specify the party responsible for costs if you are requested to take photographs. Camera and film expense can escalate.

If you self-publish, make certain you have the right to use photographs. A simple "release agreement" can be drafted to protect your interests.

Approval to use quotes from other printed material can be garnered through similar agreements. If you use quotes sparingly, provide the source of the quote and a mention in the bibliography. **If you intend to use more than a few sentences of text at a time, a release from the author, poet, and their publisher may be required.**

Free Books/Purchased Books

Publishers provide the author or poet with free books. The number will vary. They can be sold or given to friends and family.

You may purchase books from the publisher at a discount. It ranges from 40 to 55 percent. Many companies will invoice you; others require a credit card at the time of purchase.

Self-published authors and poets are free to distribute free books as they wish. **Keep track of the number given away for tax purposes.**

Next Book

Most publishers will include a "next book" clause in the publishing contract. Having invested their resources in your book, they expect you to be loyal. To guarantee this occurs, language is drafted requiring you to submit any material for a new book to the publisher. They then have a set amount of time to consider the book idea. If they decide to commit, a new agreement is negotiated in good faith. If they pass, you are free to submit the material to other publishers.

Demand that language inserted provides the publisher with "a right of first refusal based on fair negotiation." It requires the publisher to commit or pass within a short period of time.

If you self-publish and decide to employ an independent distributor to handle release of your book, be certain to restrict the representation to one book. This will permit you to seek other outlets if you are not satisfied with distributor performance.

Final Approvals

Attempt to gain final approval of title, subtitle, size and placement of cover print, front and back cover photograph or illustration, book text, author jacket biography and photograph, the photograph insert, font size and print style, and appendix materials. This may be difficult to gain, but discuss these details with the publisher or have your agent or attorney do so.

A clause ensuring no revisions will be made to any aspect of the book after you have "signed-off" is advisable. This guarantees that no editor at the publishing company will alter the text prior to the book being forwarded to the printer.

When possible, require the publisher to designate the release date for the book. Many publishers include a clause providing their right to publish the book within eighteen months of the time a final manuscript is approved. Shorten the time if you can. This is especially important if the book is tied to an anniversary or event that will provide free publicity for the book.

If you self-publish, provide enough time from the date you receive your completed book from the printer to the release date. Allow sufficient time for delivery of the book to outlets before your publicity campaign begins. Proper planning will guarantee that your book is released with a professional tone.

Important Book Contract Factors

In addition to the issues discussed above, the book publishing agreement should address the following issues:

- The agreed-upon length of the manuscript (flexibility is important)

- Manuscript or poetry collection delivery deadlines

- Royalty amounts (attempt to gain a "gross" definition)

- Royalty statement dates (quarterly basis)

- "Reserve account" amounts (publishers retain a certain percentage of revenue to cover cost of returns)

- The agency commission clause (normally 15 percent, 10 percent for television/film agents)

- Author or poet's right to audit (every six months)

- Out-of-print provisions (rights revert to author if the book is out of print for a specified period of time)

- Dispute resolution clause (arbitration alternatives may be advisable)

Literary agents and/or entertainment attorneys can advise you regarding these matters.

References

Several reference books exist regarding protection of author's or poet's rights. Among them is ***Kirsch's Guide to the Book Contract: For Authors, Publishers, Editors, and Agents.***

Jonathan Kirsch's book is helpful, but you are encouraged to seek advice from competent literary agents or entertainment attorneys. This guarantees that you will abide by **Mark's Step #10, When Considering A Book Contract, Watch Your Backside**.

Step #10 Summary

-   Remember the essential elements of a publishing contract—length of manuscript or collection of poetry, revisions, photographs, free books, purchased books, next book, final approvals, and delivery date.

-   Obtain professional advice through a literary agent or entertainment attorney regarding agency or publishing contracts.

-   Consult *Kirsch's Guide to the Book Contract*.

Epilogue

Book Report has presented one author's perception regarding the art of writing, the state of the publishing industry, and the opportunities for aspiring authors and poets to be published. I trust the ideas presented have caused you to recall the promise you repeated at the beginning of the book—**I Will Be Published!**

For those dreaming of becoming a published author or poet, consider contacting Books For Life Foundation, our not-for-profit organization created to assist your efforts. Besides utilizing this book as a guide, the foundation provides other services designed to maximize your opportunity to become published. Books For Life Foundation can be contacted through 970-544-3398, by e-mailing me at markshaw@markshaw.com or through the foundation's web site at www.booksforlifefoundation.com.

Summarizing the strategy recommended in this book, writers should follow these steps:

1. **Understand the publishing industry.**

2. **Research writing markets to see if the book idea you are passionate about is feasible.**

3. **Never forget good writing is essential to the publishing process.**

4. **Remember: great storytelling is the key to conversing with the reader.**

5. **Prepare a terrific Outline that will guide you through the writing process.**

6. **Investigate publishing alternatives and choose agents and publishers based on competent research.**

7. **Market the Query Letter and Book Proposal, not the book. (Fiction writers will prepare a manuscript in anticipation of interest from agents and publishers.)**

8. **Write a Query Letter and Book Proposal second to none.**

9. Never let rejection inhibit your quest to be published.

10. Take care when considering a book contract.

While considering steps number seven and eight, keep in mind that your goal as a writer is to answer questions in the Query Letter and Book Proposal you believe literary agents and publishers would ask if they were sitting next to you discussing your book idea. This approach keeps you focused on the information you would provide to hook their interest.

I trust my words and those of other experts quoted have both educated and inspired. I hope you have read this book and said to yourself, "Hey, if Mark Shaw, based on his background, can be published, so can I," since no one has greater respect for the world of the writer than I do. Above all, I trust you will disregard the temptation subsidy presses provide, and attempt to be traditionally published. If you are unsuccessful securing a publisher, self-publish. Either way, you are building a writing career as a professional.

Those who become published authors or poets experience a satisfaction difficult to describe. The first time I was asked "What are you doing these days, Mark?" and I was able to say, "I just had my first book published," I grinned from ear to ear. Being able to tell someone I am an author is most satisfying since being a published author or poet means I am a member of a select group.

The task from idea to publication is formidable, but the reward is significant. Besides having conveyed an important message to the world, you will discover a definite respect for those who are published. The written word is a special communication between the author or poet and readers, and to hold your book in your hand provides a special moment to remember.

To be self-published or published by traditional means arms you with a credential leading to your next book. Remember that those who have attained celebrity status as best-selling authors began by writing one book. It led to the next and the next.

With proper training, education, and a will to never give up, you can look forward to the moment when someone says, "Hey, I just read your book and I loved it." Shake their hand, say "thank you," and walk away knowing all of the hard work paid off.

William Saroyan, a gifted playwright awarded the Pulitzer Prize, sums up my belief regarding the mindset you must possess to achieve your goal of being published. In *The Writer's Handbook*, he wrote, "First, forget that you are an unpublished writer. Regard yourself, so far as you are concerned, as the only writer in the world. This is very important: it is not pride, not egotism; it is simply a necessary viewpoint for the serious writer. You must believe that you alone of all the writers in the world are writing the story of the living."

Saroyan added, "I want you to write in a way that no one else in the world has written. Any writer who is a writer can do it . . . The way not to write like anybody else is to go to the world itself, to life itself, to the senses of the living body, and translate in your own way what you see there, and hear, and smell, and taste, and feel, and imagine, and dream, and do: translate the thing or the act or the thought or the mood into your own language."

Tom Clancy's comment to *Writer's Digest* completes the thoughts of Sayoran. It sums up what I believe is the most important characteristic an aspiring writer must possess in order to realize the dream of being the author or poet of a published book.

Clancy said, "Keep at it. The one talent that's indispensable to a writer is persistence. You must write the book, else there is no book. It will not finish itself. Do not try to commit art. Just tell the damned story. If it is entertaining, people will read it, and the objective of writing is to be read." Thanks, Tom, you've said it all.

Mark Shaw

Appendix

Book Promotion Tips

Sample Non-Fiction Book Proposal

Sample Fiction Book Proposal

Sample Poetry Book Proposal

Writer's Market Agency Listing Analysis

Writer's Market Publisher Listing Analysis

Sample Agency Agreement

Sample Publisher Agreement

Agency/Publisher Submission Record

Sample Collaboration Agreement

Book Promotion Tips

Celebrate, Celebrate

The book has been written. The publishing deal is completed. The champagne celebration has produced a hangover the size of Ted Turner's Montana ranch because the long-awaited book is being released.

So what now? **Should you sit back and watch your publisher do all the work to promote the book?** Is it time for a vacation to the French Riveria to frolic on the shores of the Mediterranean?

The answer, of course, is "no," since the real work to promote the book has just begun. **Regardless of whether the publisher is large, medium-sized or small, or the book is being traditionally self-published, you are responsible for promotion, promotion, and more promotion.**

If a traditional publisher has released the book, there may be author or poet obligations regarding publicity. **Book promotion clauses are common in most publishing contracts.** They focus on what is expected of the author or poet and what is expected of the publisher when the book is released.

Without sufficient promotion, chances for success are doomed. The extent of the publicity and marketing program will depend on the size of the publisher releasing the book and the perceived importance of the book in the publisher's overall list. Having a major publisher release your book is worthy, but this does not guarantee a big promotional campaign. While negotiation is occurring, be certain to learn of the publishing company's commitment to promotion. This factor may be as important as the dollar amount of any advance being provided to you.

If there is a strong commitment to a promotion campaign, the publishing company will assign an expert in this field to coordinate the effort. The campaign may include a nationwide tour featuring television, radio, and print opportunities.

Medium-sized and smaller publishers' commitment to promotion will vary. They may or may not employ in-house experts to deal with publicity. Yours will depend on what is expected of you in tandem with efforts by the publisher.

Medium-sized and smaller publishers without an in-house promotion or publicity department rely on free-lance book promoters. These experts are hired on a project by project basis to expose the book to the media. Campaigns vary in cost depending on whether they involve print, radio, television or a combination of all three.

The publishing contract should contain specific language regarding the extent and length of the campaign and who is responsible for the cost. You may be required to expend funds to promote the book. If so, a clause should be included in the contract providing for this likelihood.

If you are willing to fund publicity or a promotion campaign for your book, consider noting this in the Query Letter and Book Proposal. A clause in the contract will provide guidance.

Book Signings

Book signings provide an opportunity for you to meet the public and sell your books. Major publishers will coordinate the appearances. Medium-sized and smaller publishers may assist, but the author or poet will assume an active role with scheduling.

The publishing contract should clarify respective roles and provide guidelines for book signing promotion, since it is essential to success. At least one month before the event, a coordinated campaign involving the author, the bookstore, and the publisher should be planned. Storefront signs and signs in the store are critical as is the announcement of the book signing in print publications and on radio and television.

Book signings must be strategically planned. Competition from other local events can impede success. Research newspaper and magazine calendar sections to discover competing events that may draw potential customers away. Discussing the best day and time for your book signing with the bookstore owner is essential. Some stores are "dead" on the weeknights; others flourish. Weather may play a part regarding scheduling. During the winter, few customers flock to book stores when there is five feet of snow on the ground. Summer months can be terrific weather-wise, but when the weather is too good, customers will stay away from their favorite bookstores.

Book signings during seasonal holidays can be advantageous. Books are great gifts for Christmas, Mother's Day, Father's Day, and Valentine's Day.

Mall bookstore signings can be terrific since there is normally a steady stream of customers walking about. Coordinating a book signing during peak hours is advisable.

For *Larry Legend*, my biography of NBA superstar Larry Bird, the publishing company arranged appearances at an unlikely venue: grocery stores. On one occasion I chuckled after being seated next to the frozen food section across from a sign reading, "Frozen Flounder, $1.99 a pound, Larry Legend $24.95."

No matter where the book signing is held, you should feel proud when your book is purchased. Thank buyers and take the time to sign the book with a personal greeting they will appreciate.

When *Testament To Courage* was purchased, I wrote, "May Cecelia's Words Inspire You," a reference to Cecelia Rexin's undying courage during the Holocaust. For youngsters whose parents bought *Larry Legend,* I wrote a message conveying how hard work and dedication helped Bird achieve success. With *The Perfect Yankee,* I wrote, "Don Larsen's achievement proves miracles do occur." *For Miscarriage of Justice*, I quoted Martin Luther King. The message read, "Injustice anywhere is a threat to justice everywhere."

Self-publishing guru Dan Poynter suggests authors and poets consider holding mini-seminars instead of book signings. In a *Writer's Digest* article, he quotes Teri Lonier, author of *Working Solo.* She stated, "An autograph party says, 'Come and appreciate me and buy a book;' a seminar says, 'Come on down, and I will give you something for free that will improve your life.'" Poynter and Lonier agree that it is important to think of "the potential benefit to the customer. How can you lure them out of the house and down to the store?"

Author Beth Crawford, a working mother, has been successful with sales of her novel through a unique approach. After she wrote *Silent Storm* and decided to self-publish it, Beth discovered the high cost of printing. Determined to continue, she and her husband purchased an inexpensive printing machine to print the book. When she became proficient at the process, Beth began promoting her novel in connection with seminars about the printing procedure. She presents a fifteen-minute speech about printing and then reads from her book. Beth also traveled throughout her home state before the release date of her book to meet people at bookstores and libraries. The result has been numerous appearances and successful sales of *Silent Storm*.

When you appear at the book signing or seminar, remember people love stories. They may be interested in the ones featured in the book, how you decided to write it, or the research tools employed. **The more entertaining you are, the greater the chances you will sell your books.**

Promotion Ideas

If the publishing company funds the promotional campaign, you will gain needed exposure. If the publishing company cannot fund the campaign, or if you are self-published, consider expending funds to cover promotional costs. **Outstanding public relations companies exist, but make certain they specialize in book promotion.** Ask for references and copies of public relations campaigns they have designed for other authors or poets.

Regardless of who is funding the promotional campaign, you must be clever to promote the book through any means possible. The saying, "The Lord helps those who help themselves," is most appropriate.

One author who splashed onto the national scene through self-promotion was Terry McMillan. When *Mama*, her first novel was published in 1987, she handled the marketing and promotion for her book. She forwarded hundreds of letters to African-American organizations requesting them to promote the book.

McMillan contacted bookstores with requests for book signings. Her efforts resulted in appearances and readings across the country. *Mama* was a moderate success, but when *Disappearing Acts*, her second book, was released, additional recognition occurred. In 1992, *Waiting To Exhale* became a bestseller. Four years later, *How Stella Got Her Groove Back* proved McMillan, the self-promoter, was a literary star.

To circulate interest about your book, keep an "address book" listing every friend and acquaintance since childhood. When book signings or other promotional appearances are scheduled, mail invitations to everyone in the area you know. You will form a group of loyal readers who will purchase future books.

Free publicity is the author or poet's best friend. Convince magazines or newspapers to print an excerpt from the book. To gain exposure, telephone radio shows, contact libraries to schedule readings, and work through local writer's centers. Public speaking also provides the opportunity to promote the book.

Author or poet Internet websites are a must in the twenty-first century. Designing them has become an art form, and there are multiple companies available to assist the writer. How fancy the site is depends on your pocketbook, but you can promote your book online to enhance sales opportunities.

To further publicize a book, consider creating a full-color flyer, brochure, or a "One-Sheet" (book cover on one side—descriptive material about the book on the other). Postcards displaying the book cover can be forwarded to media outlets, prospective purchasers of the book, and friends.

Publicizing a book not yet in the bookstores is the kiss of death. If buyers interested in the book based on media exposure visit the store and the book is unavailable, chances are they will not return to buy it. Make certain the publisher and the bookstores coordinate stocking the book at least a month before the promotional campaign begins. If you self-publish, handle the matter yourself.

Double-checking everything about your book signing is essential until the day it occurs. Make sure media exposure is secure and check the store a week or two before your book signing to see if posters are on the front window and displayed throughout the store. Most bookstores employ "community relations" managers to handle book signings, but they have many other duties. Good communication is a key to assurance that your book signing will be a success.

Regardless of how many books you sell at the book signing, request the opportunity, if it is not offered, to sign multiple books to be stocked in the store. Most stores do this as a courtesy, but publishers relish this opportunity since a signed book cannot be returned to them. This also applies to self-published authors or poets guaranteeing that you will be paid for the books left at the store.

If you are self-published, negotiate your share of the cover price with the bookstore. Splitting the revenue is fair, but many stores will permit you to keep as much as 70 percent.

If you appear for a book signing at a library or not-for-profit organization, consider donating a portion of the cover price. This promotes goodwill.

Book Promotion References

Several worthy publications will help you better understand book promotion. One is ***The Complete Guide To Book Publicity,*** written by Jodee Blanco, a seasoned professional who is also an expert on self-publishing. Using the tips she includes in her book can be very worthwhile. One discourages authors from mentioning their book more than once or twice during an interview. Another discusses what to wear for television appearances.

Blanco suggests that authors or poets write a book with promotion in mind. She believes that to successfully expose the book to the reading public, there must be a "promotional" tone, one signaling to the media that the book is timely and important. **Integrating an issue or cause into the story permits a built-in promotional package.** This permits a hook for the author or poet, the publisher, and the public relations firm representing the book.

Blanco's advice is questioned by those who believe a writer must write true to their heart and not with commercialism in mind. This "one or the other" stance fails to recognize that one can do both. Many authors or poets believing in an issue or cause convey their feelings while keeping an eye open toward promotion. As long as they don't sacrifice their beliefs, they are being true to themselves, as well as being practical.

Promotional ideas must be considered in light of expense and coverage. Make certain you are targeting the right audience for your book. Spend money wisely to reach the largest group of people who will be interested in the type of book you have written. Be creative and you will be amazed at the amount of publicity you can generate for your book.

Learning From Others

Masters of book promotion include the *Chicken Soup* authors Jack Canfield and Mark Victor Hansen. Millions of their books are sold worldwide and Canfield believes he knows the reason why.

The co-author attributes his success to good, old-fashioned research. He told *Writer's Digest*, **"I read every book I could on how to market books. It's something you have to study. It's something you have to make as important as the craft of writing."**

Canfield's interview revealed other jewels of information that can assist an author or poet. He said, **"Spend 90 percent of your time after your book comes out selling, marketing, and self-promoting."**

Canfield suggested creative methods involving marketing and self-promotion. He gave away free books to potential reviewers and the public at large while creating a web site where excerpts from the books could be downloaded at no cost. He promised to give a percentage of the retail price of the book to a charitable organization. Doing so, he said, "Created a buzz about the books."

Lessons learned from authors like Jack Canfield are essential to the continual learning process. They provide inspiration, as well as a proven game plan for success.

One strategy successful authors and poets employ is to provide free readings at libraries, high schools, colleges, and universities. Invite the media to such events as well as those who will be interested in the book topic. Canfield and others realize those attending may tell others about the book, creating an interest. Encouraging supporters to contact bookstores about the book may assist efforts to place the book there.

An avenue open to authors or poets self-publishing their book is the Internet bookstore. As stated, Amazon.com provides an "Advantage" program. It permits the author or poet, under guidelines posted on the website, to sell their book to the public. This permits wide exposure for the book especially if readers post postive reviews of the book. Asking friends and family or others who praise the book to post their review is proper. This builds creditionals for the book to those who check the website.

Building A Career

Book promotion is an important component to building a professional writing career. The goal is to create interest in both the current book and the next one. To this end, remember to act like a professional when dealing with those who take the time to visit a bookstore, chat about the book, and purchase one. Keep a mailing list so you can advise them of the next book being released.

Continued contact with the bookstores is important as well. Many authors and poets send "thank you" notes to the manager after an appearance. When the author or poet is ready for another appearance, the manager will recall the good manners with a smile.

Publishers take note of how their authors and poets handle public appearances. The writer may or may not be interested in securing the same publisher for the next book, but don't gain a reputation as someone who is difficult. The book publishing industry is small and a bad reputation with regard to promotion can impede chances regarding the next book and the next.

Above all, be proud of your book. From nothing but an idea, you have produced a bound book presenting your message to the world. Shout "hooray" and enjoy the experience.

Sample Non-Fiction Book Proposal
With Comments

Cover Page

(ten spaces)

(Book Title) **Code of Silence**
(36 Font, Bold)

(three spaces)

(Sub-title) **Melvin Belli, Jack Ruby, and the Assassination of Lee Harvey Oswald**
(24 Font, Bold)

(four spaces)

Author *(24 Font, Bold)*

(No copyright information)

(Tips—It is recommended that titles be six words or less. Titles should be symbolic of the story being told. They must be strong—unforgettable—titles sell the book.)

"He [Melvin Belli] was like a big howitzer. You had to point him in the right direction." *(14 Font, Bold, Single-spaced)*

Lawyer Frederica Sayre
(12 Font, Bold)
Chicago Tribune
(*Italicized*)

"[Belli] was gifted by nature with a velvety hypnotic voice that could charm cobras right out of their baskets."

Time Magazine

"Whatever you do, don't ask Melvin Belli about Jack Ruby. It's none of your business."

Gangster Santo Traficante to Mob Lawyer Frank Ragano, close friend of Belli's

"Something's not right. Maybe they injected Jack Ruby with cancer cells."

Melvin Belli upon learning of Ruby's death

(Tip—Short, snappy quotes are best to pique agent/publisher interest. They can be about the subject of the book (#1, 2, and 3), by the subject (#4), or drawn from the book text.)

Page 3 – additional quote – optional

"Clarence Darrow, the great defender, would have liked it. In less than an hour, [Belli] had ranged over a lifetime of learning. Like a mountain goat, he leaped unerringly from Pasteur to the hunchback of Notre Dame, to Anatole France and 'Penguin Island,' to Humpty Dumpty, to President Kennedy. Arguing before the jury, he played that voice [of his] like a symphony. It was by turns a Stradivarius, a bugle, an oboe, a snare drum racing at breakneck speed through key pages of testimony. Belli's marvelous voice glided and soared and dived - never faltering, never stumbling, never pausing except for effect. Like any skilled orator, Belli used his body as well as his voice. [He] locked his eyes on the courtroom wall, thrust out all 10 fingers straight and rigid at arm's length, like the imprecation of a mad magician."** *(14 Font, Bold, Single-Spaced)*

Harold Scarlett,
Houston Post,
describing Melvin
Bellis' final argument in
the Jack Ruby case.

(Tip—A lengthy quote from the book generates excitement and visualization. Remember—your book is like a conversation with the reader. Choose quotes that will cause an agent or editor to snap to attention.)

Table of Contents *(18 Font, Bold)*

Code of Silence *(Book Title – 24 Font, Bold)*

Book Tagline *(14 Font, Bold)*

Code of Silence chronicles the life and times of legendary lawyer Melvin Belli and his representation of Lee Harvey Oswald assassin Jack Ruby. (12 Font, Single--Spaced)

(Tip—The Book Tagline is the "hook to sell the book." In fifteen words or less, preferably less, the book should be described so readers instantly understand its content. The Tagline will be used to promote the book. Examples of superb Taglines can be discovered on the Book Page of the Thursday edition of USA Today in the bestseller list and in the Sunday New York Times Book Review. If you cannot describe your book in fifteen words or less, consider another book concept.)

Overview *(14 Font, Bold) (Summary of book—five to ten pages—double spaced)*

(Tip—Utilize text from book with description or just description. Write in present tense. Use strongest material possible to hook the reader. 12 Font—Not Bold. Double-Spaced.)

Jack Ruby's attorney, who dies at age eighty-nine in 1996, is a fun-loving eccentric who swirls fiction with fact. A self-styled dandy who sports unruly silver hair, mischievous eyes, and a devious smile, Belli wears red silk-lined suits and calf-high black snakeskin cowboy boots. "I have a penchant for all things bright and beautiful, kinky and flawed," he informs the *Los Angeles Times*, "and for good wines, great tables, wide travels, and beautiful women."

To celebrate victory in court, the Jolly Roger crossbones flag is raised high on the roof of his San Francisco office. Two booming blasts from an antique ship's roof-top cannon signal a champagne and caviar party catered for the most famous lawyer in the world. One who tells a *Paris Match* reporter during one of his whirlwind European escapades with Errol Flynn, "I was nothing until I became a screwball."

A must-see stop on the Grayline Bus tour, Belli's downtown office is a lair straight from Charles Dickens, a gallimaufry of exotica featuring an enormous Bengal tiger skin rug purchased from Elizabeth Taylor, a 17th century globe, Nepalese tapestries, hundreds of rare books, a case of aged French Burgundy, and an 18th century mahogany bar. The brick walls are dotted with autographed photographs of celebrity pals Frank Sinatra, Joe DiMaggio, Hubert Humphrey, Mae West, baseball great Barry Bonds, President Bill Clinton, and a life-sized portrait distinguished by its Napoleonic air.

To his supporters, the attorney is a true legal pioneer who causes large corporations to dread his wrath. Utilizing Clarence Darrow-type competence and William Jennings Bryan gusto, his flamboyant style becomes legendary in the courtroom when he overturns 100 years of legal precedent by assaulting Coca-Cola with a huge personal injury verdict. Victories follow in headline-making cases such as the Exxon Valdez oil spill, the Dow Corning Silicone Breast Implant case, the Tailhook Navy scandal, the Korean Airline Flight 007 crash, and the bawdy Cross-Your-Heart Bra copyright case where Belli parades a bevy of well-endowed beauties sans blouses before a spellbound jury.

During one case, Belli astounds the legal community by employing a crane to hoist his 682-pound client through a courtroom window. In another, a lawsuit seeking damages for the loss of a leg by a client in a cable car accident, Belli mystifies the jury by toting around an artificial leg wrapped in brown butcher paper during trial. As his final argument peaks, Belli drops the unraveling package on the lap of a stunned juror who believes it is the amputated leg.

When the San Francisco Giants baseball team installs faulty seat-heating devices at frosty Candlestick Park, the flamboyant lawyer who grows up in a red-light district near the gold-mining town of Sonora, California, sues the baseball club. After arguing the case in an Alaskan parka and snow boots, Belli earns a sizable judgment the Giants refuse to honor. Undaunted, the cantankerous attorney secures a lien on the body of future Hall of famer Willie Mays and team owner Horace Stoneham's private stock of Scotch. The Giants honor the judgment the next day.

Belli's fame spreads when the first of his *sixty-two* books, *Modern Trials* (sales: three million copies and counting) becomes the bible for every trial lawyer. This volume and subsequent works remain popular through the efforts of the 10,000-plus members of the Belli Society, a prestigious club of lawyers earning million dollar-plus verdicts.

While many praise him as the father of modern personal injury law and an astute criminal defense attorney in the tradition of F. Lee Bailey, Edward Bennett Williams, and Luis Nizer, critics allege Belli is a bizarre, shameless, self-promoting ambulance chaser who should be disbarred. One former colleague, Frederica Sayre, swears Belli is misunderstood. He tells the *Chicago Tribune*, "[Belli] is like a big Howitzer. You have to get him pointed in the right direction."

A reporter for the *San Francisco Chronicle* is puzzled by the loquacious attorney, observing, "He allows a burning ego to eclipse a first-class legal mind," while pointing out that the burly barrister is responsible for several legal milestones. Among them: the use of advertising by lawyers, the utilization of "day in the life" films to depict a victim's depraved condition, the employment of aerial photos and models to educate juries, and the introduction of demonstrative evidence featuring "Elmer," the plastic human skeleton and Belli's courtroom sidekick.

Like his friend, film idol Errol Flynn, Belli is a lady-killer. Married *six* times, he accuses fifth wife Lia of being a "merciless tramp." He alleges she had an affair with Bishop Desmond Tutu and is guilty of throwing Momba, one of his prized greyhounds, off the Golden Gate Bridge. The divorce becomes known as "The Lia Wars." As it proceeds, the *San Francisco Chronicle* polls readers as to which "parent" is titled to custody of the dogs.

Despite Lia's accusations that Belli is the "nastiest man in the world," Jack Ruby's attorney is an international personality, a crusader for legal reform. He appears at White House dinners accompanied by glamorous models, in Star Trek movies, and as a regular on the *Johnny Carson Show*. This prompts one pundit to observe, "Mel [is] the real thing, a Barnum and Bailey original."

(Tip—Remember—the first few sentences of the Overview must be superb to hook the reader. Be creative, visual, brief, and clear. Ask yourself—If I were an editor or publisher reading this material, what would I want to know about the book so as to decide whether to read further?)

(Note: subsequent text in the Overview details Belli's representation of Jack Ruby.)

(Comment: This latter section of the Overview presents an example of descriptive narrative detailing the intended story you want to tell. Make certain to provide a good beginning, middle, and end so the agent or editor realizes you are a competent storyteller. Include the highlights of the book to entice the reader to say, "This is a book I must represent or publish.")

(Tip—Be careful not to exaggerate or attempt to boost the material. Facts, facts, facts—are the key. They should speak for themselves. Agents and editors are turned off by those who promote instead of tell the story and let it stand on its own.)

Author Biography *(14 Font, Bold, 4-6 paragraphs at most)*

A featured speaker at the annual JFK Assassination researcher's convention in Dallas, the author is a former criminal defense lawyer and investigative journalist who has written books analyzing the Mike Tyson trial and the Jonathan Pollard case. *Code of Silence* represents more than three years of research probing every detail regarding Belli and the theory that underworld figures ordered him to represent and, in effect, silence Ruby.

(Tip—Above text provides author "credentials" or "platform" to write the book.)

The author's unique perspective of the tragic events in Dallas in 1963 stem from his courtroom experience as a trial lawyer. He was also associated with Melvin Belli in the mid-1980s.

(Tip—Details mini-biography of author. Key elements include expertise to write the book (knowledge of subject matter, association with subject, and education), publishing credits, and brief personal information about the author.)

(Tip—Write in third person to avoid use of "I this" and "I that." Above text provides personal association with the subject matter of the book.)

When the author questioned Belli regarding the Jack Ruby case, he was stymied. Curious as to why Belli, known as the proverbial chatterbox, was closed-mouthed about the Ruby case, the author began to research Belli's life and investigate the attorney's involvement in the Ruby case. To that end, exclusive interviews with Belli's legal colleagues, friends, and family members including his sixth wife, Nancy, who has designated the author as Belli's biographer, occurred. The author also obtained Belli's FBI file under the Freedom of Information Act. He is also privy to exclusive jury notes compiled throughout the Ruby trial.

(Comment: Above all, The Author section must answer the one question that the agent or editor will be asking, "Why are you the one person in the world to write this book?")

The author's interest in headline-making legal cases began when he covered the Claudine Longet trial as a correspondent for *ABC's Good Morning America.* He analyzed the Mike Tyson trial and wrote an investigative book about the case titled *Down For The Count.* The author provided legal commentary on the O. J. Simpson and Jon Benet Ramsey cases. He has appeared on *ABC, CNN, CBS, BBC*, and *Australian Channel Four.*

(Tip—Above text provides author media exposure. Agents and editors understand promotability advantages.)

Included among the twelve books the author has written are *Forever Flying*, the memoir of aviation hero R. A. "Bob" Hoover, *Larry Legend*, a biography of NBA legend Larry Bird, *Testament to Courage*, the Holocaust memoir of angel of mercy survivor Cecelia Rexin, *Miscarriage of Justice, The Jonathan Pollard Story* and *The Perfect Yankee*, the story of Yankee pitcher Don Larsen's perfect game in 1956. Eighteen editions of the author's books, including five in paperback and one printed in Japanese, have been published. More about Mark Shaw can be discovered at www.markshaw.com.

(Tip—Above text provides author writing credentials. If none, detail interesting aspects of your life that will be of interest to agent or editor.)

Curiosity regarding the publication of **Code of Silence** has been apparent to the author during author tours for his most recent books. Without exception, interviewers and radio listeners have requested information regarding Belli's participation in the Jack Ruby case. Thirst for fresh insight regarding conspiracy theories surrounding the JFK and Oswald assassinations will continue for years to come.

(Tip—Above text provides information regarding author curiosity and book subject and research techniques. The agent or editor must know that the author is a research expert.)

Book Audience *(14 Font, Bold, 4-5 paragraphs)*

As conspiracy theories continue to abound, a broad audience exists for this book since it not only includes those fascinated with the investigations of the JFK and Lee Harvey Oswald assassinations and conspiracy theories but the millions of readers familiar with Melvin Belli's legal career. Readership should be popular with the 10,000-plus members of the Belli Society, founded by the attorney. Their annual convention is held in Atlanta.

(Tip—Audience—Who is going to purchase and read the book? Be as specific as possible regarding groups, and organizations. The broader the potential readership, the better.)

Similar Successful Books

In addition to being written in the spirit of such best-selling biographies as *Lindbergh, Truman,* and *Cohn,* this book joins Gerald Posner's *Case Closed* and Frank Ragano's *Mob Lawyer* to provide an historical re-creation of the chilling events in Dallas in November 1963. It will appeal to those fascinated with several mob-related conspiracy publications such as *Contract On America, The Mafia Murder of President John F. Kennedy, Mafia Kingfish, The Hoffa Wars,* and *Who Was Jack Ruby?*

These publications were successful, but no author has presented a chronicle of the Jack Ruby case, before, during, and after the trial, through the eyes of his attorney. Exclusive access to information contained in the Ruby trial files, examination of Belli's FBI file, and fresh material gained through interviews with Belli's legal colleagues, friends, and family provide a unique perspective of one of the greatest attorneys who ever lived.

> *(Tip—Agents and publishers relish comparing a book under consideration with a successful one. List as many as possible, but be certain to explain why yours is better. Terminology such as "This is the first book to . . . is suggested.)*

> *(Sources to discover similar successful books include: Bookstores, Publisher's Weekly, Books In Print, Publisher's Trade List Annual, and Forthcoming Books. Similar books may have a bibliography that will list other similar books.)*

Promotional Ideas

Based on author visibility, multiple opportunities for promotion of the book exist. During his research on the book, the author has become known as an expert on Belli and theories surrounding whether he was recruited by the Mafia to silence Ruby.

> *(Tip—Publishers seek authors who have the ability to gain media attention for the book. Be certain to provide creative examples of how the book can be promoted.)*

Format/Manuscript Status *(14 Font, Bold, 2-3 paragraphs)*

Code of Silence's format presents extensive background material regarding Melvin Belli, a chronology of the Jack Ruby trial, historical references to the life and times of Belli following the Ruby trial, references to Belli's FBI file, and depiction of Belli's association with organized crime. Based on the latter and examination of facts never before revealed regarding evidence that Belli lied about his participation in the Jack Ruby case, questions are raised regarding whether he was hired to discredit and, in effect, silence Lee Harvey Oswald's assassin.

(Tip—Format—Provide the agent or publisher with the means by which you intend to tell your story. Be as succinct as possible, but clarity is essential.)

The Prologue and two sample chapters are presented with this proposal. The manuscript will be completed within six weeks of a publishing agreement.

(Tip—Manuscript status—Provide information concerning what material is presented with the proposal and when you contemplate completing the book. This permits the agent or publisher to monitor your progress and request that more material be presented for review.)

Book To Film *(14 Font, Bold, one to two paragraphs)*
The larger than life persona of Melvin Belli translates to film in the spirit of such motion pictures as *Hoffa, Cohn* (attorney Roy Cohn), *Fidel* (Castro), and *JFK*. Like them, Belli was a twentieth century icon whose exploits spanned the globe.

(Tip—For a book that possesses film or television potential, provide information regarding similar motion pictures. If there is interest, a "treatment" will be drafted outlining the theme of the film.)

(Tip—The Tagline used to describe the book will be utilized to "pitch" the film concept to interested parties.)

Outline *(14 Font, Bold)*
(Tip—Agents and publishers need to know that the writer is organized and has completed a book outline. Headings are provided along with "snippets" of text topics. Brevity is key, but clarity is essential.)

Prologue
Belli addressing the Jack Ruby jury.

Book I
Chapter 1—Preliminaries
Opening of Ruby trial—Dallas—March, 1964. Descriptions of Belli and Ruby. Information on Dallas and trial judge. Discord with Kennedys by labor and mob. Belli participation in Trial of the Century.

Chapter 2—Jack Ruby's Lawyer
Belli's famous cases—San Quentin convict, artificial leg trial, breast disfigurement case, fattest man in the world, Willie Mays v. San Francisco Giants trial. Description of Belli's offices. Life Magazine dubs Belli *King of Torts*.

(Note: The remainder of Book I, and Book II, III, IV, and the Epilogue would follow in similar fashion.)

Sample Text *(14 Font, Bold)*
(12 Font, double-spaced, suggested length 30 pages)
(Most writers choose the Prologue, if there is one, and the first two or three chapters of the book. Some choose the first two and the final one, but continuity and clarity can be a problem. Make certain that this material is the best of the best you have written. Edit it so many times that you have the material memorized. The text can be single-spaced.)

Book One *(18 Font, Bold)*

Prologue *(18 Font, Bold)*

"When I arose from the counsel table in the dead silence of the expectant courtroom, the fetid odors striking from nostrils, the lights over-head glaring down on the haze from cigarette and cigar smoke, I caught a curious look of anticipation in Judge Joe Brown's eye. I walked the five miles from counsel table to jury rail. It took me several hours. I felt like Alice in Wonderland falling down the hole. My feet didn't seem to touch the floor. I was about to make my plea for Jack Ruby's life."

Melvin Belli's description of the final few moments preceding his final argument in the wee hours of the morning of March 14, 1964 marked his most famous moment in history. With millions watching on television, the lawyer *Life Magazine* called "The King of Torts" began to address the jury on behalf of Jack Ruby, the assassin of Lee Harvey Oswald in the only live television broadcast of a murder in history.

Forty-plus years later, there remain questions about Belli's motives in representing the cold-blooded killer of the man who allegedly assassinated President John F. Kennedy, but experts agreed Belli's final argument was a command performance worthy of a Broadway Tony Award. When the barrister had completed his plea for Ruby in the packed Dallas courtroom during what the media called "The Trial of the Century," no one could say that he hadn't delivered anything but a sterling performance leaving those who witnessed it gasping.

For fifty-eight minutes, Belli was evangelical, the conductor of the symphony, THE king of the court. Majestically, he cast his vote in favor of reason, of sympathy, for a client he believed was truly mentally ill.

Regarding the attorney for Jack Ruby's oratory skills, reporter Harold Scarlett of the *Houston Post* wrote, "Belli was gifted by nature with a velvety, hypnotic voice that could charm cobras out of their baskets." Whether he could "charm" twelve jurors into supporting his call for a verdict of not guilty by reason of insanity remained to be seen.

(Further text from the Prologue, and Chapters One and Two would follow.)

Appendix

Unique Photographs, If Any *(14 Font, Bold)*

(Provides agent or publisher with relevant photographs that may be included in the photograph insert. Beware—book photographs are expensive so be certain to indicate whether

you have the rights to them. Less is better since many
agents and publishers shy away from books that will require
too many photographs.)

Author Publicity Material

(If appropriate, include newspaper and/or magazine articles
about you or the subject matter of the book. You may also
include brief articles written by you to provide further writing
samples.)

Sample Fiction Book Proposal
With Comments

Cover Page

(Ten spaces)

(Book Title) **No Peace For The Wicked**
(36 Font, Bold)

(four spaces)

(Sub-Title) **A Sordid Tale of Injustice In Redding County**
(24 Font, Bold)

(four spaces)

Author
(24 Font, Bold)

(no copyright information)

(Tips—It is recommended that titles be six words or less. Titles should be symbolic of the story being told. They must be strong— unforgettable—titles must sell the book.)

An unrectified case of injustice has a terrible way of lingering, restlessly, in the social atmosphere like an unfinished question.
(14 Font, Bold, Single-spaced)

Mary McCarthy
(12 Font, Bold)
American Novelist

There is no crueler tyranny than that which is perpetrated under the shield of law and in the name of justice.

Montesquieu
1742

(Tip—Short, snappy quotes are best to pique agent/publisher interest. They should be symbolic of the book theme.)

Page 3 – Contents (Optional)

Contents *(18 Font, Bold)*

No Peace For The Wicked
(Book Title, 24 Font, Bold)

Book Tagline *(14 Font, Bold)*
A lawyer facing disbarment seeks redemption for two mentally retarded men imprisoned for a murder they did not commit.
(12 Font, Not Bold, normally double-spaced)

(Tip—The Book Tagline is the "hook to sell the book." In fifteen words or less, preferably less, the book should be described so readers instantly understand its content. The Tagline will be used to promote the book. Examples of superb Taglines can be discovered on the Book Page of the Thursday edition of USA Today in the bestseller list and in the Sunday New York Times Book Review. If you cannot describe your book in fifteen words or less, strongly consider another book concept.)

Synopsis *(14 Font, Bold) (Summary of book—five to ten pages)*
(Tip—Use text from book plus description or just description. Written in first person. Use strongest material possible to hook the reader. 12 Font—not bold. Single or double-spaced.)

Lawyer Luther Parsons sits in his black Audi in 101 degree Arizona heat deciding whether to dive into demon drink or resist the temptation and continue his life on the run. His sojourn from Manchester, Ohio, a bedroom suburb of Cincinnati, left behind a $350,000 judgment destined to plunge him into bankruptcy, a wife poised to divorce a drunk, and a past filled with memories of a client gone mad who beheaded a DEA agent and then killed three teenagers.

Just as Luther decides Jack Daniels is the answer to all his problems, longtime friend Sonny Burk, the leader of an erstwhile band of do-gooders called the 18th Street Irregulars, calls. It seems two borderline mentally retarded men convicted of a murder they did not commit have been released from prison. Sonny's plea—return and serve a good dose of justice to those responsible for the injustice.

After a Jeff Gordon fan reminds Luther that it is the downtrodden who need his services more than anyone, he returns to Ohio and agrees to represent Ike Fellows, who suffers from Elephant Man disease, and Homer Kendrik, a slow learner who was putty in police officers' hands. Luther's motive is simple – the large amount of money he believes can be retrieved from city, county, and state coffers for the acts of retribution committed against his clients.

Reconciliation with wife Jessie occurs as both agree that Luther will cease his drinking. Together with Sonny, and the Irregulars, Luther begins his investigation, one focusing on detective Bud Hodges, a maniacal, out-of-control officer who controls law enforcement in Manchester. This investigation broadens to include other police officers, the county prosecutor, and a county judge. In the clear appears to be Rex Caldwell, Ike Fellows' public defender, the son of Senator Otis Caldwell, a Presidential aspirant.

When Luther, a former legal analyst for national trials, sues for fifty million dollars, the media, including *The New York Times* and *CNN*, spotlight the case while referencing the potential connection to Otis Caldwell. As the case progresses, Luther overcomes several obstacles while continuing to battle his drinking problem. His maturation is seen as he fends off a cover-up designed to protect the powers-that-be in Manchester.

A month before trial, Luther decides to settle the case in the best interest of Ike Fellows, whose severe psychological problems stem from being raped while in prison. Just before a settlement is reached, Ike decides he wants those who persecuted him punished and Luther resumes his crusade not only for the legal fees he will earn but to clear the names of Fellows and Kendrick.

As the trial date nears, tragedy occurs when Sonny is killed by Luther's enemies. Armed with new determination and with revealing evidence provided by a former CIA operative who has electronically reproduced the illegally obtained confessions of Fellows, Luther decides he will not only prove his client's innocence but finger the true killer of the drug dealer Ike and Homer were supposed to have killed.

During testimony from detective Bud Hodges, Luther sets him up for the playing of the incriminating audio tape. Confronted with having killed the drug dealer, Hodges turns on Rex Caldwell and accuses him of the murder. Caldwell is taken into custody and both he and his President-to-be father, implicated in providing hush money, are indicted.

When the jury returns with their verdict, Ike and Homer are awarded twenty-five million dollars. Luther and Jessie celebrate with two men whose story proves that there is no peace for the wicked.

> *(This sets up the story – descriptive text to provide the beginning, middle, and end of the story along with character descriptions, plot points, etc.)*

The Author *(14 Font, Bold, 4-6 paragraphs at most)*
> *(Tips—Details mini-biography of author. Key elements include expertise to write the book (knowledge of subject matter, etc.), publishing credits, and brief personal information about the author. Question you want to answer is: Why am I the one person in the world to write this book?)*

K. J. Fitzgerald is the pen name for Mark Shaw, a former defense lawyer turned television legal analyst and author of fifteen published books. His most recent, *Miscarriage of Justice, The Jonathan Pollard Story*, has been optioned as a film by Twentieth-Century Fox Television.

A veteran of more than 100 jury trials, most of them murder cases, the author has drawn upon his experiences in the courtroom to write *No Peace For The Wicked.* Inspired by a true story, the book presents a fresh look at how the legal system treats those too weak to defend themselves.

The author's media credits and continuing media exposure include his current coverage of the Kobe Bryant case for *ESPN* and *USA Today.com*. He has also analyzed the Mike Tyson, O. J. Simpson, and Claudine Longet trials.

The author's publications include *From Birdies To Bunkers*, to be released by HarperCollins in Spring, 2004, *Down For The Count*, chronicling the Mike Tyson case, *Forever Flying*, the autobiography of famed aviator R. A. "Bob" Hoover, and *Larry Legend*, a biography of NBA legend Larry Bird. More about the author can be learned at www.markshaw.com.

Book Audience *(12 Font, Bold, 4-5 paragraphs.)*

(Tip—Presents potential readers for the book. Also suggests that there is a built-in audience for the book based on the author's previous work. Tip—If warranted, sales figures from the previous books could be mentioned.)

During the past few years, hundreds of men and women have been released from prison based on the discovery of new evidence proving their innocence. In the spirit of this theme, **No Peace For The Wicked** will appeal to readers interested in a disturbing, yet inspiring story of one lawyer's crusade to right a terrible wrong. Readers will also be intrigued with the love story between the lawyer and his wife as she deals with his alcohol tendency, ones that threaten to destroy their marriage and his career.

The inside look at the legal system through the eyes of a former trial lawyer will appeal to readers fascinated with how the system can be manipulated by powerful individuals with no concern for the less fortunate. A realistic reaction from those reading the book may very well be, "But for the grace of God go I," based on the realization that what occurred to Ike and Homer could easily happen to them.

Similar Successful Books

(Tip—Compares the book to others that have been successful. Also details why this book is even better.)

No Peace For The Wicked is written in the spirit of mystery legal thrillers such as *Presumed Innocent* and *The Verdict*. The unique aspect of the book deals with its raw inside look at a legal system manipulated by a chosen few who have no hesitation to destroy the lives of two innocent men. Unlike other books in the same genre, *No Peace For The Wicked* grabs the throat of the criminal justice system and won't let go until redemption occurs.

Format/Manuscript Status *(14 Font, Bold, 2-3 paragraphs)*

> *(Tip—Provides agent or publisher with suggested format for book. Permits them to realize that you are organized.)*

No Peace For The Wicked chronicles a flawed lawyer's attempt to secure redemption for the wrongful arrest, conviction, and imprisonment of two mentally retarded men for a murder they could not possibly have committed. It details their story from beginning to end while documenting the escapades of the trial lawyer, one threatened with disbarment. The culmination of the book features a scintillating trial where the men's reputations are restored while the true killer is revealed.

A 395 page manuscript is available upon request.

> *(Tip—Details progress with book. Permits agent or publisher to monitor status of book and potential completion date. Remember that publishers are not interested in "works in progress" books that will need nurturing. They want as close to the finished product as possible.)*

Book To Film *(14 Font, Bold, one to two paragraphs)*
No Peace For The Wicked translates easily to film since it features strong drama (Ike and Homer, two innocent men imprisoned for a murder they did not commit), a lead character with a dubious past (lawyer Luther Parsons), and his feisty wife (Jessie), who attempts to keep him from drinking himself to death. The courtroom ending provides a thrilling climax when the true murderer is revealed. Similar films of interest are *A Civil Action, The Verdict*, and *The Firm*.

(Tip—Presents agent or publisher with concept that additional revenue from book may be possible. Remember the tagline for the book will be used to promote the book.)

Outline *(Chapter Headings 14 Font, Bold, Text 12 Font, Not-bold))*

(Tips—Provides the agent or publisher with a snapshot of the chapter titles and potential text. Tip—Titles must be provocative and snippets of text exciting and descriptive.)

Prologue

Ike Fellows' release from jail. He is hounded by an out-of-control cop determined to send him back to prison. Ike slithers through the streets intent on making it home safely.

Book I
Chapter One – Call For Help

Lawyer Luther Parsons reaches a crossroads while on sabbatical in Arizona. Confronted by demons intent on destroying his life through alcohol, he must decide whether to return to Ohio to help two border-line mentally retarded men imprisoned for a murder they did not commit.

Chapter Two – Help Me

Ike Fellows visits Luther and discusses background of case and potential representation.

Chapter Three - Call For Help

Ike Fellows visits the offices of Luther Parsons, *the* defense lawyer in Manchester, Ohio, located near Cincinnati. Ike pours out his story—one depicting his having been persecuted for a crime he did not commit.

Chapter Four - Ike's Journey

Background re Ike—disclosure of Elephant Man's disease, absence of education, family history, trouble with the law.

Chapter Five - The Lawyer

Background re Luther Parsons, family, law school, rise to prominence as a defense lawyer. Hint of trouble with a case that may lead to disbarment proceedings.

(Note—Remainder of chapters will provide similar text to disclose snippets of information to be relayed to the reader. See Outline in Non-fiction Proposal for more examples.)

(Note—Books II, III, and Epilogue would follow.)

Sample Text *(14 Font, Bold)*

(12 Font, Not-bold, double-spaced, suggested length 30 pages)
(Tip—Most writers choose the Prologue, if there is one, and the first two or three chapters of the book. Some choose the first two, and the final one, but continuity and clarity can be a problem. Make certain that this material is the best of the best you have written. Edit it so many times that you have the material memorized. The text can be single- spaced.)

Prologue

"Get your stuff, retardo. You're going home."

The moon-faced matron stuffed a deck of cards into her denim shirt pocket, shoved her puffy hand through the Redding County jail cell door, and tossed in a folded garbage bag. It floated to the concrete floor in front of Ike Fellows's bunk.

Ike looked up, confused by the abrupt intrusion. Alice Porkman stood there sneering, one hand twirling a set of keys and the other lodged in the folds of her thick waist.

"Had to interrupt a game of cards to deal with your no good ass," Alice said. "Waste of my damn time."

Ike was lying on his bunk, dreading the moment when he would be called out for a shower. Though his long brown hair was dull and stringy, and his body odor offensive even to him, he pretended to be asleep to avoid going since showering brought back memories of Armington State Prison. Bad memories.

Her voice rising an octave, Alice repeated her words. "Ya hear me, retardo? I said pack up your shit. You're goin' home."

His keeper had used this ploy to trick him before, but having no choice, Ike, whose patchy beard and missing front teeth made him appear older than his thirty-five years, hurriedly gathered up the photo-booth picture of his sister and her kids. As Alice scraped her keys across the metal cell bars, he stuffed the photograph in the bag with his extra set of prison clothes and a wooden cross a child molester had whittled for him.

As an air raid siren cut the silence, Ike tried to move quickly. He heard the clank of the cell door key against the lock, but his hands were shaking, his movements clumsy. Alice opened the door and he obediently shuffled down the corridor, two steps behind his guardian, sucking in the smell of disinfectant spread in the cell block earlier that morning.

At a desk just beyond the cell block, Alice grabbed a clipboard. She shoved a pen in Ike's face, pointing to a space on the paper.

"Sign," she ordered, her voice dull and cold.

Ike grabbed the pen, laboriously inking his mark on the line as the foul odor of the nearby latrine lingered in the air. Alice yanked the pen away, gripped his right shoulder and shoved him toward the back door. She opened it with her free hand and pushed him out onto the wooden back steps of the jail as the door thumped closed behind him.

The fading rays of the late summer sun dipped beyond the landscape as Ike stood in the shadow of the jail, gathering the confidence to walk away. He followed the sun's descent with his wary eyes before focusing on a chirping Bob White perched on the limb of a nearby tree, then to parched red roses trailing along a neighboring fence. Across the street, he spied a worn "Bush For President" sign tacked to a pockmarked telephone pole. Beside it another read, "Manchester is G.O.P. Country."

Ike smelled the grassy scent in the thick Ohio air and tugged at the too tight collar on his blue work shirt. For the first time in eighteen months, he could breathe without the stench of urine and mold, of unclean men in a world behind steel bars.

Ike was wearing his prison-issue jeans, the work shirt stamped with his D.O.C. number, and black, crepe-soled oxfords. The matron hadn't given him his ID or any money. Not even the $75 "gateage" inmates normally received at their release. He considered returning to ask for it, but feared being locked up again.

Ike tripped and stumbled down the jail steps. His rolling gait was the result of neurofibromatosis, Elephant Man's disease. Lumpy clusters moguled his face, hands, and arms. His shoe splayed below a pant leg cut to allow room for the huge protuberance above his left ankle. The ribbing of his dirty white cotton sock stretched tautly over the swelling.

Inmates who had come and gone during his three week stay at the jail called him "retardo" and "one leg." When the lump festered and cracked, pus stained his sock, giving inmates more reasons to taunt him.

Though the afflicted leg slowed his pace, Ike pushed ahead, suddenly anxious to put distance between himself and the jail. With every step, he glanced over his shoulder to see if anyone was following. He trusted no one, especially policemen.

Ike walked with his head lowered, avoiding eye contact with anyone on the sidewalk and a few passing cars traveling the Manchester streets at dusk. "I gotta get to Sharon's house," he repeated as a mantra. She was his sister and only living relative.

Ike was two blocks from the jail when an unmarked, black Dodge patrol car rolled to the curb less than twenty feet from him. He quickened his step, but he couldn't out-pace the car as it crawled alongside.

The shrill sound of a familiar voice caused Ike to trip and fall. "Hey, you dumb retard," the agitator spat, his voice booming across the vacant street.

Ike didn't look, but now he was certain his release was a trick. He was going back to prison.

"Hey, retard, look at me when I talk to you," the agitator barked as Ike heard a car door slam. "You and me got some business to take care of."

Ike froze, his only possessions clutched against his chest. Tears welled. He felt helpless, sprawled on the sidewalk, afraid to move.

Seconds later, Ike felt his tormentor's presence hovering over him and the sound of handcuffs clanking in the air.

"You crazy wimp," the voice scolded as handcuffs appeared in front of Ike's eyes. "Did you really think I was gonna let your sorry gimp ass walk around *my* town?"

Text from Chapter One and Two would follow.

Appendix
Unique Photographs, if any
Publicity Materials

(Include newspaper and magazine articles about the subject matter, author, etc., and other pertinent material)

Sample Poetry Book Proposal
With Comments

Cover Page
(Ten spaces)

(title) **Parade of Ladies**

(36 Font, Bold)

(three spaces)

(poet) **Diana Meadows**

(24 Font, Bold)

(No copyright information)

(Tip—It is recommended that titles be six words or less. Titles should be symbolic of the story being told. They must be strong—unforgettable—titles sell the book.)

Parade of Ladies *(18 Font, Bold)*

Tagline *(14 Font, Bold)*

A Parade of Ladies is a collection of poems that depict a time gone by when respect for the fair sex was the call of the day.

> *(Tip—clarity is a key. If someone asked you what your book is about, what would you say?)*

Synopsis *(14 Font, Bold)*

"Where have all the ladies gone?" I ask in a tone familiar to that of a professor addressing his students. Have males forgotten that the fair sex is to be pampered with love and affection and not demeaned for standing up for their rights? Whose to say that those women that choose to stand up for what they believe in still aren't as feminine as the ones that stay at home, keep their mouths shut, and raise children?

Twenty-five years ago, women were respected for their opinions and not chastised as "feminists" on the prowl. But all that changed when men, threatened by the strength shown by their wives, girlfriends, and sisters, decided enough was enough. Soon women were being looked down upon and laughed at for speaking their minds. Too often they were threatened with reprisal, sexual or otherwise, unless they promised to shut up.

In *A Parade of Ladies*, this poet tells stories of those women, unknown though they are, who stood their ground and said "Take me as I am or leave." Woven through the collection is a theme of pride and believing in oneself despite the odds. In "John Waterford's Wife Carol," the woman of the house tells her husband that she is applying for college since their four children have left the nest. In "Rex Walter's Girlfriend," Olivia decides to join the NAACP despite warnings from her spouse that she will be pigeonholed as a "communist sympathizer." In "Ralph Johnson's Sister," Sidney Anne Johnson is a mother of eight that intends to leave her abusive husband in spite of threats that he will kill her.

Twenty-four poems are presented featuring twenty-four women with stories to tell, each essential to *A Parade of Ladies*.

(Tip—Outlining the theme of the poetry collection is imperative. Catch the interest of the agent or publisher with an exciting overview of the stories to be told by the poems.)

Poet Biography

Diana Meadows is a single parent to six children, ages four to eighteen. After being abandoned by her husband, she worked sixteen-hour days while studying for her bachelor's degree in education on the weekends.

Diana began writing poetry to suppress spousal abuse. After her husband left, she began to write in earnest. One poem from her self-published first collection, *A Family of Flowers*, was printed in *Poets and Writers Magazine*. Other poems have appeared in the *Village Voice* and various newspapers. In September of 2002, she received first prize in the poetry and prose competition conducted by Books For Life Foundation.

Ms. Meadows, a first grade teacher at Northwest School in Louisville, Kentucky, resides with two of her children, four dogs, and five cats, in the woods near Lexington, Kentucky.

(Tip—Presenting the poet's credentials, her platform for speaking through her poetry is essential. Any agent or publisher will realize this lady knows about the subject matter being featured.)

Book Audience

Women interested in overcoming any self-doubt will be readers of *A Parade of Ladies*. Inspirational in nature, the material is hard-boiled but right on point. Through the women featured, readers will understand that the poet is expressing her thoughts regarding the state of womanhood today. The *Louisville-Courier Journal* properly dubbed the poet's first collection of poetry, *A Family of Flowers*, "the hard knocks of family life." *A Parade of Ladies* promises a similar hard-edged style while making women stop and think about whom they really are.

(Tip—Publishers seek the largest audience possible for a book. Attempt to show that there may be multiple readers that will be interested in the poetry.)

Similar Successful Books

A Parade of Ladies is written in the spirit of *Ollie's Fables*, a series of poetry books emphasizing the rights of women. This collection is unique because it examines the subject matter in an objective manner based on the poet's personal experiences.

Another similar collection is *Peace On Earth*, by Elouise Johnson. *A Parade of Ladies* compares favorably with this book, but extends the subject matter.

Promotion Ideas

Through her exposure as a leading advocate of women's rights, and a monthly newsletter sent throughout the country to battered women, the poet has a built-in audience for her collections of poetry. A *Family of Flowers* was promoted through the poet's web site at www.standonyourown.com and more than three thousand copies were sold. *A Parade of Ladies* will be promoted through the newsletter and the wesite and at the poet's speaking appearances.

> *(Tip—Attempt to validate that the poet has readers interested in the book either through previous works or media exposure. Agents and publishers know sales are dependent on promotion, promotion, and promotion.)*

Collection Status

The poet has written sixteen of the poems for the collection. The remaining eight will be completed within two weeks of contract.

> *(Tip—Provide the agent or publisher with the status of writing. This shows professionalism and good organizational skills.)*

Outline
(Partial List of Poems)

John Waterford's Wife Carol
Peggy First, A Woman Alone
Rex Walter's Girlfriend
Pink Dye's Older Sister
Wilma Pam's Dead Lover
Ralph Johnson's Sister

Olivias Creek's Missing Husband
Bart Black's Dead
Have You Seen Christina Applebaum?
Poor Little Red Chambers

(Tip—Provides agent or publisher with thumbnail sketch of poetry. Titles are catchy, easy to remember.)

Sample Poems

(Tips—Sample poems will be typed one to a page. If a Cover page is not used, then type in upper left hand corner name, address, telephone number, and e-mail address. Space down six lines or so, center, and print the title of the poem in 18 Font, Bold. The poems will be single-spaced, double-spaced between stanzas. If the poem stretches beyond one page, continue to the next by indicating your name, a keyword from the title of the poem, and the page number at the upper top left-hand corner of the page.)

John Waterford's Wife Carol *(18 Font, Bold)*

She was a lovely thing, you see,
When John Waterford spied her in the bar.
He was smitten like never before,
Carol was his dream come true.

The wedding was a day to recall,
Special feelings all around,
Four children soon filled the household,
John and Carol, the perfect couple.

But Carol wasn't certain who she was,
A high-school graduate but nothing more,
She wanted to find herself,
When the children left the nest.

An ad for a college caught her eye,
But John laughed at the idea.
Carol raised her voice,
John raised his fist.

Months went by,
Carol afraid to try,
John the roadblock,
To self-respect, a chance to change.

Then God paved the way,
When John was hit by a truck.
She was sad to see him go,
But not that sad.

And then the day arrived,
College student Carol,
How proud she was to be in class,
Her dream instead of his fulfilled.

Six years hence,
And Carol found her way,
She loves life,
Most of all herself.

(Tip—Use strong words, words that improve pacing of the poem. Remember that all good stories are love stories.)

(Note: Between five and ten poems would follow this one.)

Appendix

(Includes photographs, illustrations, media coverage for the poet, etc.)

Explanation/Analysis of *Writer's Market* Agent Listing

Agent Listing:

Christopher Bloomburg Literary Agency *(name of agency)*

4567 Avenue of the Stars, Suite 300
New York, New York 23003 *(address)*
212-546-8797 *(telephone number)*, 212-546-8798 *(fax)*
Cboomburg@aol.com *(e-mail address)*

Agents—Christopher Bloomburg, Liz Dahling, Bill Book *(Contacts at small agency)*

Established, 1980 *(Two decades-plus existence—above average for literary agencies)*

Member AAR *(Association of Authors Representatives—good organization—Indicates professionalism for the agency)*

Represents seventy-five clients *(Good client base)*, 15 percent new/unpublished authors *(Not a large percentage, but there is hope for the aspiring author)*

Currently handles Fiction, Non-Fiction, and Poetry *(Provides a wide range of representation)*

Mr. Bloomburg has been a literary agent for twelve years. He was an editor for Doubleday and an assistant editor at HarperCollins before that. *(Agent/agency background—experience at publishers good indication of expertise)*

Represents: Non-fiction books, novels. Considers these non-fiction areas, popular culture, biography, and memoirs. Considers these fiction areas: Horror, fantasy, science fiction, romance. *(Indicates* specific fields of agency interest. *Tip—It is unprofessional to contact the agency with other genres of writing.)*

How To Contact: Query Letter, Book Proposal, Manuscripts. *(Type of material that may be submitted)* SASE. *(Requests self addressed, stamped envelope accompany material.)* Accepts fax queries but not e-mail. *(Proper procedure to submit material. Tip—Does not say the agency won't accept unsolicited material. Some agencies will not.)* Considers simultaneous queries. *(Understands that writer may be submitting to several agents at one time.)* Responds in six weeks on queries, ms three months. *(Permits writer to understand time element for consideration.)* Obtains most new clients through recommendation from others, solicitation, conferences *(Provides new client information base. Tip—This appears to be an excellent agency for unpublished authors—very open-minded.)*

Needs: Agency seeking Hispanic romance and science fiction, World War II novels, Sports Biographies *(Indicates type of material agency seeking.)*

Recent Sales: Sold 125 books last year. Seventy-five to major publishers. Examples: *Two Can Make A Family*, by John Dunwiddy (Scribner), *Perfect World, A Novel,* by Emily Partridge (Dutton) *I Knew The Babe,* by Arthur Blogges (Sports Publishing), and *My Girlfriend Was A Boy, A Novel*, by Rex Roost (HarperCollins) *(Provides proven agency track record. Tip—Watch for books sold similar to the same genre you are considering.)*

Terms—Agency received 15 percent on domestic sales, 20 percent foreign sales. *(Standard in the industry. Tip—Film and television agents will charge 10 percent.)* Written contact required. *(Some agencies require contract, some don't. Tip—Better to have one to protect interests)* Charges clients for photocopying and mailings *(Many smaller agencies charge for expenses. Tip—Never hire an agent that charges you a fee to represent you. This is very unprofessional.)*

Writers' Conferences—Aspen, Maui, Summerfield, Hidden Valley *(Provides conferences attended by agent or associate.)*

Tips—Thoroughly research the genre you are contemplating. Visit bookstores to see what is selling and who is publishing the bestsellers. Attend writers' conferences to hone your craft and meet industry people. Complete manuscript of novel before submitting query letter or book proposal. Not necessary re non-fiction. *(Guidance from agent. Tip—Excellent advice. Indicates that agent is knowledgeable of literary industry.)*

Explanation/Analysis of
Writer's Market Publisher Listing

Publisher Listing:

Aardvark Publishing Company *(name of publisher)*

350 Fifth Avenue, New York New York 23003 *(address)*, 212-787-5432 *(telephone number)*, 212-787-5433 *(fax number)* Web site: www.aardvark.com. *(web site)*, **Aardvark@aol.com.** *(e-mail address)*

Acquisitions: Patricia Longfellow, Executive Editor (romance, mystery, thrillers), Clancy Purdue, Editor (sports, adventure), Ilene Puffbottom, Executive Editor (self-help, art, music), Stacy Stillwagon, Editor (historical romance, erotic), Paul Butterbaugh, Editor (true crime, general fiction), Abe Lincoln, Senior Editor (pop, culture, spiritual, health), Augustina Soprano, Editor (historical novels), Amy Lain, Editor (gay and lesbian, health, cookbooks), John D. Dannon, Editor (alternative health, general non-fiction, self-help). *(Provides contact information for alternative genres. Tip—Telephone to make certain an individual is still with the company and in same category since literary industry people change jobs and positions at a high rate. Also—if your specific genre is not listed, check with the agency to see whether they handle it. If not, do not waste time by submitting material.)*

Publishes 250 titles/year. *(Provides information regarding publishing quotas.)*, Receives 4,000 submissions/year. *(Provides idea of titles purchased vrs. titles received.)* 10 percent from first-time authors, 20 percent from un-agented writers *(Indication that company is open to aspiring authors whether agented or not.)*

Pays 10-15 percent royalty on hardcover, 8-10 percent on paperback—royalty based on retail price. *(Industry standard. Tip—Royalty basis should be pinned down to avoid misunderstandings.)* Pays $2,000 to $25,000 advances. *(Indicates that company will pay hefty advance but not comparable to largest publishers.)*

Publishes book 9-18 months after acceptance of manuscript *(There are exceptions but this time frame is standard. Tip—Gearing your book to event or to current topic permits better promotion tie-ins. Books are normally published fall/winter and spring.)*

Accepts simultaneous query letters, book proposals, manuscripts *(No rule against submitting material to other publishers.)* Responds in 4 weeks to queries and book proposals, 4 months to manuscripts. *(Permits you to know when to follow up if no word.)*

Book catalog online at www.aardvark.com. *(Permits inspection of type of books company publishes. Tip—Check out books similar to yours.)*

Book Specialties: Non-fiction—military/war, true crime, women's issues/studies, travel, cooking/foods, humor, how-to, gifts, psychology, current events, gay/lesbian, nature/environment, pop culture, philosophy, animals, business economics, biography, memoirs, history, hobbies. Fiction—thrillers, mysteries, erotica, occult, suspense, horror, westerns, contemporary, romance. *(Specifies various genres appealing to publisher. Tip—If your book idea is not listed, don't submit material.)*

Recent Titles: *The Happy Horses, A Novel,* James Harrold, *Typewriters and My Mother-In-Law,* Humor, Oliver Cup, *Please Don't Eat the Dogs,* Humor, Arthur Loser, *Teddy Roosevelt, Was He Gay?* Earl Putts, *London on $5000 a Day,* travel, Pete Piper, *The Prince and the Frog, A Novel,* Jason Underbucket, *Who Stole The Kitty? A Novel,* Happy Grimes. *(Permits you to review publisher's titles.)*

Tips: Prefer agent submissions, but will consider well-conceived query letter and book proposal. Do not send unagented manuscripts. Do send SASE. *(Latter good suggestions for aspiring authors.)*

Sample Agent Agreement With Legal Tips

(Tips—If you are offered a literary agent agreement, hire a competent entertainment lawyer. He or she can best represent your interests. Regardless, familiarizing yourself with the basic outline of an agent agreement can be helpful.)

Representation Agreement

This letter of agreement will confirm the arrangement between us by which you have appointed Scarborough Literary Agency as your exclusive agent in the sale, lease, license, and/or other disposition of literary and related rights to any and all works penned by you during the term of this agreement.

(Standard language detailing the representation during a defined period.)

You understand such appointment to cover the active marketing throughout the world of all your literary rights, including but not limited to, publishing, motion pictures, electronic, stage, radio, television, recording rights, and generally to advise you professionally.

(Details specifics of representation. Tip—Keep language as specific as possible to avoid confusion. The clause, "Generally to advise you professionally"—should be left out if possible.)

Scarborough Literary Agency will actively market and represent your best interests to the best of its ability utilizing its contacts throughout the entertainment industry. The agency will not enter into an agreement on your behalf without your written consent.

(Provides language requiring agency to act in your best interest, but restricts their ability to enter into agreements without your having final approval. Tip—This latter language is essential to protecting you against acts by agent that are adverse to your interests.)

You agree that Scarborough Agency will collect for you revenues due from the marketing of any and all works covered by this agreement. Said revenues will be forwarded to you within fifteen days of receipt by the agency.

(This language authorizes your agent to act as your depository for monies earned. Tip—Learn when the reporting periods are for your publishers and be certain to check as to whether revenues are due.)

In consideration of Scarborough Agency's representation, it will retain a fifteen percent commission of all revenues collected in the United States of America and twenty percent of all revenues collected from foreign sources.

(Standard fees for literary representation. Tip—Attempt to include the word "gross" as in gross revenues so there is no doubt of the amount
being commissioned. Tip—When dealing with theatrical agencies, the commission will be ten percent.)

When marketing your literary work, Scarborough Agency will incur certain out-of-pocket expenses including photocopying, postage, messengers, and overnight courier services. You agree to reimburse the agency for said expenses within ten days of billing. Any other expenses must be approved by you in advance. Scarborough Agency agrees to keep all expenses to a minimum.

(Specifies your responsibility to pay for out-of-pocket expenses. Tip—Insert "under one hundred dollars" after the word "expenses" in line four. This protects you against excessive overruns.)

This agreement is effective as of the date both parties have signed below. It will continue to be valid for a period of one year unless cancelled by either party with sixty days written notice.

(Details term of agreement. Tip—Stay away from any agreement longer than one year. Also—watch for language

that continues agreement indefinitely subject to one party or the other cancelling.)

Regardless of the cancellation by either party to this agreement, Scarborough Agency will continue its representation and collection of revenues for all works initiated or completed during the term of representation.

(Standard language protecting agency after cancellation of agreement. Tip—If possible, limit collection of revenue to five years.)

This agreement is binding under the laws of the State of _____. All parties agree that in the event of dispute, the matter shall be subject to arbitration under the auspices of the American Arbitration Association.

(Specifies mechanism for legal matters. Tip—Attempt to designate your state as venue.)

Agreed to by all parties designated below this ___ day of ____, ____.

_____

Maude Bonderbast, President Scarborough Literary Agency

_____

Author

Sample Publisher Agreement With Legal Tips

(Tips—If you are offered a publishing agreement, hire an entertainment lawyer or utilize the services of a literary agent to represent you. They can best protect your interests. Regardless, familiarizing yourself with a publishing agreement can be helpful.)

Publishing Agreement:

This is an agreement between Author (hereafter referred to as "author") and Afterlife Publishing Company (hereafter referred to as "publisher") regarding the publication of the book titled, *Guardians of the Heavens*.

(Sets out parties to the agreement and subject matter.)

Author and Publisher agree:

The author will write for publication a book tentatively titled *Guardians of the Heavens*. To the publisher, the author grants all rights including but not limited to the exclusive right to publish, sell, create derivative works and distribute the book during the full term of the copyright and renewals thereof throughout the world and in all languages. The author reserves the electronic rights and the motion picture and television rights.

(Details the issuance of rights to book from author to publisher. Tip—Delete the words, "including but not limited to" if possible. This will prevent confusion. Also—If all rights are not being transferred, specify exact countries where publisher can market book. Also—It is important to reserve motion picture and television rights for later sale.)

The publisher shall have the right to copyright the book in the name of the author.

(Important that copyright remains in the name of the author. Tip—Never give up that right.)

The author will complete and submit to the publisher a manuscript of not more than 250 pages by _____. After the manuscript is accepted by publisher, it shall be published at the publisher's own expense within eighteen months. The publisher reserves the right to prevent publication due to circumstances beyond its control. If they do not publish the book within eighteen months, all rights revert to the author.

(Details the conditions for publication including length of manuscript and due date. Also specifies period of time within which publisher can publish book. Tip—Attempt to shorten period of time for publication to one year or less. If possible, pin down publication date. Also—be certain that the reversion clause is included to protect your interests.)

Publisher will pay to the author an advance against royalties in the amount of $10,000. Half will be paid upon acceptance of the manuscript and half will be paid on the date the book is published.

(Sets terms for the advance to be paid to author. Tip—Attempt to obtain as much of advance as possible up front. Also—if possible, add clause specifying that no portion of the advance will be returned to the publisher if they do not publish book.)

Publisher will pay to the author royalties based on retail price of the book. The breakdown for such payments shall be: 10 percent of revenues produced by sale of 10,000 books, 12½ percent of revenues produced by the next 5,000 books, and 15 percent of revenues thereafter.

(Details standard revenue-sharing terms for most books. Tip— Attempt to negotiate "retail price" or "invoice price" as

standard for measuring royalties. "Net revenues" will provide less money due to discounts.)

No royalties shall be paid to author on copies given to or purchased by the author, sample copies, damaged copies, returned copies, or copies given away for publicizing the work or to promote sales. Royalties on non-trade special sales may be independently negotiated with the mutual consent of the author and the publisher.

(Specifies books that will not be subject to royalties. Tip— Limit this category as much as possible.)

The publisher shall have the right to reserve a percentage of royalty payments, not to exceed 20 percent, in anticipation of copies of the works being returned by its customers. If the author has previously submitted to the publisher a work that was subsequently published by the publisher, then publisher has the right to combine royalty statements for multiple works written by the author for the publisher. If the author has purchased books from the publisher and has not paid the publisher's invoice, the publisher may deduct the amount due on the invoice from the amount of the royalty due the author during any royalty payment period.

(Protection language for the publisher. Tip—Restrict the reservation amount as much as possible. Attempt to bring all revenues owed current after two years.)

Net proceeds derived from the disposition of "subsidiary rights" shall be divided equally between publisher and author. They include: digest, abridgment, condensation or selection, book club first and second serialization, reprint edition through another publisher, syndication, translation and foreign language book publication, publication in the English language outside the United States, the right to public display, the right to grant reprints and other uses to third parties, and all other rights and uses now known or hereinafter to become known.

(Sets out other potential sources for sale of book. Tip— Restrict this clause as much as possible. Delete general languages such as final phrase above concerning "all other rights.")

The publisher will report on the sale of the work by providing royalty statements on a quarterly basis. All balances due author shall be paid at that time.

(Denotes publisher obligation regarding earnings statements. Tip—Even thought most publishers report twice a year, attempt to secure quarterly reporting.)

The author is responsible for submitting the manuscript (electronically/floppy disk, and hard copy) including a Table of Contents, Foreword, Epilogue, Appendix materials, and Bibliography. The author shall also submit suggested photographs applicable to the book. Publisher shall be responsible for all costs of printing the book, including the inclusion of photographs.

(Details materials to be submitted by author. Tip— Photographs can be expensive so make certain the cost is the responsibility of the publisher.)

The author warrants that he or she is the owner of the work and has full power and authority to copyright it and make this arrangement. He or she asserts further that the work does not infringe any copyright, trademark, trade secret, or other intellectual property, violate any property rights, or right of privacy, or contain any scandalous, libelous, or unlawful matter. The author agrees to defend, indemnify, and hold harmless the publisher against all claims, suits, costs, damages, and expenses that the publisher may sustain by reason of any scandalous, libelous, or unlawful matter contained or alleged to be contained in the work, or any infringement or violation by the work of any copyright or property right; and until such claim or lawsuit has been settled or withdrawn, the publisher may withhold any sums due to the author under this agreement.

(Asserts publisher's rights if publication is challenged. Tip— publishers will insist on this clause. It will be a deal breaker.)

The publisher shall have the right to edit the work for publication, but the author shall have final approval of the text prior to release of the book. The author shall also have final right of approval over the cover art and text, back, front, inside front, and inside back, and the photographic insert, if any.

(Language re approvals. Tip—Many publisher agreements do not provide author with final approvals. Seek to gain this right.)

The publisher shall provide twenty-five copies of the book free to the author.

(Author free copies. Tip—Attempt to induce publisher to provide as many free copies as possible for give-aways as well as personal use.)

If the work is not in print for a period of six months or the publisher declares that the work is no longer worthy of print for continued sale, all rights revert to the author. He or she may purchase all remaining copies of the book at publisher's cost. He or she may also obtain from publisher all plates, books, sheets, and photographs.

(Out of print circumstances. Tip—Require publisher to relinquish rights to book if it does not sell a certain amount of copies per year.)

The author agrees that during the term of this agreement he or she will not agree to publish a work on the same subject that will conflict with the sale of this book.

(Key terminology is "conflict with the sale of this book." Tip— Make certain language is definitive regarding this point.)

The author agrees to submit his or her next work first to publisher for their evaluation. Publisher shall have thirty days to either agree to negotiate in good faith a publishing agreement or decline to do so.

("Next book" language. Tip—Avoid if possible.)

The author agrees to provide publisher with an eight-by-ten snapshot. He or she also agrees to promote the book as requested by the publisher. This includes interviews for newspaper, radio, television, book signings, and other promotional events. Publisher shall be responsible for all expenses incurred by author to promote the book. Publisher agrees to expend $___ to promote and market the book.

(Sets out author obligation. Tip—Keep language as broad as possible. Attempt to bind publisher to expend x dollars to promote book.)

The author designates Sleepy Time Literary Agency as his or her author representative. All revenues due author and other correspondence with the agency shall be forwarded through its address at 345 Park Avenue, New York, New York 20002.

(Designates author's literary representative.)

This agreement constitutes the entire agreement between the parties. It supercedes any oral or written proposals, negotiations and discussions. The agreement may not be altered in any form without the express, written consent of all parties to the agreement.

(Standard language)

This agreement is binding and shall inure to the benefit of the heirs, executors, administrators, or designees of the author and to the assigns of the publisher. The author may assign their rights under this agreement as they wish. The publisher cannot do so without the written consent of the author.

(Specifies future rights. Tip—If possible, do not permit the publisher to assign the rights to the book with your consent.)

This agreement shall be binding under the laws of the state of Massachusetts. Any and all conflict shall be first submitted to the American Arbitration Association.

(Provides guidelines re conflict resolution. Tip—Attempt to include languages providing your state as governing body for law.)

Signed this ____ day of ___, ____.

_____

Scarborough Publishing Company

_____

Author

Agent/Publisher Submission Record

Document: Book Proposal—*Las Vegas, A Novel*
(Tip—Prepare one sheet for each submission. Print and collect in loose-leave notebook marked "Submissions.")

Submission Date -   June 12, __

Agent/Publisher Information -   Rosalie Thompkins Agency
                                                    56 West 57th Street
                                                    New York, NY 20002
                                                    212-789-7890
                                                    RThompkinsAgency@aol.com

Contact at Agent/Publisher -   Jeanette Furber, Agent

Four – Six Week Reaction -   No response, telephoned agency.
                                                    Spoke with Furber's assistant.
                                                    Proposal in stack to be read.
                                                    Estimated time—two weeks.

Follow-up - 6/17—Furber's assistant telephoned. Requested full manuscript.
Forwarded by Fed Ex.

Revisions, if an   _____
                                                    _____

Decision -   Hooray! Jeanette has agreed to
                                                    represent book. Suggested revisions
                                                    being forwarded.

Outcome -   Revisions completed. Submitted to
                                                    Jeanette. She submitted it to four
                                                    publishers. Riverhead books' offer
                                                    accepted. Hooray again!

(Tip—First submit material to four or five literary agents. Follow-up, keep four to five in play at a time. If no positive response, then repeat process to selected editors at publishing companies. Continue process until successful, but keep good records for future use.)

Sample Collaboration Agreement
With Comments

(Tips—If you are asked to collaborate on a book, or wish to work with a collaborator on your book, hire an entertainment lawyer or utilize the services of a literary agent. Regardless, familiarizing yourself with a collaboration agreement can be helpful.)

Agreement

Eugene Fixbaker ("Fixbaker") and Anne Spellbinder ("Spellbinder") hereby agree to collaborate on a book with the working title, ***Around The World In Twenty-Six Days*** ("work") under the following terms and conditions:

(Sets out the parties and the book covered by the agreement.)

Fixbaker will provide research for the work and his writing expertise and Spellbinder her writing expertise and use of her literary agent to solicit interest in the work. The parties agree to collaborate on the text for the work with Fixbaker having final approval.

(Details the respective responsibilities of the parties and the contribution of each party. Tip—Be as specific as possible to avoid conflict.)

The work will be written in first person detailing travel tips for completing a trip around the world in twenty-six days. The length of the completed manuscript will approximate 250 pages. Spellbinder agrees to provide photographs from a recent trip abroad for the work.

(Specifies the theme of the book, the length, and one author's responsibility to provide photographs. Tip—Book description essential. Make certain the parties understand clearly the book that is being written.)

The parties agree that an acceptable draft of the manuscript, subject to Fixbaker's final approval, will be completed on or before September 1, ____. At that time, the manuscript will be submitted to Afterburner Literary Agency for evaluation by Spellbinder's agent. Revisions shall be performed by the parties forthwith so that the manuscript and accompanying query letter can be submitted by the agent to selected publishers by October 1, ___.

> *(Details the completion date for the manuscript, one party's right to approval, and a timetable for submission to the agent and potential publishers. Tip—Be realistic as to deadlines so that there is no rush to forward material before its time. You only get one shot with agents and publishers—make certain the material is the best of the best.)*

The parties agree that they shall be fifty-fifty partners in the work. To that end, all expenses and any and all revenues from all sources for the work shall be shared. The parties designate Afterburner Literary Agent as their sole literary representative.

> *(Sets up financial arrangement between the parties. Tip— Essential to any agreement so there is no question of who gets what. Most collaborations are fifty-fifty but others may be tilted toward one party.)*

Credits for the work shall read, "Around The World In Twenty Six Days" by Eugene Fixbaker and Anne Spellbinder. The parties agree to perform all services, including promotion and marketing of the book, under the auspices of any contract with a publisher. Fixbaker shall have final approval over the selection of the said publisher.

> *(Specifies credits for the respective authors and the right of one author to have final approval. Tip—Detailing credits is as important as the financial arrangements. Be clear so there are no misunderstandings and hard feelings. Also—providing one party with final approval provides solution when disputes arise.)*

If the work is not acquired by a publisher, the parties agree to consider alternative means of publishing, including self-publishing. The parties agree to negotiate in good faith the particulars of such an endeavor. If no publisher is selected and self-publishing is not attempted, the parties agree to shelve the project for a one-year period of time. When that has expired, the parties agree that new submissions may be made, but if none are, the work becomes the property of Fixbaker.

(Provides out-clause in event manuscript is not publishable.)

The parties agree that all decisions made regarding the work shall be with the consent of the other subject to the approvals mentioned above. This agreement shall not be revised without the written consent of the parties. The parties agree that in the event of any disputes the law of Ohio shall govern and that said dispute shall initially be submitted to the American Arbitration Association for resolution.

(Covers boilerplate details regarding essential elements of the agreement.)

Signed this _____ day of ___, ____.

_____
Eugene Fixbaker

_____
Anne Spellbinder

Bibliography

Balzac and the Little Chinese Seamstress, Dai Sijie, Random House, New York, 2001

Book, The Magazine For The Reading Life, July/August, 2001

Down and Out In London and Paris, George Orwell, Harcourt, New York, 1933

Every Saint Has A Past, Every Sinner Has A Future, Terry Cole-Whitaker, Putnam, New York City, 2001

How To Write a Book Proposal, Michael Larsen, Writer's Digest Books, Cincinnati, Ohio, 1997

Jack Kerouac, Selected Letters, Edited by Ann Charters, Penguin, New York, 1996

Novel Ideas, Barbara Shoup and Margaret Love Denman, Alpha Books, Indianapolis, Indiana, 2001

On Writing, Stephen King, Scribner's, New York City, 2001

On Writing Well, William Zinser, HarperCollins, New York, 2001

Presumed Innocent, Scott Turow, Warner Books, New York, 1987

Seabiscuit, Laura Hillenbrand, Ballantine, New York, 2001

1,818 Ways To Write Better and Get Published, Scott Edelstein, Writer's Digest Books, Cincinnati, 1991

The Complete Guide To Book Publicity, Jodee Blanco, Allworth Press, New York, 2000

The First Five Pages: A Writer's Guide to Staying Out of the Rejection Pile, Noah Lukeman, Simon and Schuster, 2003

The Writer's Chapbook, George Plimpton et al, The Modern Library, New York, 1999

Twentieth Century Dictionary of Quotations, Edited by The Princeton Language Institute, The Philip Lief Group, Bantam Doubleday Dell Publishing Group, New York City, 1993

Various Issues – Writer's Digest Magazine

Writer's Guide To Book Editors, Publishers, and Literary Agents, Jeff Herman, Prima Publishing, 2002

Writing Down The Bones, Natalie Goldberg, Shambhala, Boston and London, 1986

Your Novel Proposal, From Creation to Contract, Blythe Camenson and Marshall J. Cook, Writer's Digest Books, Cincinnati, Ohio, 1999

Resources

Daniel Alderson, *Talking Back To Poems: A Working Guide for the Aspiring Poet*

Briggs, John, *Fire in the Crucible: The Self-creation of Creativity and Genius*

Brande, Dorothea, *Becoming A Writer*

Burroway, Janet, *Writing Fiction: A Guide to Narrative Craft*

Buzan, Tony, *Use Both Sides of the Brain*

Epel, Naomi, *Writers Dreaming*

Forster, E. M., *Aspects of a Novel*

Hartwell Fiske, Robert, *The Dictionary of Concise Writing: 10,000 Alternatives to Wordy Phrases*

Hemingway, Ernest, *A Moveable Feast*

Hirsch, Edward, *How to Read a Poem and Fall in Love with Poetry*

Keyes, Ralph, *The Courage To Write; How Writers Transcend Fear*

Maisell, Eric, *Staying Sane In The Arts*

May, Rollo, *The Courage to Create*

Nachmanovitch, Steven, *Free Style Improvisation in Life and Art*

Perry, Aaren Yeatts, *Poetry Across the Curriculum*

Rico, Gabrielle Lusser, *Writing the Natural Way*

Uleland, Brenda, *If You Want To Write*

Welty, Eudora, *One Writer's Beginnings*

Notes

To Order Copies of Book Report, Poetry Report, Grammar Report, My Book Proposal, or DVD Copies of Mark Shaw's "How To Become A Published Author or Poet: A to Z Seminars:"

Telephone Books For Life Foundation 970-544-3398

E-mail at: help@booksforlifefoundation.com

Visit Books For Life Foundation at 450 South Galena Street, Aspen, Colorado

Write Books For Life Foundation at P. O Box CC, Aspen, Colorado 81611

Seminars,
Speaking Engagements

Mark Shaw and other Books For Life Foundation staff members and advisors are available to conduct seminars focusing on writing tips, publishing strategies, and storytelling ideas at high schools, colleges, universities, libraries, writer's centers, writer's groups, youth groups, senior centers, corporations, and legal organizations. For more information, visit www.booksforlifefoundation.com.

Mark Shaw

Mark Shaw is a former lawyer turned author with fourteen published books. They include *Book Report, Grammar Report, Poetry Report, From Birdies To Bunkers, Miscarriage of Justice, Let The Good Times Roll, The Jonathan Pollard Story, Larry Legend, Testament To Courage, The Perfect Yankee, Bury Me In A Pot Bunker,* and *Forever Flying*.

Mr. Shaw is a literary consultant, and creative director of Books For Life Foundation. Along with his canine pal, Black Sox, he lives in Aspen Colorado. More about Mark Shaw and contact information is available at www.markshaw.com or www.booksforlifefoundation.com

Printed in the United States
17854LVS00005B/1-54